Best Bike Rides
Portland, Oregon

Help Us Keep This Guide Up to Date

Every effort has been made by the authors and editors to make this guide as accurate and useful as possible. However, many things can change after a guide is published—roads are detoured, phone numbers change, facilities come under new management, and so forth.

We welcome your comments concerning your experiences with this guide and how you feel it could be improved and kept up to date. While we may not be able to respond to all comments and suggestions, we'll take them to heart, and we'll also make certain to share them with the authors. Please send your comments and suggestions to the following address:

Globe Pequot
Reader Response/Editorial Department
246 Goose Lane
Guilford, CT 06437

Or you may e-mail us at:
editorial@falcon.com

Thanks for your input, and happy riding!

BEST BIKE RIDES® SERIES

Best Bike Rides
Portland, Oregon

Great Recreational Rides
in the Metro Area

AYLEEN CROTTY AND LIZANN DUNEGAN

GUILFORD, CONNECTICUT
HELENA, MONTANA

An imprint of Rowman & Littlefield
Falcon and FalconGuides are registered trademarks and Make Adventure Your Story is a
trademark of Rowman & Littlefield.

Distributed by NATIONAL BOOK NETWORK

Copyright © 2016 by Rowman & Littlefield
Maps: Alena Pearce © Rowman & Littlefield

British Library Cataloguing-in-Publication Information available

Library of Congress Cataloging-in-Publication Data

Names: Crotty, Ayleen, author. | Dunegan, Lizann, author.
Title: Best bike rides, Portland, Oregon : great recreational rides in the
  metro area / Ayleen Crotty and Lizann Dunegan.
Description: Helena, Montana : FalconGuides, 2017.
Identifiers: LCCN 2016032776 (print) | LCCN 2016032859 (ebook) | ISBN
  9780762784462 (pbk. : alk. paper) | ISBN 9781493014262 (ebook) | ISBN
  9781493014262 (e-book)
Subjects: LCSH: Cycling—Oregon—Portland Metropolitan Area—Guidebooks. |
  Bicycle touring—Oregon—Portland Metropolitan Area—Guidebooks. |
  Portland Metropolitan Area (Or.)—Guidebooks.
Classification: LCC GV1045.5.O72 P674 2017 (print) | LCC GV1045.5.O72 (ebook)
  | DDC 796.609795/49—dc23
LC record available at https://lccn.loc.gov/2016032776

∞™ The paper used in this publication meets the minimum requirements of American
National Standard for Information Sciences—Permanence of Paper for Printed Library
Materials, ANSI/NISO Z39.48-1992.

The authors and Rowman & Littlefield assume no liability for accidents happening to, or injuries sustained by, readers who engage in the activities described in this book.

Contents

Overview

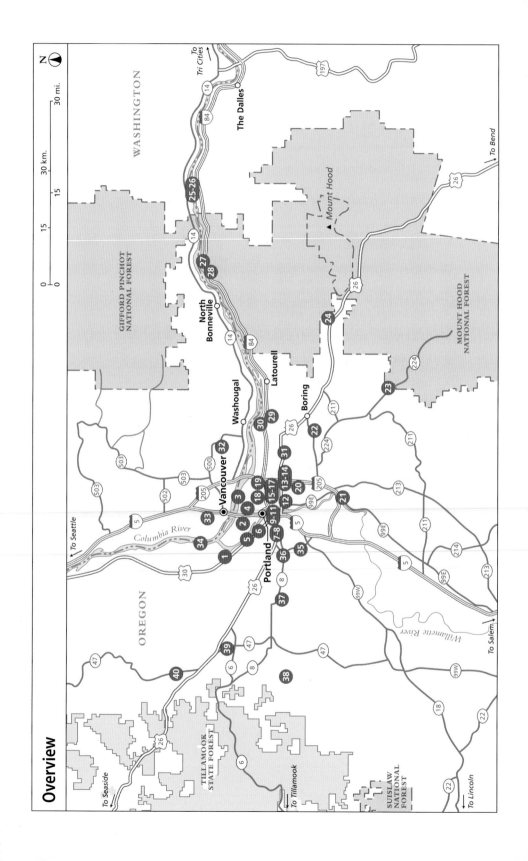

Southeast of Portland

East of Portland and the Columbia River Gorge

North of Portland

West of Portland

Acknowledgments

Considerable thanks go to the many Portland cyclists who helped shape this book by offering route advice, sharing their favorite spots, and riding alongside the authors. Thanks also to Stephanie Edman, Brian Hinsley, Greg Larson, Kiran Limaye, Lisa Luna, Matt Stefanik, and Ride with GPS.

—A. C.

Thanks to my cycling friends who accompanied me on many of the rides in this book, as well as to the bike shop owners who helped with route questions and offered suggestions for new routes to explore.

—L. D.

Introduction

Cycling is by far the best way to see Portland. A vast network of low-traffic streets, bike lanes, and off-road paths makes it easy to snake around the city in search of adventure. We've put together a series of forty routes that will help you explore the region by bike. There's a little something for everyone in here, no matter your age, riding experience, or endurance.

Portland is internationally regarded as one of the world's most bike-friendly cities, and has been honored with the "Platinum Status" designation from the League of American Bicyclists. In the urban core, many streets are designated as "greenways," with traffic-calming features that allow cycling in an environment more relaxed than the busy nearby streets. It's easy to navigate the city safely from east to west and north to south on low-traffic roads and in designated bike lanes, even while crossing the Willamette River, which divides the city, or traversing over the I-84 freeway, which cuts through the city from east to west.

A whopping 7 percent of Portlanders bike to work—a national high—and daily bike commute numbers are proudly showcased on the digital display boards of bike counters mounted on several of the popular bridges that span the Willamette River. It's not uncommon to see moms on cargo bikes toting kids to school, dogs riding in trailers, and cyclists of all stripes streaming down the streets of Portland rain or shine. In fact, on sunny summer days you may even find yourself behind a stop light traffic jam of more than 20 people on bikes—affectionately known locally as a "commuter peloton."

Over the years, the city of Portland has worked hard to make Portland bike friendly by installing road infrastructure that makes it safer and easier to ride a bike in the increasingly busy urban center, but other factors have also

Bear and Tiz enjoying their DoggyRide bike trailer designed especially for dogs. PHOTO BY LIZANN DUNEGAN

contributed to Portland's active transportation success: Retail, advocacy, and bike fun.

Bike shops abound so you're never too far from supplies and friendly service, where the staff will assist you in answering questions or getting your bike in tip-top shape.

The local bike advocacy organization is the Bicycle Transportation Alliance. The alliance works hard to raise awareness about cycling at the state level and in government.

Since 2000, Portland has had a vibrant bicycle culture that started around that time with monthly casual group rides, and has blossomed into weekly offerings of rides and activities for people who love all types of riding. Whether you're looking for gravel-grinding off-road excursions, picnics by bike, or group rides with your little ones, you'll find an event to join.

Every June, a grassroots network of cyclists hosts hundreds of events over the course of three weeks for the Pedalpalooza festival, and nearly all the events are free. If you find yourself in the city during this time, be sure to catch at least one event during this impressive spectacle. Though they brave rain for eight months out of the year, Portland cyclists love to have fun on two wheels, and their efforts have inspired a rich community of cycling.

Safety

"Share the road" is the Portland way to ride, meaning all road users have a right to be on the road. We can all contribute to safe roads by being respectful. Follow the rules of the road, make eye contact, and ride predictably. Signal your turns clearly by pointing in the direction you want to turn.

The Metro Bike There! map is a handy way to navigate the city as its color-coded streets indicate various bike-friendly features. The weather-resistant map is available at most bike shops and some environmentally friendly grocery stores.

If you are ever unsure of where you are going, slow down, move to the side of the road and stand on the shoulder or sidewalk. Portlanders are a friendly lot, so don't be shy about asking for directions. If you find yourself on a busy road without a bike lane that doesn't feel safe, pull over and consult your map. Usually there are calm side streets just a block or two away. You can also look for the green navigational signs that indicate bike-friendly routes and the mileages to get to various neighborhoods and destinations.

Oregon law requires helmets for youths fourteen and younger, but it's a good idea for cyclists of all ages to wear a helmet. The law also requires a white front light and a rear reflector, but we recommend a bright rear light. When riding at night, ensure your lights are charged up and ride with the understanding that it's not easy for other road users to see you, especially when it's raining. You never know where your adventure may take you, or where you'll want to linger after the ride, so pack your lights just in case you wind up staying out late.

In Oregon, cyclists are allowed full use of a lane of traffic, meaning you do not need to concern yourself with squeezing onto the very edge of the road. Often it's safer to ride in the lane so you are visible. On rural roads with no shoulder or bike lane, position your bike where a right car tire would be. The law—and etiquette—dictates that riders form a single file whenever cars are approaching from behind.

It is illegal to ride on the sidewalk in the downtown core of Portland, and riding on the sidewalk can be dangerous in other parts of the city. It's best to choose low traffic routes and ride in the street.

Many Portland roads have tracks for the Portland Streetcar and the MAX light rail. Avoid riding near the tracks if possible, and cross tracks at a right angle. It's easy for a bike wheel to get caught in the tracks, but it's also easy to avoid such accidents by riding with care.

When riding on trails, be respectful of other trail users. Cyclists must yield to walkers, hikers, and horse riders. It's also a good idea to give fair warning of your approach so you don't startle people or horses, and to say hello to foster friendly relations with other trail users. When riding on crowded paths, slow down and give a wide berth when passing other trail users. In some instances, it may even be prudent to dismount and walk your bike.

When riding on trails, avoid skidding, riding off the trail, or otherwise disrupting the surface more than necessary. This type of abuse can cause ruts and washouts that harm the environment and the condition of the trail. When riding on a narrow path or singletrack, the uphill rider has the right of way.

Cycling is becoming increasingly common, and drivers are learning to be on the lookout for cyclists. As all work toward sharing the road, your presence on the bike plays an important role. When we follow the rules of the road, ride predictably, and are friendly toward other road users, we foster an improved environment for everyone. Smile and wave, acknowledge kind gestures (such as when a car allows you to proceed first through a four-way stop), and be thoughtful about how your maneuvers affect those around you. By riding respectfully, you can set a great example.

Ride to Eat, Eat to Ride

Portland is a fantastic food city with no shortage of delicious options, too abundant to list them all here. It's generally advisable to eat one hour prior to your ride to ensure your food is well digested before you begin vigorous activity. But if you're on a pleasure cruise, eating along the way is no problem at all.

Beyond formal sit-down establishments, Portland has a wealth of food carts that make it easy to stay with your bike as you grab an affordable bite to eat. We also highly recommend a post-ride nosh and drink session, the perfect way to wind down, discuss the day, and relax.

Weather

July, August, and September are gorgeously dry and warm months in Portland, and the rest of the year it can be rather wet. It rains nearly nine months out of the year in Portland, but that doesn't deter the stalwart population from commuting by bike in droves. Riding in the rain isn't for everyone, but a hot drink or warm bath afterward makes for a sweet reward.

In the summertime, the temperature usually hovers in the 80-degree Fahrenheit range and the peak time of day is about 5 p.m. Portland's climate rarely dips down below 40 degrees, and most winter days are fairly mild, though wet. When riding October through April, it's best to bring along rain gear: Even if the morning looks clear, it will likely be raining by afternoon.

If you find yourself with a sunny winter day, seize that opportunity to go for a long, clear ride, but be forewarned that the weather is likely to shift later in the day.

Typical rainy riding gear includes:

- Fenders to keep you dry, and avoid spraying the riders behind you
- Rain pants or a rain cape that shields your legs
- A breathable rain jacket or thick wool sweater to keep the rain at bay
- Waterproof gloves
- Shoe covers
- A small soft cloth for drying off your glasses and face when you arrive at your destination

Low-cost emergency plastic rain suits are available at some convenience stores and at army surplus stores like Andy and Bax, and are a suitable option if you're caught unprepared.

On wet roads, use caution when riding over leaves and metal surfaces such as sewer covers as they can be slick.

Equipment and Gear

Other than when it's raining, you shouldn't need any special clothing to ride a bike in Portland. It's common to see cyclists riding in all types of outfits, from office attire to street clothes to Lycra racing kits. Wear whatever is most comfortable, so long as it won't drape down and get caught in your wheels or your gears. For most of the rides in this book, a road-style bike with gears is recommended. Bring a lock to secure your bike if you stop, even if you're just running inside a store quickly. You may also want a rear rack so you can attach a pannier to carry items or the layers of clothing you shed as you warm up on your ride. It's easier to ride with your gear on the bike instead of on your back in a backpack, as your back will get sweaty and the pack may cause strain on your neck and shoulders.

Most bikes come outfitted with a water bottle cage, so bring along a water bottle or two to stay hydrated during your ride.

Getting There and Parking

Portland has an excellent public transportation system, so for many of the rides we've included directions for taking the MAX light rail or a bus to the start location. Consult the easy-to-use TriMet.org website for the most up-to-date fares and schedule. We've listed public transportation options when they provide a relatively easy way to access the trail start. If no options are listed, it may still be possible to use public transportation to get to the trailhead. Consult the TriMet website to determine if transfers from one route to another can get you to the start point.

Bikes are welcome on Portland MAX light rail and buses, but there is limited capacity. Only two bikes fit on a bus, and occasionally when the bus arrives the rack already contains bikes. To become familiar with the process of bringing your bike on the MAX or bus, consult the TriMet website.

Rides begin in a variety of locations, from private parking lots to city parks. Consult the parking signage to ensure you're in compliance with regulations, and consider how long you will be out riding if you need to pay by the hour for parking.

Using This Guide

Portland has a variety of terrain, and it's surprisingly easy to find serene natural areas just on the edge of the urban core. Most rides in this book are 5 to 30 miles long with no significant climbing, though a few standout rides feature challenging climbing. We've offered opportunities to explore urban routes, bike lanes, off-road bike paths, rail-trail paths, wide gravel paths, rural roads, and thrilling singletrack mountain biking.

These rides are all designed to be a special experience, one that allows you to explore a region and sink into the environment, whether that means watching birds, swimming in the river, or stopping at cafes. The time listed is an estimate, and we encourage you to enjoy the journey. If a ride has an extensive number of opportunities to stop along the way, we've tried to indicate that in the estimated time section. Take into consideration the features of the ride and pack your gear accordingly, so you can fully explore what's offered on the route, such as bringing along a bathing suit and towel for rides that go past beaches.

For such an outdoorsy city that also loves bikes, there is a surprising lack of mountain biking access in the Portland area. We mapped a few suggested routes in each trail system, but part of the fun is studying the trailhead maps and choosing your own adventure based on the type of off-road riding you want to do, and how far you want to ride.

Key to icons used in this edition:

 Road Bike   Mountain Bike   Hybrid

Ride Finder

BEST PAVED TRAIL RIDES

13 Springwater Corridor: Southeast Foster Road to Downtown Boring

23 Clackamas River Cruise

27 Historic Columbia River Highway State Trail: Cascade Locks to Moffett Creek Bridge

32 Lacamas Lake Path

33 Burnt Bridge Creek Greenway Trail

34 Frenchman's Bar Trail

39 Banks–Vernonia State Trail

BEST FOR MOUNTAIN BIKING OR RIDING ON GRAVEL ROADS

5 Saltzman Road and the Majestic St. Johns Bridge

6 Leif Erikson Drive

22 Cazadero State Park Trail

24 Sandy Ridge Mountain Bike Trail System

28 easyCLIMB at Cascade Locks

40 L. L. Stub Stewart State Park

BEST RIDES FOR URBAN SIGHTSEEING

11 Family Friendly Fountain Tour

12 Tilikum Crossing: The People's Bridge

14 Springwater Corridor: Sellwood–Hawthorne Loop

17 Southeast Neighborhoods Tour

18 Five "Quadrants" Ultimate Portland Loop

BEST FOR WILDLIFE

1 Sauvie Island

2 Nature in the City: North Portland Loop

5 Saltzman Road and the Majestic St. Johns Bridge

6 Leif Erikson Drive

10 Tryon Creek Natural Area and Portland Bridges Loop

13 Springwater Corridor: Southeast Foster Road to Downtown Boring

14 Springwater Corridor: Sellwood–Hawthorne Loop

22 Cazadero State Park Trail

35 Fanno Creek Greenway Trail

BEST FOR RIDING WITH CHILDREN

9 Eastbank Esplanade–Tom McCall Waterfront Park Loop
11 Family Friendly Fountain Tour
12 Tilikum Crossing: The People's Bridge
23 Clackamas River Cruise
28 easyCLIMB at Cascade Locks
32 Lacamas Lake Path
33 Burnt Bridge Creek Greenway Trail
34 Frenchman's Bar Trail

BEST FOR RURAL SERENITY

5 Saltzman Road and the Majestic St. Johns Bridge
25 Hood River Valley Loop
26 Historic Columbia River Highway State Trail: Hood River to The Dalles
29 Columbia River Gorge Waterfall Tour
35 Fanno Creek Greenway Trail
36 North Plains Ramble
37 Mini Farm Tour
38 Hagg Lake Ramble

BEST FOR NEW RIDERS

9 Eastbank Esplanade–Tom McCall Waterfront Park Loop
12 Tilikum Crossing: The People's Bridge
13 Springwater Corridor: Southeast Foster Road to Downtown Boring
14 Springwater Corridor: Sellwood–Hawthorne Loop
15 Mount Tabor Park
17 Southeast Neighborhoods Tour
19 Northeast Portland Neighborhood Loop
23 Clackamas River Cruise
28 easyCLIMB at Cascade Locks
31 Gresham–Fairview Path
32 Lacamas Lake Path
33 Burnt Bridge Creek Greenway Trail
34 Frenchman's Bar Trail
35 Fanno Creek Greenway Trail
37 Mini Farm Tour
38 Hagg Lake Ramble
39 Banks–Vernonia State Trail
40 L. L. Stub Stewart State Park

BEST FOR UNIQUELY PORTLAND FEATURES

11 Family Friendly Fountain Tour
12 Tilikum Crossing: The People's Bridge
14 Springwater Corridor: Sellwood–Hawthorne Loop
17 Southeast Neighborhoods Tour
18 Five "Quadrants" Ultimate Portland Loop

BEST FOR A HILL CLIMB CHALLENGE

BEST FOR BIKING WITH SIDE ACTIVITIES

Map Legend

═══ 205 ═══	Interstate Highway	■	Building/Point of Interest
─ 26 ─	US Highway	⋀	Campground
─ 14 ─	State Highway	†	Cemetery
▬ 14 ▬	Featured State/Local Road	—	Dam
─────	Local Road	🍴	Dining
▪▪▪▪▪▪	Featured Bike Route	!	Gate
▪▪▪▪▪▪	Bike Route	17.1 ◆─	Mileage Marker
─────	Trail/Unpaved Road	🏛	Museum
┝─┼─┼─┥	Railroad	🅿	Parking
▬▬▬▬	Airfield/Runway	ᴙ	Picnic Area
─ ·· ─ ·· ─	State Line	▲	Peak
～～～	Small River or Creek	👥	Restroom
⬭	Body of Water	⦕	Scenic View/Viewpoint
▭▭▭	National Forest/Park/Wilderness Area	♠	Small Park
▭▭▭	State Park/Forest/Preserve Recreational Area	①	Trailhead
		⊢━━⊣	Tunnel
✈	Airport	❓	Visitor/Information Center
▭	Bench	🚰	Water
⛵	Boat Launch	≋	Waterfall
⌣	Bridge		

Portland Area

Want to know what Portland is really like? The best way to see the city is on a bike! The routes in this section will offer a mix of remote, urban, hilly, flat, short, and long routes. There is definitely a little of something for everyone here, including a family-friendly fountain tour!

You'll have an opportunity to thoroughly explore Forest Park, Portland's forested oasis on the edge of the city. Some of the routes climb high for gorgeous, sweeping city views; others stay low around the river for glimpses of

Shady Leif Erikson Drive makes for an enjoyable ride on a hot summer's day. PHOTO BY LIZANN DUNEGAN

wildlife in the city and opportunities to jump in the restored Willamette River, which flows through the heart of the city.

You'll definitely cross plenty of bridges, too. Portland's east and west sides are divided by the Willamette River, but connected by twelve bridges, nine of which can be traversed by bike, and most of which are included in this book. Be sure to stop at the tops of the bridges to take in gorgeous river and cityscape views.

It's easy to get around Portland by bike, with many bike lanes, designated low-traffic streets, and a generally friendly population of road users. Many of these routes begin from the urban core, making it easy to take public transportation or ride your bike to the beginning of the ride. The routes here will give you a chance to explore some of the most intriguing sections of Portland. Be sure to bring your appetite, as you're sure to pass some great eating and drinking establishments along the way—that's what Portland is known for.

Sauvie Island

Located just minutes from Portland, this ride takes you on a tour of the rural land-scape of Sauvie Island, which is filled with small farms, nurseries, and wild, open spaces. You'll have the chance to see hawks soaring above open fields, bald eagles nesting, and migratory waterfowl from the wildlife viewing areas that are pres-ent on this route. In the summer months, you also have the opportunity to stop and pick berries and try other locally grown produce at some of the local farms. On a clear day you'll also have gorgeous views of prominent Cascade volcanoes, including Mount Rainier, Mount Saint Helens, Mount Adams, and Mount Hood.

Start: The paved parking area off NW Gillihan Loop Road on Sauvie Island. Sauvie Island is approximately 10 miles north of Portland off US 30.

Length: 18.0-mile lollipop

Approximate riding time: 3 hours with stops

Best bike: Road bike

Terrain and trail surface: Rural paved roads that are flat and fast, with a variety of twists and turns.

Traffic and hazards: The shoulder on this ride varies from 1 to 2 feet at the start of the ride to no shoulder at all for rest of the ride. The summer traffic can be thick on this route, and there are many blind curves where you will need to exercise extreme caution. As a common courtesy, always ride single file. Also note there are many places where you can pull off the road to let traffic by, which allows you more time to soak in the great views of the many picturesque farms and abundant bird life on the island.

Things to see: Berry picking at local farms; bird-watching; Howell Territorial Park

Map: USGS Sauvie Island

Getting There: By car: From I-405 in Portland, take the NW Industrial Area/Saint Helens/US 30 west exit and follow the signs for Saint Helens. Drive 8.8 miles north on US 30 until you see a sign indicating Sauvie Island wildlife area. Exit to the right and cross the bridge to the island. After crossing the bridge turn left onto NW Gillihan Road, then take another immediate left into a large circular paved parking area.

By public transportation: From the bus mall in downtown Portland, board the bus labeled "16 Front Ave/St. Helens Rd. to Sauvie Island". Get off at NW Gillihan Road. Your ride begins from the large circular paved parking area where the bus stops. GPS: N45 37.731' / W122 48.912'

THE RIDE

This 18.0-mile ride takes you through the quiet, rural landscape of the 24,000-acre Sauvie Island, which is located at the confluence of two of Oregon's major rivers: the Willamette and the Columbia. Sauvie Island is the largest island in the Columbia River and one of the largest freshwater islands in the world. At 4 miles wide and 15 miles long, it is made up of fertile farmland, shallow lakes, marshes, sloughs, and groves of cottonwood, willow, and ash. The island is home to more than 300 species of animals, including raccoons, beavers, mink, and black-tailed deer. Sauvie Island is located on the Pacific Flyway, which attracts thousands of migrating birds each year.

The northern half of Sauvie Island is comprised of a 12,000-acre wildlife area managed by the Oregon Fish and Wildlife Service. This vast refuge has designated viewing areas where you can see a variety of bird species. During the fall more than 150,000 ducks congregate in the wetlands on the island. You may see mallards, ruddy ducks, green-winged teals, buffleheads, pintails, and wigeons. Other additions to this cast of characters include sandhill cranes, blue herons, Canada geese, snow geese, and tundra swans. Bald eagles can also be seen roosting in trees on the island from December through March. This rich variety of bird life attracts not only birders but also hunters. The wildlife area is generally closed from October 1 through the middle of January for hunting season.

If you are riding during the summer months, bring along a container for collecting fresh berries. There are several u-pick berry farms on the island, and you'll likely pass by swaths of wild blackberries as well.

Sauvie Island is filled with small farms, where you may see horses and other livestock.
PHOTO BY LIZANN DUNEGAN

A group of Native Americans called the Flatheads were the first inhabitants of the island. They mainly subsisted on a diet of the tuberlike plant called *wapato*. This nutritious plant gained the attention of Lewis and Clark, who named the island Wapato when they passed through the area from 1805 to 1806. This name was later changed to Sauvie after a French-Canadian named Laurent Sauvé, who worked for the Hudson's Bay Company on a dairy farm in the early 1800s. You'll hear the name of the island pronounced as *Soh-vee, Sah-vee,* or *Sah-vees.* A lifelong islander once commented that all three pronunciations are correct.

In the mid-1850s much of the island was turned into large farms by settlers who were part of the great Oregon Trail migration. Today the farming tradition continues, and much of the southern half of the island is composed of nurseries, small farms, farmers' markets, and rural residences.

Begin this route by pedaling south on Gillihan Loop Road for a short distance. The road then swings north, taking you through a rolling landscape of open fields and pastures, nurseries and large country homes. A variety of raptors can be seen soaring above the open landscape, including red-tailed hawks, Cooper's hawks, kestrels, and rough-legged hawks. Dotted along the route are many farm markets, which are fun to explore during the summer season and offer opportunities to pick up a variety of fresh, organic berries, and gather seasonal produce and island-made goods like honey and jam. On a clear day you will have a magnificent view to the north and west of Mount Rainier, Mount Saint Helens, Mount Adams, and Mount Hood.

After 6.0 miles you'll turn right onto NW Reeder Road and continue your journey north. Along this section you'll pass by different wildlife area access points and you can check out some of the island's great sandy beaches. Stop by the Reeder Beach Resort to get recommendations for beach access.

At 8.9 miles you'll arrive at the wildlife-viewing platform that contains informative displays about the geology, history, and bird life of the island. This is your turnaround point.

Bike Shops

21st Avenue Bicycles: 916 NW 21st Ave., Portland, OR 97209; (503) 222-2851; 21stbikes.com
Block Bikes: 7238 N Burlington Ave., Portland, OR 97203; (503) 819-6839; blockbikespdx.com

When you are ready to continue on the route, follow NW Reeder Road back (south) to the junction with NW Gillihan. Stay right (south) on NW Reeder Road and continue to the intersection with NW Sauvie Island Road. Turn left and continue pedaling south, where you'll pass more open fields and farms. At 17.0 miles be sure to stop and admire the architecture of the Bybee-Howell House, located in the 120-acre Howell Territorial Park. This two-story, Classical Revival-Style house was built in the mid-nineteenth century.

If you plan on exploring the island more via car, be sure to pick up a day-use parking permit for a small fee at Sam's Cracker Barrel Store (you'll pass this store on your right at 17.8 miles), which is required at all wildlife-viewing parking areas on the island and at the main beach, Collins Beach.

MILES AND DIRECTIONS

0.0 Start by turning left (south) out of the parking area onto NW Gillihan Loop Road. Watch for traffic as you exit out of the parking area.

6.0 Turn right onto NW Reeder Road.

6.5 Pass a gravel parking area on your left, which is an access point to the Sauvie Island Wildlife Area. There is a portable restroom in this parking area.

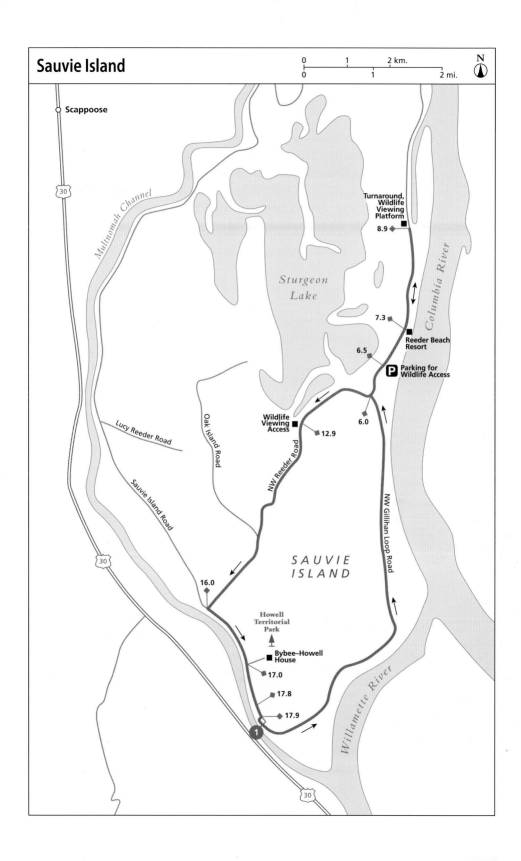

Sauvie Island

Scappoose

Turnaround, Wildlife Viewing Platform
8.9

Sturgeon Lake

Multnomah Channel

Columbia River

7.3

Reeder Beach Resort

6.5

Parking for Wildlife Access

Wildlife Viewing Access
12.9

6.0

Lucy Reeder Road

Oak Island Road

NW Reeder Road

NW Gillihan Loop Road

Sauvie Island Road

SAUVIE ISLAND

16.0

Howell Territorial Park

Bybee–Howell House

17.0

17.8

17.9

Willamette River

7.3 Pass Reeder Beach Resort on your right. This is a good place to stop for snacks and drinks. There are portable restrooms and a pay phone here.

8.9 Come to a wildlife-viewing platform with interpretive signs and restrooms. From this viewing platform you'll have the opportunity to view mallard, pintail, wigeon, and green-winged teal ducks; blue herons; tundra swans; and sandhill cranes. This is your turnaround point. To return to your starting point, follow NW Reeder Road back to the junction with NW Gillihan Loop Road.

11.8 At the Y junction, turn right (south) and continue riding on NW Reeder Road.

This old red truck makes a curious roadside attraction. PHOTO BY LIZANN DUNEGAN

12.9   Pass another wildlife-viewing area on the right, with restrooms.

16.0   At the T intersection, turn left onto NW Sauvie Island Road.

17.0   Pass the historic Bybee–Howell House on your left.

17.8   Pass Sam's Cracker Barrel Store on your right. This is another good place to stock up on drinks and snacks. A pay phone is available.

17.9   Turn right onto NW Gillihan Loop Road.

18.0   Arrive back at your starting point on the left.

RIDE INFORMATION

Local Events/Attractions
Providence Bridge Pedal: 1631 NE Klickitat St., Portland, OR 97212; (503) 281-9198; blog.bridgepedal.com. This annual event (held in mid-Aug) is a noncompetitive bike ride crossing Portland's historic bridges: Morrison, Sellwood, Hawthorne, Ross Island, Marquam, Burnside, Broadway, Steel, St. Johns, and Fremont.

The Bybee–Howell House: Howell Territorial Park, 13901 NW Howell Park Rd. on Sauvie Island; (503) 797-1850; oregonmetro.gov/index.cfm/go/by.web/id=152. This historic house built in 1858 gives you a glimpse at what life was like here in the mid-nineteenth century.

Restrooms
There are restrooms adjacent to the parking area at the start/finish of the ride. Restrooms are also available at mile 6.5, mile 7.3, and mile 12.9.

Nature in the City: North Portland Loop

This amazingly flat route packs a punch with plenty of spectacular ride features and natural wonders. The route is filled with many interesting highlights and hangout spots, so plan to spend your time exploring a region that is teeming with wildlife alongside an active industrial hub. Because of this juxtaposition, you'll ride next to a little bit of truck traffic at times, but always with a wide, off-the-road paved path for safe passage. Be well prepared for your excursion by packing a picnic lunch, ample water, binoculars, a beach towel, and your swimsuit.

Start: North end of Kenton Park

Length: 18.4-mile loop

Approximate riding time: About 2 hours of riding, plus 1 to 3 hours to explore the region

Best bike: Road bike

Terrain and trail surface: Paved city streets with a tiny bit of gravel

Traffic and hazards: 0.1 mile of walking along the grass on the side of the road

Things to see: Smith and Bybee Lakes; Kelley Point Park; Willamette River; Columbia River; Columbia Slough; Chimney Park (dog park); Pier Park (disc golf mecca); historic Kenton; downtown St. Johns; Cathedral Park/St. Johns Bridge; Willamette Bluffs

Maps: USGS Portland; Metro Bike There! map

Getting There: By car: From downtown Portland, head north on I-5 for 7.5 miles. Take exit 306A and loop around on Columbia Boulevard to Argyle Street. Continue on Argyle Street 0.2 mile to North Brandon Street and look for parking. Your ride begins from the corner of North Brandon at Argyle Street, at the north end of Kenton Park.

By public transportation: Take the MAX Yellow Line to the Kenton station and head west 2 blocks to Kenton Park. Your ride begins from the corner of North Brandon at Argyle Street, on the north end of Kenton Park. GPS: N45 35.067' / W122 41.364'

THE RIDE

You will begin and end your journey in the quaint neighborhood of historic Kenton, where food and drink options abound. Three-fourths of the way through this ride you'll pass through the large neighborhood of St. Johns, but between Kenton and St. Johns there is very little in the way of amenities (other than restrooms), so you'll want to plan ahead.

A 0.5-mile walking trail brings you to a serene bird-viewing platform tucked in the woods.
PHOTO BY AYLEEN CROTTY

Restoring the Columbia Slough

It may not look like much, but the Columbia Slough, a tributary of the Columbia River, is an important Portland waterway.

Sloughs have a long history of use among native people for safe canoe passage and accessible fishing and hunting that's not as intense as a major river. The Lewis and Clark expedition traveled along the Columbia Slough and complained there was too much noise due to reasons quite different from today's city din: They encountered massive numbers of geese and swans residing in the area.

In the early 1920s, a levee was constructed along the Columbia River to prevent flooding from the annual spring rains. According to the Columbia Slough Watershed Council, as this area was developed "what was once a wildlife-rich mosaic of sloughs, wetlands and lakes was transformed into a highly managed system of channels, agricultural lands, industrial development and residences." And thus began a long history of environmental decline.

Today the slough is being rediscovered, thanks to groups like the Columbia Slough Watershed Council with support from the city of Portland's Environmental Services department. After extensive restoration, this urban watershed now provides recreation, green space, drainage, and abundant wildlife habitat. The Columbia Slough Watershed Council website notes the slough "is home to 4,200 businesses, 170,000 people, a marine terminal, and two airports . . . the streams, sloughs, wetlands, grasslands, and woodlands here provide wildlife corridors and migratory routes for more than 175 species of birds." The Columbia Slough Watershed Council also notes that mink, river otter, beaver, coyote, and sensitive species like bald eagle, peregrine falcon, willow flycatcher, and Western pond and Western painted turtles rely on the slough habitats. An impressive twenty-eight fish species call the Columbia Slough home.

Restoring the slough means enticing the wildlife back by creating habitat and planning a waterway that will eventually develop naturally.

This ride features a lot of smooth, off-the-road paved riding. Begin by heading toward the Columbia Slough Trail (mile 0.5). The approach can be tricky, but once you're on the path, you'll be sailing on a freshly paved berm above the Columbia Slough waterway. It may not look like much, but this important waterway provides crucial habitat for a variety of wildlife, and various groups have been working to restore it to a more natural state (see the sidebar). Look for the engineered log stacks that provide habitat for steelhead,

A view of the Columbia Slough with an engineered logjam for wildlife habitat.
PHOTO BY AYLEEN CROTTY

Areas of water grass have been planted to create safe zones for the fish and other aquatic creatures. Young salmon, in particular, favor the calm waters of the slough over the powerful Columbia River as they navigate their way to the Pacific Ocean. Steelhead, coho, and Chinook frequently travel through here.

Engineered logjams formed from stacks of logs provide additional protective areas for wildlife. Trees have been planted along the shoreline to provide shade that cools the water. Over time, these trees will create natural logjams as the Columbia Slough begins to return to a more natural state.

coho, and Chinook salmon who favor the calm waters of the slough over the intense current of the Columbia River.

Continue along to Smith and Bybee Lakes, the largest urban wetland wildlife refuge in the United States, and home to 100 bird species. At mile 3.4, you can take a break at the boat launch and walk to the water's edge with your bike. From this vantage point, you'll easily spot the abundant flocks of graceful great blue heron. Birders will delight in looking for bald eagle, osprey,

Bring your swimsuit and a good book! Kelley Point Park has the best beaches in Portland.
PHOTO BY AYLEEN CROTTY

pileated woodpecker, willow flycatcher, marsh wren, savannah sparrow, and peregrine falcon, among others.

For a woodsy stroll, lock your bike at the bike rack (mile 4.1) and walk along the 0.5-mile walking path to the viewing platform. Shhh . . . allow yourself to get lost in the forested canopy of birdsong that drowns out the din of the city.

Your next stop is Kelley Point Park, at the confluence of the Willamette and mighty Columbia Rivers, Portland's two main waterways. A paved path winds around the peninsula and you can ride your bike for the entirety of the path, or securely lock your bike in the parking lot and walk if you don't want to bring your bike down onto the sandy beach.

There is beach access along both rivers, but the Willamette side, accessed from the first parking lot, affords calmer waters for wading in. This natural area is becoming a popular, though rustic, beach hangout spot. Roll out your beach towel, strip down to your bathing suit, pull out the snacks, and crack open a good book for a serene afternoon break. The river is always perfectly cool from June through September, making this halfway point a perfect destination on a hot day.

Best Bike Rides Portland, Oregon

As you ride back out of Kelley Point Park and take a right onto Marine Drive, nature study comes to a close and it's time to wind your way back into the city. At mile 11.1, the bike lane abruptly ends. The safest way to continue is to walk on the grass shoulder for about 600 feet, continue on the sidewalk for 600 feet, then you'll be at Chimney Park. The driveway in Chimney Park is rough, loose gravel for less than a quarter-mile stretch. Chimney Park is one of dog-friendly Portland's many off-leash dog parks, a fun spot to stop and watch the dogs romp around. A bridge over the railroad tracks connects you to Pier Park, an expansive forested park that features an extensive and popular disc golf course.

The route takes you past Cathedral Park, with dramatic views of the majestic St. Johns Bridge that looms overhead. For extra points and extra mileage, you can ride down to the water and hang out at the park, but it is a steep climb back out. You might prefer to appreciate the view from up top.

Bike Shops

Kenton Cycle Repair: 2020 N McClellan St., Portland, OR 97217; (503) 208-3446; kentoncyclepdx.com
Block Bikes: 7238 N Burlington Ave., Portland, OR 97203; (503) 819-6839; blockbikespdx.com

You'll exit St. Johns onto Willamette Boulevard, a lovely winding road. Cathedral Coffee (mile 14.0) makes for a nice stop along the way. Willamette Boulevard winds along the Willamette Bluffs, which overlook Swan Island, home to many of Portland's industrial operations and the site of Portland's first airport. You'll also glimpse spectacular river views, the cityscape, and the West Hills of Portland. If the timing works out right, this stretch is best ridden at dusk (with bike lights brightly flashing at the front and rear of your bike), as the sun goes down and the city begins to light up. This is one of the best nighttime views of Portland.

Finish in the cute neighborhood of historic Kenton for post-ride drinks and tasty food. As you wander around this fun neighborhood, look for the gigantic Paul Bunyan statue on North Interstate Avenue—a popular spot to snap a photo. Your journey ends back at Kenton Park.

MILES AND DIRECTIONS

0.0 Start on the north end of Kenton Park on N Brandon Street at N Argyle Street. Turn right on N Argyle Street.

0.2 Turn left on N Denver Avenue.

0.5 Make a slight right onto the Schmeer Road bikeway and loop under N Denver Avenue on the bike route.

2

0.7   Turn left onto the Columbia Slough Trail.

2.4   Continue north on the Columbia Slough Trail as it parallels N Portland Road/Swift Highway.

3.1   Cross N Portland Road/Swift Highway with caution, and continue past the gates to stay on the trail.

3.5   You can't swim in Smith and Bybee Lakes, but there is an optional walk down the boat launch path (500 feet) for a spectacular view of Smith Lake teeming with birds. Bring your bike with you.

4.4   Continue through Smith and Bybee Lakes Wetlands Natural Area to the broad sidewalk along the south side of Marine Drive.

6.4   Cross Marine Drive and enter Kelley Point Park.

6.9   Turn left into the parking lot and stay left to enter the trail through the gate. Loop around the park on the trail. (**Option:** The mileage for this route includes a ride through the park on the pathway. You can also explore the waterfront by walking along the beach; simply head down any one of the access paths on your left. If you don't want to bring your bike with you on the sand, lock it up securely in the parking lot before you reach the park trail.)

7.9   Continue onto the main park road to exit the park.

8.6   Turn right onto Marine Drive.

8.8   You will see a left turn lane for bikes. Cross Marine Drive and turn right onto the sidewalk path.

11.0   Continue straight at the stoplight to continue onto N Columbia Boulevard. (**Note:** Just after the intersection, the bike lane abruptly ends. Move your bike onto the grassy shoulder and walk 500 feet to the entrance of the park.)

11.3   Enter Chimney Park and follow the park driveway past the gates onto the gravel. Watch out for loose gravel on this rutty road.

11.6   Take the pedestrian overpass bridge and continue on the smooth bike path to the Pier Park entrance and restrooms.

11.9   At the edge of the park, turn left onto N James Street.

12.1   Turn right on N Reno Avenue and continue through the school lot to stay on Reno.

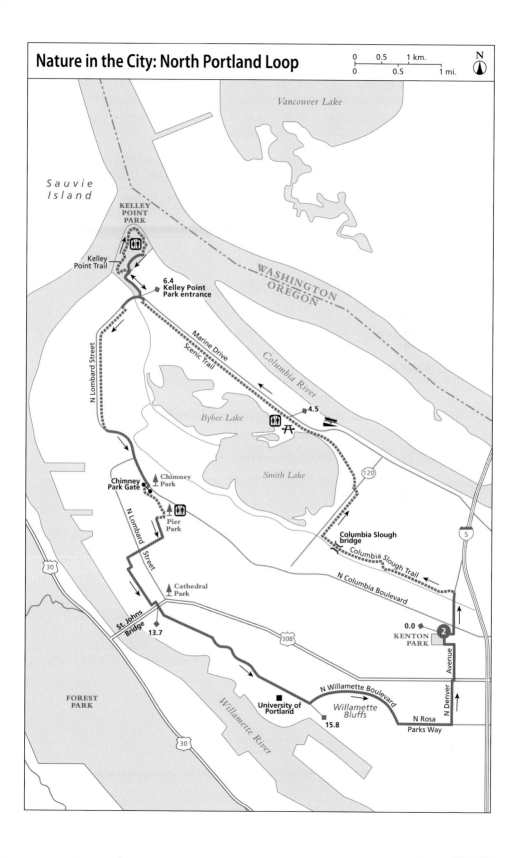

Nature in the City: North Portland Loop

0   0.5   1 km.
0   0.5   1 mi.

N

Vancouver Lake

Sauvie Island

KELLEY POINT PARK

Kelley Point Trail

6.4 Kelley Point Park entrance

WASHINGTON
OREGON

Columbia River

Marine Drive Scenic Trail

4.5

Bybee Lake

Smith Lake

N Lombard Street

Chimney Park Gate

Chimney Park

Pier Park

(120)

(5)

Columbia Slough bridge

Columbia Slough Trail

N Lombard Street

N Columbia Boulevard

Cathedral Park

St. Johns Bridge

13.7

FOREST PARK

(30)

(30)

(30B)

Willamette River

University of Portland

15.8

N Willamette Boulevard

Willamette Bluffs

N Rosa Parks Way

0.0

2

KENTON PARK

N Denver Avenue

12.6 Turn left onto N Willamette Boulevard.

12.7 Turn left onto N Edison St. This road will take you to the top of Cathedral Park. From the top of the park, ride under the bridge up the hill to meet back up with N Willamette Boulevard.

13.3 Turn right on N Willamette Boulevard. You will stay on Willamette for a while. Enjoy the view along the Willamette Bluffs, a high area overlooking Swan Island, the river, downtown Portland, and the West Hills. This is a busy road with a bike path that's well used by other cyclists. Use caution if you stop to take a photo (which you should!).

16.7 Continue onto N Rosa Parks Way.

17.3 Turn right onto N Denver Avenue.

18.2 Turn left onto N McClellan Street.

18.4 Finish your ride back at Kenton Park.

RIDE INFORMATION

Local Events/Attractions

Paul Bunyan Statue: N Interstate Avenue just before it intersects Denver. The towering statue is a popular spot to take photos.

Kenton Farmers Market: Fridays from 3 p.m. to 7 p.m. The market runs June 5 to Sept. 25 and is located at N McClellan Street and N Denver Avenue; portland farmersmarket.org.

Restrooms

Restrooms are located at the ride's start and finish in Kenton Park; at mile 3.8 (Smith and Bybee Lakes); at miles 7.4 and 7.8 (Kelley Point Park); and at mile 11.9 (Pier Park).

3

Marine Drive Bike Path

Located along NE Marine Drive, this route follows a paved bike path along the shores of the Columbia River. You can enjoy river scenery, views of Mount Hood, and watch planes take off and land at the Portland airport. You will also see a variety of wildlife on this urban tour, including great blue herons and osprey.

Start: M. James Gleason Memorial Boat Ramp off NE Marine Drive

Length: 15.0 miles out and back

Approximate riding time: 1.5 to 2.5 hours with stops

Best bike: Road bike or mountain bike

Terrain and trail surface: Paved multiuse path and bike path along NE Marine Drive

Traffic and hazards: Heavy commuter traffic on NE Marine Drive

Things to see: Views of the Columbia River and Mount Hood; Portland International Airport; and wildlife viewing

Map: USGS Camas

Getting There: By car: From the intersection of I-5 north and I-84 in Portland, travel north for 5.0 miles and take exit #307 for Marine Drive/Delta Park. Continue 0.4 mile, then go right and follow signs toward Marine Drive East. At the end of the off-ramp, turn left toward Marine Drive East. Follow Marine Drive east for 2.9 miles to the M. James Gleason Memorial Boat Ramp located on the left side of the road. GPS: N45 36.029' / W122 37.077'

THE RIDE

This route is part of a 40-mile loop that connects parks and green spaces in Portland. The Olmsted Brothers, well-known landscape architects, originally proposed the 40-mile loop in 1903. In a report to the Portland Parks and Recreation board, the Olmsteds said, "Parks should be connected and approached by boulevards and parkways . . . they should be located and improved to take advantage of beautiful natural scenery. The above system of scenic reservations, parks and parkways and connecting boulevards would . . . form an admirable park system for such an important city as Portland is bound to become." This original trail idea has been expanded, and when completed a network of more than 140 miles will connect more than thirty Portland parks and green spaces.

The scenic Columbia River is host to an abundance of wildlife and, at 1,243 miles, is the longest river in the Pacific Northwest region. PHOTO BY LIZANN DUNEGAN

Osprey nests are a common sight on this route during the spring and summer months.
PHOTO BY LIZANN DUNEGAN

This route starts at the M. James Gleason Memorial Boat Ramp, which has water and restrooms. Follow the paved path that starts in the southeast edge of the parking area.

The trail parallels the majestic Columbia River, which flows west until it reaches Hayden Island in North Portland, where it turns north. The river then continues northward to join the Willamette River at the southern tip of Sauvie Island, located 10 miles north of Portland off US 30. From that point the river travels in a northwest direction for 80 miles to Astoria, where it empties into the Pacific Ocean.

As you ride you'll see fishing boats and sailboats navigating the river. This is the most heavily fished section of the Columbia River, and spring Chinook salmon and sturgeon are the main catch. You will also mostly likely see great blue herons fishing in the shallow waters near the shore. Osprey are

Bike Shops

Community Cycling Center: 1700 NE Alberta St., Portland, OR 97211; (503) 288-8864; communitycyclingcenter .org

Upcycles: 909 NE Dekum St., Portland, OR 97211; (503) 388-0305; upcyclespdx.com

Marine Drive Bike Path

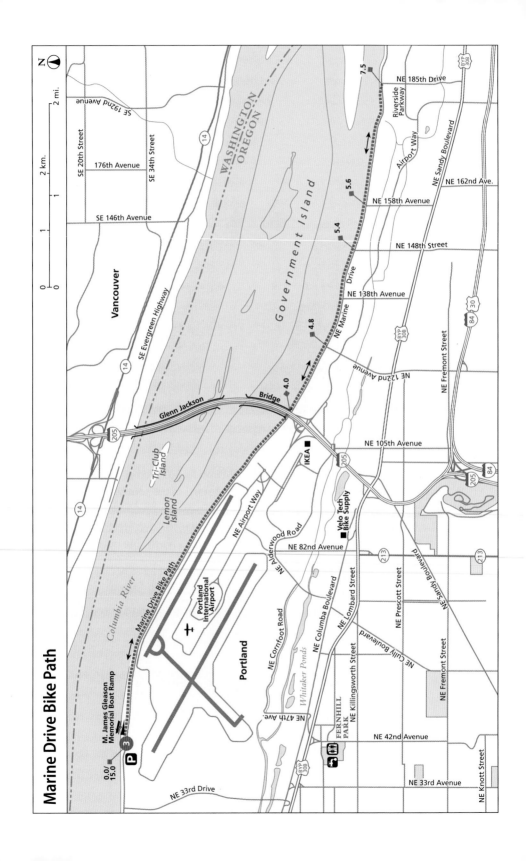

another common sight. In the spring and summer months, look for nesting platforms on the electrical towers that parallel NE Marine Drive.

MILES AND DIRECTIONS

0.0 Start at the M. James Gleason Memorial Boat Ramp by following the paved sidewalk located in the southeast corner of the parking lot until it intersects with the Marine Drive paved path. Turn left (east) and follow the paved path as it parallels the Columbia River.

3.2 Arrive at a trail junction. Continue to the left. The trail that goes right takes you to the Portland International Airport and Gresham.

4.0 Cross NE Marine Drive using the crosswalk and continue riding on the paved bike path on the other side of NE Marine Drive.

4.8 Cross NE 122nd Avenue and continue on the paved bike path that parallels NE Marine Drive.

5.4 Continue straight and cross 148th Avenue, staying on the paved bike path.

5.6 Cross NE Marine Drive and continue on the paved bike path.

7.5 The paved bike path ends. This is your turnaround point. Retrace the same route back to your starting point.

15.0 Arrive back at the M. James Gleason Memorial Boat Ramp.

RIDE INFORMATION

Local Events/Attractions
Providence Bridge Pedal: 1631 NE Klickitat St., Portland, OR 97212; (503) 281-9198; blog.bridgepedal.com. This annual event (held in mid-Aug) is a noncompetitive bike ride crossing Portland's historic bridges: Morrison, Sellwood, Hawthorne, Ross Island, Marquam, Burnside, Broadway, Steel, St. Johns, and Fremont.

Restrooms
Restrooms are available at the start/finish of the ride at M. James Gleason Memorial Boat Ramp.

Two States, Two Bridges

Vancouver, Washington, is a city unto its own in an entirely different state, but it is also very much a suburb of Portland—just 10 miles away from downtown Portland. Vancouver residents work and play in Portland, constantly crossing over the wide Columbia River on one of two elevated interstate bridges, the I-5 Bridge and the Glenn Jackson Bridge (I-205). As you cross from one state to the other on these towering bridges, high above the world, you'll have a bird's eye view of both cities and sweeping views of the river.

Start: Woodlawn Park on NE Dekum Street at NE Claremont Street

Length: 22.0-mile loop

Approximate riding time: About 3 hours

Best bike: Road bike or hybrid

Terrain and trail surface: Paved city streets

Traffic and hazards: This is a low traffic route with safe street crossings. The I-5 Bridge sidewalk is narrow with guardrails on either side. Ride at a slow pace so you maintain control of your bike.

Things to see: Vancouver Land Bridge; Fort Vancouver; Renaissance Trail; Stanger House; Jane Weber Evergreen Arboretum; historic Evergreen Highway; Glenn Jackson Bridge bike crossing; broad Columbia River views

Map: USGS Portland

Getting There: By car: From downtown Portland, head north on I-5 for 7.0 miles. Take exit 305A and continue east on North Lombard Street. Turn right on NE 11th Avenue, which brings you to Woodlawn Park. Park anywhere on the street along the park, then head south one block along Claremont Avenue (the small bridge over the park) to begin your ride on the south end of the park, on NE Claremont Avenue where it intersects NE Dekum Avenue. Parking is free with no restrictions.

4

By public transportation: Take the number 8 bus north and get off on NE Dekum Avenue at the Claremont stop. This intersection is the start of the ride. GPS: N45 34.308' / W122 39.256'

THE RIDE

This ride begins in the quirky, historic Woodlawn neighborhood, where diagonal streets, originally oriented to a long-defunct streetcar line, create intriguing blocks and the "Dekum Triangle" commercial district. Food and drink options abound in this tightly knit, burgeoning neighborhood. There are few amenities along this ride.

The I-5 Bridge spans the mighty Columbia River, connecting Oregon to Washington.
PHOTO BY AYLEEN CROTTY

At the beginning of this ride, travel along Vancouver Avenue, then Vancouver Way, as you wind your way to Vancouver—a relatively easy route to remember! An intentionally designed pathway assists cyclists in crossing the first stretch of the Columbia River to Jantzen Beach, a shopping district (technically an island) and residential area packed with big box stores and chain restaurants. Carefully follow the bike directional signs "To Vancouver," and it's an easy approach to the I-5 Bridge.

A somewhat steep incline along a narrow but safe sidewalk brings you to the apex of the I-5 Bridge, with striking views of the Columbia River from up high. Stop for photos and to take in the sights. As you descend the bridge, use caution and maintain a comfortable speed, as the sidewalk is narrow and several gates jut out into the walkway, making for a tight squeeze in a few places.

Bike Shops

Upcycles: 900 NE Dekum St., Portland, OR 97211; (503) 388-0305; upcyclespdx.com

Velotech (parts, apparel, and accessories only; no repairs services): 5741 NE 87th Ave., Portland, OR 97220; (503) 342-9981; velotech.com

Once you exit the bridge, quickly jump onto the Discovery Historic Loop, a pathway leading through Fort Vancouver. The first section of this path is the Land Bridge, an impressive feat of engineering that connects Fort Vancouver to the Columbia River to offer the same access once traveled by native people. The route creates a safe and serene passage over both the busy WA 14 highway and train tracks. As you enter the Land Bridge, pause to take in the gorgeous welcome gate designed by Native American artist Lillian Pitt.

The route winds through Fort Vancouver, a 366-acre national historic site where most of the attractions are free. Stop into the visitor center for more information about the historic site's features.

Continue on the pathway through the Fort Vancouver property and you'll arrive at WA 14 again. This crossing isn't nearly as pleasant as the Land Bridge, so follow the pedestrian signage for safest way to navigate this congested area.

Turn left onto Columbia Way to begin your tour of the Renaissance Trail, an easy, flat, 5.0-mile trail that parallels the Columbia River. This off-the-road trail begins as a wide sidewalk along the road, then tucks into the trees. The Renaissance Trail comes to an end at Wintler Park, a relaxing beach spot with picnic tables and restrooms. This is a nice stopping point along the ride, where you can dip your toes in the river, go for a swim, catch glimpses of osprey soaring overhead, and take in the view.

A brief and intense climb from sea level brings you up to the historic Evergreen Highway, a wonderful road with very little traffic that parallels the Columbia River. Architecture buffs will delight in the varied older home styles. This beloved neighborhood features mostly older homes with some lots being newly developed. The residents work in harmony to preserve their historic neighborhood, and have recently raised funds to expand the Renaissance Trail along the Evergreen Highway. When complete, this will be a spectacular way to pedal all the way from I-5 to I-205 along a river-view trail. Take your time and look closely: Some of the most intriguing structures are hidden in the trees.

The celebrated Stanger House, the oldest residential structure in Clark County, is situated along Evergreen Highway. Stop to tour the expansive Jane Weber Evergreen Arboretum, and to view the notable Stanger House.

Eventually you'll reach the Glenn Jackson Memorial Bridge, where I-205 crosses the mighty Columbia River. The bridge is named for Glenn Jackson, a

A view of the unique Glenn Jackson Bridge bike path, situated in the very center of I-205.
PHOTO BY AYLEEN CROTTY

businessman and influential transportation planner affectionately known as Mr. Oregon. A unique multiuse path allows cyclists and pedestrians to safely cross this busy interstate bridge. As you climb the hill to approach the bridge, it seems as though the pathway is bound for the woods, but as it continues to ascend, the trail eventually emerges in the very middle of I-205, with four lanes of traffic barreling by in either direction. Concrete walls with guardrails and wide shoulders keep you safely separated from the traffic, but this is certainly a crossing you'll remember forever. This stretch of your ride is extremely loud, especially in contrast to the serenity of the historic Evergreen Highway behind, but 1.5-mile, flat, smooth passage goes by surprisingly quickly.

You'll exit on the Oregon side and meander along NE Alderwood Road near the Portland International Airport, as planes soar overhead. For a portion of your ride you'll be on NE Cornfoot Road, with no shoulder but limited traffic. The cars move at a moderate pace and it's a safe road, but you'll still want to ensure you ride on the far right to allow ample room for cars to pass.

From NE Cornfoot Road, you will turn onto NE 47th Avenue and pass by Whitaker Ponds Natural Area (mile 17.3), an access point to the Columbia Slough waterway and a serene stopping point. Be sure to check out the lovely gazebo, covered in a roof made of living plants. The two ponds are surrounded by a black cottonwood forest that has been enhanced over the years to include thousands of native plants. A wildflower meadow flourishes near the park entrance, an important source of habitat for local pollinators. The Lewis and Clark Garden, near the gazebo, highlights plant communities from the western United States.

A short hill brings you up to NE 42nd Avenue, and then onto quiet residential NE Holman Street, your route back into the historic Woodlawn neighborhood, where plenty of food and drink options will provide respite after this fantastic ride. You'll end at Woodlawn Park, where the ride started.

MILES AND DIRECTIONS

0.0 Head west on NE Dekum Avenue.

0.7 Turn right on NE Vancouver Avenue.

1.8 Turn right onto NE Vancouver Way.

3.4 Turn left onto N Marine Way.

3.5 Enter the multiuse path on your right. You will see freeway exit traffic; stay to the right for the path. Follow the path signs for Vancouver, and wind your way around the cloverleaf and onto the overpass.

Two States, Two Bridges

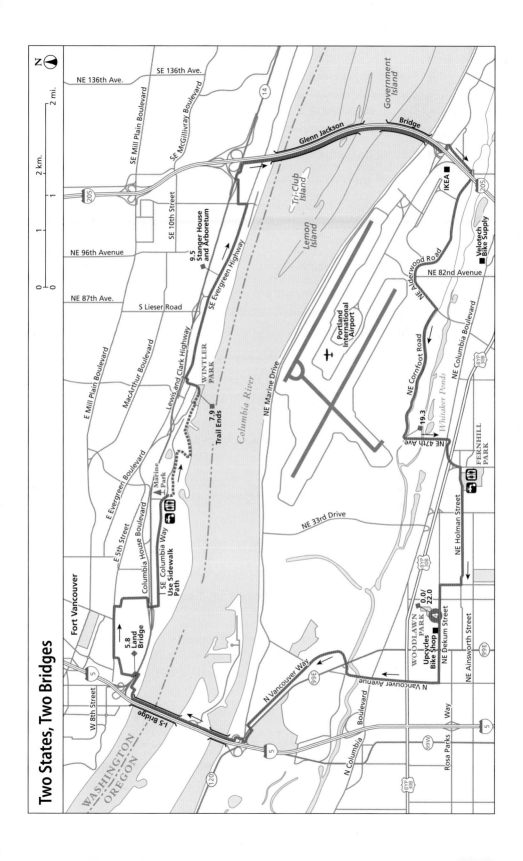

4.4 At the sidewalk curb cut, carefully cross N Tomahawk Island Drive to continue on the road toward the bridge. Follow the bike directional signs to Vancouver. At the next intersection, cross the road toward the bridge. Follow the path up onto the bridge and head across the river.

5.3 Take the first path exit to the right off the bridge.

5.5 Turn left onto Columbia Way.

5.6 Turn left onto the path under the train tracks. Follow the sign to Fort Vancouver and the Land Bridge. Continue on the path, staying right the entire time.

6.3 Turn right onto E 5th Street.

6.8 Just after S Street, turn right onto the path and continue to WA 14, a busy highway. (***Note:*** Use the pedestrian crossing to safely make your way to SE Columbia Way.)

7.5 Turn left onto SE Columbia Way and use the wide sidewalk path.

8.7 At Marine Park Way, turn right and onto the multiuse path. Continue on this path along the river until you reach Wintler Park. Continue through Wintler Park until the path ends.

10.3 Turn left toward SE Topper Drive.

10.4 Turn left onto SE Topper Drive.

10.4 Continue onto SE Chelsea Avenue.

10.6 Turn right onto SE Evergreen Highway.

12.6 Turn left onto SE Ellsworth Road.

12.7 Turn right onto SE 23rd Street.

13.0 Turn left to enter the I-205 multiuse path. Cross over the Columbia River on I-205.

15.7 Pass the path exit to Airport Way Northbound.

16.2 Turn right on NE Alderwood Road.

17.9 Turn right onto NE Cornfoot Road.

19.3 Turn left onto NE 47th Avenue.

19.9 Cross NE Columbia Boulevard; the road continues as NE 42nd Avenue.

20.3 Turn right onto NE Holman Street.

21.8 Turn right onto NE 13th Avenue.

22.0 Turn left onto NE Dekum Street.

22.0 Arrive back at Woodlawn Park.

RIDE INFORMATION

Local Events/Attractions

Fort Vancouver: 750 Anderson St., Vancouver, WA; (360) 816-6230; fortvan .org. This ride takes you through the heart of Fort Vancouver, built in 1825 by England's Hudson's Bay Company. Later, the US Army built an outpost by Fort Vancouver to protect settlers who followed the Oregon Trail to its end on the river. The fort also became an important sawmill site during World War I. Today, you can tour an interpretive center and other attractions. Access to the park is free, but there is a fee to enter the reconstructed fort.

Free Summer Concert Series: July through Aug on Wed from noon to 1 p.m. and Thurs from 6 to 8 p.m. at Esther Short Park, 415 W 6th St. in Vancouver; and on Sun from 1 to 3 p.m. at the Columbia Tech Center, 1498 SE Tech Center Dr. in Vancouver; (360) 487-8630; cityofvancouver.us/parksrec/page/special-events.

Jane Weber Evergreen Arboretum: 9215 SE Evergreen Hwy., Vancouver, WA; theintertwine.org/parks/jane-weber-evergreen-arboretum. This is the site of the historic Stanger House, the oldest home in Clark County. The house was built in 1867 and is an example of Pioneer Plank construction. The arboretum is open to the public, with no fee. When groundskeepers are present, they will occasionally offer impromptu tours. The site is managed by Washington State Parks and maintained by volunteers. The arboretum and home are both part of a long-range plan to restore the property and make it a significant historical attraction.

Woodlawn Farmers Market: Sat from 10 a.m. to 3 p.m., 7200 NE 11th Ave., Portland, OR; (614) 361-3027; facebook.com/woodlawnneighborhoodfarmers market.

Restrooms

Water is available at the ride's start/finish at Woodlawn Park, and restrooms are available in the summer. Restrooms are also available at mile 8.7 (Marine Park); at mile 10.3 (Wintler Park); and at mile 20.5 (Fernhill Park).

Saltzman Road and the Majestic St. Johns Bridge

Forest Park is a lush, 5,000-acre network of dense forest located on the west side of Portland, just on the edge of the city. Most of the trails are closed to cycling, but Saltzman Road is a gorgeous and fortunate exception. The floor of the steep trail is old pavement that has been covered with hard-pack pea gravel, making for very easy gravel riding. Forest Park is stunning year-round, but Saltzman Road is especially picturesque in the fall, when leaves gently blanket the trail and autumnal tones paint a colorful landscape. This route also includes a thrilling descent and a ride over the towering St. Johns Bridge. On the weekends, Saltzman Road can be crowded with a mix of trail users, so head out on a weekday if you want to have more of the trail to yourself.

Start: Southwest corner of the St. Johns Plaza at N Lombard Street and Philadelphia Avenue

Length: 16.9-mile lollipop

Approximate riding time: 1.5 to 3 hours

Best bike: Road bike with wide tires, hybrid, or mountain bike

Terrain and trail surface: A mix of smooth pavement and hard-packed gravel that's easy to ride on

Traffic and hazards: Mostly low- or no-traffic routes except for a few miles along US 30, which is busy but has a very wide shoulder. Newberry Road is a steep, winding descent. Saltzman Road is crowded with hikers and dogs on the weekends.

Things to see: River views; Douglas fir, western hemlock, and western red cedar; Oregon grape; abundant wildlife; birds; and gigantic sword fern

Maps: USGS Portland; Metro Bike There! map

Getting There: By car: From downtown Portland, take I-405 north to US 30 toward Saint Helens. Turn left onto NW Bridge Avenue to approach the St. Johns Bridge. Continue onto N Philadelphia Avenue. At N Lombard Street, turn left and look for parking. Your ride begins from southwest corner of the St. Johns Plaza at N Lombard Street and N Philadelphia Avenue. Head southwest on N Philadelphia to being riding.

By public transportation: From downtown Portland, take bus 16 or 44 to St. Johns. Get off at N Lombard and N Burlington, and walk across the street to the St. Johns Plaza at N Lombard and N Philadelphia. GPS: N45 35.405' / W122 45.308'

THE RIDE

This ride begins in St. Johns, a peninsula of land formed by the confluence of the Willamette and Columbia Rivers. This section of Portland was originally

The majestic St. Johns Bridge is your gateway to Forest Park. PHOTO BY AYLEEN CROTTY

an independent city, and joined with Portland in 1915. To this day, St. Johns maintains a distinct feel and unique identity within Portland.

You'll depart St. Johns and ride over the Willamette River over the St. Johns Bridge, which features dramatic Gothic supports that frame a view into Forest Park, your main destination on this ride. You can ride on the road or on the sidewalk, depending on your comfort level with traffic.

Bike Shop

Block Bikes: 7238 N Burlington Ave., Portland, OR 97203; (503) 819-6839; blockbikespdx.com

From the bridge, ride downhill on US 30 until you reach Saltzman Road, an unassuming road in an industrial area. The initial section of Saltzman leads to isolated homes tucked into the hillside, and it's here that you begin your climb. Eventually the road peters out and is closed to motorized traffic, but continues as a paved and gravel trail through Forest Park.

The lush, forested trail is a mellow and rewarding uphill climb. PHOTO BY AYLEEN CROTTY

Forest Park is one of Portland's most treasured areas, a protected forested land that reflects Portland's love of the outdoors. It is one of the largest urban forests in the United States, and features second-growth and old-growth forest, and 70 miles of recreational trails. Shade-loving plants flourish under the lush canopy of Douglas fir, western hemlock, and western red cedar.

The entirety of your ride along Saltzman Road is an incline for 3.5 miles, with grades averaging 3.5 to 5 percent, making for a slow and steady climb with very few intense switchbacks. You will encounter downhill cyclists and some hikers and runners, but for the most part you will be treated to a solitude that seems impossibly tranquil given your proximity to the city. Branches crack in the distance as the abundant wildlife moves through their home, and birds soar overhead. Saltzman Road is a heavenly opportunity to relax your mind and soak in the scents and sights of the forest while working your muscles.

Saltzman Road exits Forest Park at NW Skyline Boulevard, a lovely winding road that snakes along a ridge of the West Hills of Portland. Turn north and work your way toward NW Newberry Road, a steep, sharply winding descent that brings you back down to the Willamette River. Newberry is a fast road, with downhill grades of, at times, 10 to 12 percent. Ride cautiously, at a speed where you always feel in control of your bike. Some of the turns are tight, and it's best to approach them at a slower speed than you might imagine. As you feel comfortable descending, open up your ride a little and enjoy that downhill—you certainly earned it! Newberry comes out at US 30, and you'll have a broad shoulder to ride on, traveling alongside busy traffic for a few miles before climbing back up to the St. Johns Bridge and returning to the plaza where the ride started.

MILES AND DIRECTIONS

0.0   Head southwest on N Philadelphia Avenue.

0.5   Continue onto NW St. Johns Bridge.

0.9   Continue onto NW Bridge Avenue.

1.5   Make a slight right onto NW Saint Helens Road/US 30.

2.6   Turn right onto NW Saltzman Road.

6.4   Turn right onto NW Skyline Boulevard.

10.9   Turn right onto NW Newberry Road.

13.0   Turn right onto NW Saint Helens Road/US 30.

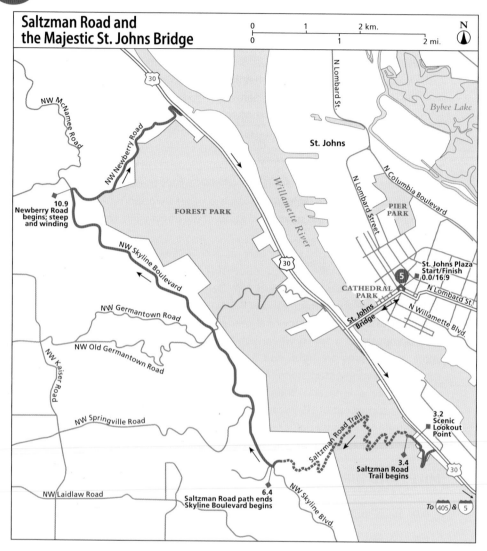

Saltzman Road and the Majestic St. Johns Bridge

0   1   2 km.
0   1   2 mi.

N

NW McNamee Road

NW Newberry Road

30

N Lombard St.

Bybee Lake

St. Johns

N Columbia Boulevard

10.9
Newberry Road
begins; steep
and winding

FOREST PARK

Willamette River

N Lombard Street

PIER
PARK

NW Skyline Boulevard

NW Germantown Road

30

St. Johns Plaza
Start/Finish
0.0/16.9

NW Old Germantown Road

CATHEDRAL
PARK

N Lombard St.

NW Kaiser Road

St. Johns
Bridge

N Willamette Blvd.

NW Springville Road

3.2
Scenic
Lookout
Point

Saltzman Road Trail

NW Laidlaw Road

3.4
Saltzman Road
Trail begins

6.4
Saltzman Road path ends
Skyline Boulevard begins

NW Skyline Blvd.

30

To 405 & 5

15.6   Turn right onto NW Bridge Avenue.

16.0   Turn left onto the St. Johns Bridge.

16.4   Continue onto N Philadelphia Avenue.

16.9   Arrive back at St. Johns Plaza.

RIDE INFORMATION

Local Events/Attractions

Cathedral Park: Located under the St. Johns Bridge along the east side of the Willamette River, this park is a pretty and relaxing spot to enjoy looking out over the river.

St. Johns Farmers Market: Open Sat from 9 a.m. to 2 p.m. in St. Johns Plaza, located on N Philadelphia Avenue between N Lombard and N Ivanhoe Streets. The market runs May 30 through Oct 24.

St. Johns Parade: This parade takes place on the second Sat in May, beginning at noon. The St. Johns Parade has been a tradition in the North Portland area since 1962, and every year some forty to sixty groups are showcased at this festival event.

Restrooms

There are no designated public restrooms on this ride.

Leif Erikson Drive

This route takes you on a 16.0-mile out-and-back section of Leif Erikson Drive, a gravel multiuse trail that journeys through Portland's famous 5,000-acre Forest Park. You will pedal within a landscape of shady big-leaf maple and alder trees carpeted with sword fern, Oregon grape, and red elderberry. Along the way there are viewpoints from which you can see the Columbia River and downtown Portland.

Start: The end of NW Thurman Drive in Northwest Portland

Length: 16.0 miles out and back (with longer options)

Approximate riding time: 3.5 to 5 hours with stops

Best bike: Mountain bike or road bike with wide tires

Terrain and trail surface: Multiuse gravel road

Traffic and hazards: This route can be very crowded on the weekends with walkers, runners, and dogs.

Things to see: Views of the Willamette River and downtown Portland; deciduous forest, wildflowers, and wildlife

Maps: USGS Portland; Metro Bike There! map

Getting There : By car: From I-405 northbound in Portland, take the US 30 West–Saint Helens exit (exit 3). At the end of the off-ramp, stay in the right lane, which turns into NW Vaughn Street. At the first stoplight, turn left on NW 23rd Avenue. Go one block and turn right onto NW Thurman Street. Continue 1.4 miles to the end of the road and park near the green metal gate. Leif Erikson Drive starts at the gate. GPS: N45 32.368' / W122 43.489'

THE RIDE

There aren't many city parks where you can pedal through a 5,000-acre forest that is home to more than sixty-two species of mammals and 112 species of birds. But, as one of the largest city parks in the world, Portland's Forest Park is one such place. Thanks should go to those who lived in Portland at the turn of the century, and who had the foresight to secure what is today a wonderful park system enjoyed by mountain bikers, runners, and hikers alike.

Forest Park is part of a forested ridge local Native Americans referred to as "Tualatin Mountain." As settlements sprang up along the Willamette River and the west side of the mountain in the early 1800s, the original Indian routes over the mountain were improved and expanded. These improvements allowed farmers on the west side of Tualatin Mountain to take advantage of the export opportunities and expanding settlements along the Willamette River. It also allowed for extensive logging on the mountain. What was once an evergreen forest of Douglas fir, western hemlock, and western red cedar is now covered with a canopy of mostly red alder and big-leaf maple.

In the Olmsted report of 1903, John C. Olmsted, a landscape architect from Brookline, Massachusetts, recommended to the Municipal Park Commission of Portland that the woodlands of Tualatin Mountain be purchased for a public park. Unfortunately, between 1915 and 1931, the land became embroiled in shifty real estate schemes. As a result, more than 1,400 acres of residential lots were forfeited to the city of Portland and the additional land on Tualatin Mountain was acquired by Multnomah County due to delinquent taxes. No land was purchased for park use. Finally, in 1947 and 1948, Multnomah County and the city of Portland

A cyclist gets a good workout on Leif Erikson Drive.
PHOTO BY LIZANN DUNEGAN

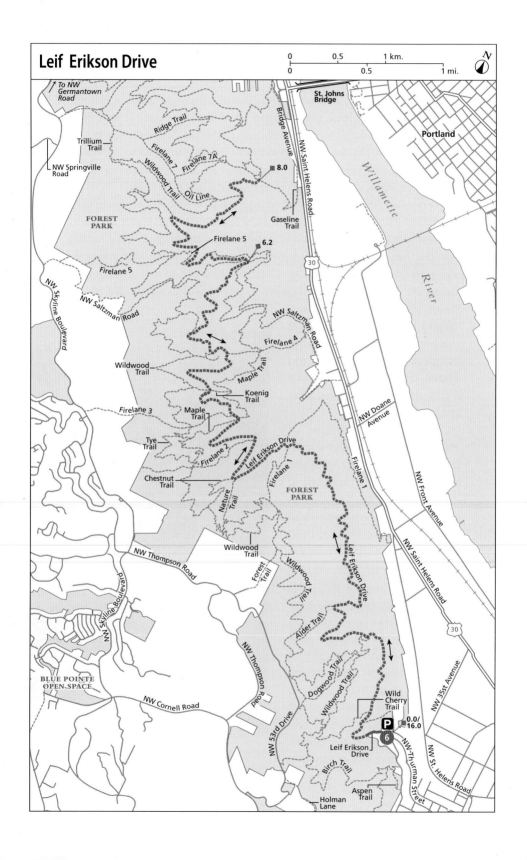

Leif Erikson Drive

0   0.5   1 km.

0   0.5   1 mi.

N

To NW
Germantown
Road

Ridge Trail

Trillium
Trail

Firelane 7

Firelane 7A

NW Springville
Road

Wildwood Trail

Oil Line

8.0

FOREST
PARK

Firelane 5

Gaseline
Trail

Firelane 5

6.2

NW Skyline Boulevard

NW Saltzman Road

NW Saltzman Road

Firelane 4

Wildwood
Trail

Maple Trail

Koenig
Trail

Firelane 3

Maple
Trail

Tye
Trail

Firelane 2

Leif Erikson Drive

Chestnut
Trail

Firelane 1

Firelane 1

NW Doane
Avenue

NW Front Avenue

NW Saint Helens Road

FOREST
PARK

Nature
Trail

Wildwood
Trail

Leif Erikson Drive

NW Thompson Road

Forest
Trail

Wildwood Trail

Alder Trail

NW Skyline Boulevard

BLUE POINTE
OPEN SPACE

NW Cornell Road

NW Thompson Road

NW 53rd Drive

Dogwood Trail

Wildwood Trail

Wild
Cherry
Trail

0.0/
16.0

P

6

Leif Erikson
Drive

NW Thurman Street

NW St. Helens Road

Birch Trail

Aspen
Trail

Holman
Lane

St. Johns
Bridge

Portland

Willamette

River

Bridge Avenue

NW Saint Helens Road

30

30

NW 35st Avenue

transferred 2,500 acres of this land back to the Portland Parks & Recreation department. Forest Park was then dedicated in September 1948.

This scenic ride takes you through a shady canopy of big-leaf maple and red alder trees. In the spring months, you can see trillium blooming along the roadside.

At 6.2 miles you arrive at the junction with NW Saltzman Road. Continue straight (right) on Leif Erikson Drive. You will notice that this section of the road is quieter and offers more solitude. Continue riding to the junction with Firelane 7, which is the turnaround point for this route. You have the option of continuing another 3.2 miles to the road's end at NW Germantown Road.

MILES AND DIRECTIONS

0.0 Start the ride by going around the green metal gate and riding on the doubletrack Leif Erikson Drive. There is a sign with a map of Forest Park trails and a drinking fountain just past the green gate on the right side of the road.

0.2 Pass a blue portable restroom on the right side of the road.

6.2 Arrive at a four-way intersection (NW Saltzman goes left). Continue straight (right) on Leif Erikson Drive.

8.0 Turn around at the junction with Firelane 7. You have the option of continuing another 3.2 miles to the road's end at NW Germantown Road.

16.0 Arrive back at the trailhead at NW Thurman Street.

RIDE INFORMATION

Local Events/Attractions
Providence Bridge Pedal: 1631 NE Klickitat St., Portland, OR 97212; (503) 281-9198; blog.bridgepedal.com. This annual event (held in mid-Aug) is a noncompetitive bike ride crossing Portland's historic bridges: Morrison, Sellwood, Hawthorne, Ross Island, Marquam, Burnside, Broadway, Steel, St. Johns, and Fremont.

Restrooms
There is a portable restroom available at mile 0.2.

Skyline Loop

This route takes you on a tour of scenic Skyline Boulevard, which winds northwest along the ridge crest of the Tualatin Mountains and offers magnificent views of the Tualatin Valley. This hilly ride will challenge you as it takes you past expensive executive homes in Portland's West Hills; through the great expanse of Forest Park; and then through a rural landscape filled with mature forests, century-old farms, vineyards, and agricultural crops.

Start: At the junction of SW Knights Boulevard and SW Kingston Boulevard

Length: 42.3-mile loop

Approximate riding time: 4 to 6 hours

Best bike: Road bike

Terrain and trail surface: Paved city streets

Traffic and hazards: Skyline Boulevard is a busy street with many blind curves and little or no shoulder. Some sections of Skyline Boulevard also have speed bumps. As you travel farther northwest on Skyline Boulevard, the route takes you into a more rural area and there aren't as many cars. Watch for traffic when you cross NW Cornelius Pass Road at 12.1 miles. Rock Creek Road is bumpy and has some potholes. At 13.1 miles you'll have to stop for a railroad crossing. There are no railroad traffic lights, so you need to rely on your own judgment to look for trains before crossing the tracks. The rest of the roads on this ride have little or no shoulder and light to moderate traffic (depending on the time of day). This ride is best completed at midday or on a weekend. Avoid this ride during morning and evening rush hours.

Things to see: Downtown Portland skyline; views of the Tualatin Valley, Mount Saint Helens, and Mount Hood; the Willamette River; the Oregon Zoo; Washington Park

Maps: USGS Linnton, Hillsboro, Dixie Mountain, and Portland

Getting There: From downtown Portland drive 1.8 miles west on US 26 toward Beaverton. Take exit 72 for the Oregon Zoo and the World Forestry Center. At the end of the off-ramp, turn right on SW Knights Boulevard and drive through the Oregon Zoo parking area. After 0.4 mile you'll pass the World Forestry Center on your left. At 0.6 mile turn right into a parking area directly across from the Vietnam Memorial, at the intersection of SW Knights Boulevard and SW Kingston Boulevard. There is a fee to park at this location. GPS: N45 30.778' / W122 43.020'

THE RIDE

The ride starts by meandering through the green expanse of 332-acre Washington Park, which is crisscrossed with hiking trails that wind through a lush, fern-filled forest. This park was established in 1871 and was originally only 40 acres. Over the years, adjacent lands were purchased until it reached its present size.

After almost a mile of climbing, turn northwest onto Skyline Boulevard. This twisty road snakes along the crest of the Tualatin Mountains, which run in a northwest direction separating Portland and the Willamette River to the east from the Tualatin Valley to the west. As you pedal on this winding road, you'll have many opportunities to stop and admire the views to the southwest of the Chehalem Mountains and the Tualatin Valley.

At the 2.0-mile mark, you'll pass Willamette Stone State Park, located on the west side of Skyline Boulevard. This 1.6-acre park has a small monument commemorating the important surveying point where the Willamette meridian and the Willamette baseline meet. This site was the origin for sectioning all of the land in Oregon and Washington.

> **Bike Shops**
>
> **Bike Gallery:** 1001 SW 10th Ave., Portland, OR 97205; (503) 222-3821; bikegallery.com
> **21st Avenue Bicycles:** 916 NW 21st Ave., Portland, OR 97209; (503) 222-2851; 21stbikes.com

As you continue riding on Skyline Boulevard, pass the great expanse of Forest Park to the east. Originally, Native Americans established routes over this vast ridge. As the area around Portland was settled these routes were improved, allowing settlers on the east side of Tualatin Mountain an easier passage to bring their goods to the growing city of Portland. Skyline Boulevard was a result of this expansion.

Beautiful fall foliage appears in Washington Park. PHOTO BY LIZANN DUNEGAN

Continue pedaling northwest on Skyline Boulevard until you reach the 12.1-mile mark, where you'll cross busy NW Cornelius Pass Road. As you continue heading northwest, the landscape opens up and becomes more rural. At 12.4 miles, turn onto NW Rock Creek Road. The road surface starts out a bit rough and you'll have to dodge some potholes. This road takes you on a roller-coaster descent through a forested canyon, and past several small farms where you might see horses, sheep, or cattle grazing. After the descent be ready for some steep climbing back to NW Skyline Boulevard at 17.7 miles.

The rest of this route has many steep ups and downs as it winds through rural Helvetia hill country. This countryside is filled with century-old farms, wineries, and elaborate homes. Just past 27 miles you'll pass Helvetia Tavern, a highly recommended local watering hole. This tavern serves delicious hamburgers and homemade fries. If you want to check out another local hangout, pedal a half-mile farther and stop at Rock Creek Tavern.

After you've had a chance to check out the local color, pedal back up to Skyline Boulevard and return to your starting point.

MILES AND DIRECTIONS

0.0 Start by turning right out of the parking area onto SW Knights Boulevard. The route winds through Washington Park.

0.3 At the T intersection turn left onto SW Fairview Boulevard.

0.9 Turn right onto SW Skyline Boulevard.

1.4 At the T intersection turn left onto West Burnside.

1.6 At the Y intersection stay to the right, following the signs for NW Skyline Boulevard.

2.0 Pass Willamette Stone State Park on your left. Watch for speed bumps over the next 0.5 mile.

3.3 At the four-way intersection and stop sign, go straight (crossing NW Cornell Road) and continue on NW Skyline Boulevard. If you want to stop for some good burgers and shakes, Skyline Restaurant is located on your left at this intersection.

4.2 At the four-way intersection and stop sign, go straight (crossing NW Thompson Road) and continue on NW Skyline Boulevard.

5.4 Pass Skyline Memorial Gardens on your left. This is a good place to stop and admire the view of the Tualatin Valley to the west.

Skyline Loop

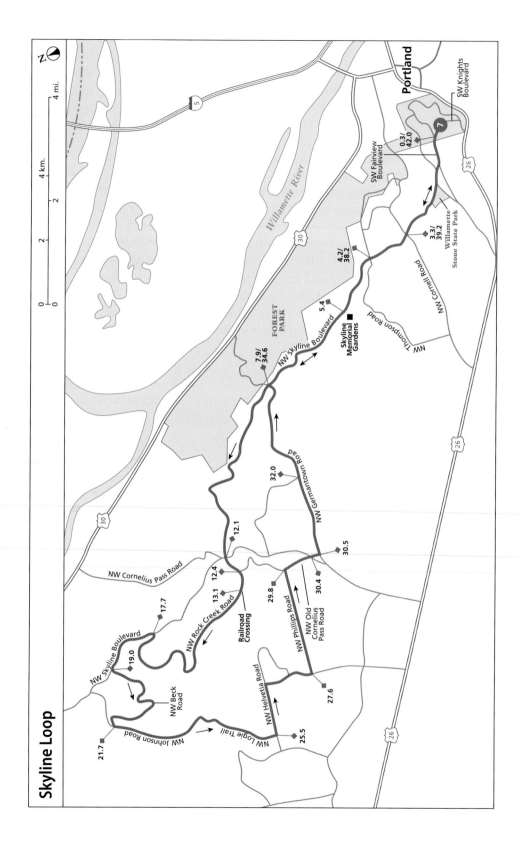

7.7   Pass Skyline Tavern on your left. This is one of many good local watering holes you'll discover on this route.

7.9   At the four-way intersection and stop sign, continue straight (crossing NW Germantown Road) on NW Skyline Boulevard.

12.1   At the four-way intersection and stop sign, continue straight (crossing NW Cornelius Pass Road). Be cautious of the heavy traffic on this road. After crossing the highway you'll come to a stop sign. Turn left onto NW Old Cornelius Pass Road.

12.4   At the Y intersection turn right onto NW Rock Creek Road. Note that this road is rough and has multiple potholes.

13.1   Stop for a railroad crossing.

16.8   At the Y intersection, go right and continue on NW Rock Creek Road.

17.7   At the T intersection and stop sign, turn left onto NW Skyline Boulevard.

19.0   Turn left onto NW Beck Road.

21.7   At the T intersection and stop sign, turn left onto NW Johnson Road. Note that NW Johnson Road eventually turns into NW Logie Trail.

25.5   At the T intersection and stop sign, turn left onto NW Helvetia Road.

27.2   Pass Helvetia Tavern on the right.

27.6   Turn left onto NW Phillips Road.

29.8   At the next T intersection, turn right onto NW Old Cornelius Pass Road. Pass by Rock Creek Tavern at this intersection.

30.4   At the four-way intersection and stop sign, continue straight (crossing NW Cornelius Pass Road).

30.5   At the T intersection and stop sign, turn left onto NW Germantown Road.

32.0   At the four-way intersection and stop sign, continue straight on NW Germantown Road (crossing NW Kaiser Road).

34.6   At the four-way intersection and stoplight, turn right onto NW Skyline Boulevard.

38.2   At the four-way intersection and stop sign, continue straight on NW Skyline Boulevard (crossing NW Thompson Road).

39.2 At the four-way intersection and stop sign, continue straight on NW Skyline Boulevard (crossing NW Cornell Road).

40.9 At the Y intersection and stop sign, turn left onto West Burnside Street.

41.1 Turn left onto SW Skyline Boulevard.

41.7 Turn left onto SW Fairview Boulevard.

42.0 Turn right onto SW Knights Boulevard.

42.3 Turn left into the parking lot where the ride started.

RIDE INFORMATION

Local Events/Attractions:

Oregon Zoo: 4001 SW Canyon Rd., Portland, OR 97221; (503) 226-1561; oregonzoo.org. Visit the zoo and see a variety of animals in their natural environments.

Providence Bridge Pedal: 1631 NE Klickitat St., Portland, OR 97212; (503) 281-9198; blog.bridgepedal.com. This annual event (held in mid-Aug) is a noncompetitive bike ride crossing Portland's historic bridges: Morrison, Sellwood, Hawthorne, Ross Island, Marquam, Burnside, Broadway, Steel, St. Johns, and Fremont.

World Forestry Center: 4033 SW Canyon Rd., Portland, OR 97221; (503) 228-1367; worldforestry.org.

Restrooms

Restrooms are located at mile 7.7 (Skyline Tavern); at mile 27.2 (Helvetia Tavern); and at mile 29.8 (Rock Creek Tavern).

Heights of Portland: Washington Park to Council Crest

Washington Park is a 410-acre urban park connected to Portland's beloved Forest Park, creating a huge network of forested land. Nestled within the trees are many of Portland's favorite destinations: the Oregon Zoo, the International Rose Test Garden, the Portland Japanese Garden, the World Forestry Center, the Children's Museum, and Hoyt Arboretum. You could easily spend days exploring this region, and this ride will give you a taste of these features. This ride is combined with a climb up to Council Crest, the highest point in the Tualatin Mountains (also known as the West Hills) that flank Portland's west side. This ride features big climbs and outstanding views on very low traffic routes.

Start: Gravel pullout parking area by the Portland Japanese Garden

Length: 10.2-mile loop

Approximate riding time: 1.5 to 2.5 hours of riding, plus additional time to relax and explore the area

Best bike: Road or hybrid bike

Terrain and trail surface: Smooth pavement

Traffic and hazards: A low-traffic route; steep climbs

Things to see: Striking glimpses of Mount Hood framed by the cityscape; the Oregon Zoo; the International Rose Test Garden; the Portland Japanese Garden; the World Forestry Center; the Children's Museum; Hoyt Arboretum; lush forested areas with towering trees

Maps: USGS Portland; Metro Bike There! map

Getting There: By car: From downtown Portland, take US 26 west toward Beaverton. Take the Oregon Zoo exit. Follow the signs toward Hoyt Arboretum. Drive past the paid parking lots and look for the first pullout parking area (free) before the Portland Japanese Garden.

By public transportation: From downtown Portland, board the Max red or blue line to Hillsboro and exit at the Oregon Zoo. Ride the elevator to the top and turn right onto SW Kingston Drive. Continue on SW Kingston Drive for 0.7 mile to the first gravel pullout and the beginning of your ride. Turn left onto SW Kingston Drive to follow the route accurately, though you will be backtracking the 0.7 mile you just rode. GPS: N45 30.730' / W122 42.571'

THE RIDE

This ride takes you on several rewarding climbs for breathtaking views of the city and shady forested lanes that meander through quiet neighborhoods.

You'll begin from Washington Park near the Oregon Zoo. Once you exit Washington Park, you'll parallel US 26 on a path that affords safe passage over the highway and into the Southwest Hills neighborhood. Continue along the relaxing SW Hewett Boulevard, with towering trees and very little traffic. Your gentle 5.0-mile climb to Council Crest begins here, and SW Hewett Boulevard is the perfect route to get you there as it winds through the serene neighborhood at a gentle incline never steeper than a 4-percent grade.

It is said that Native Americans perhaps once held councils atop Council Crest, and that in 1898 delegates to the National Council of Congregational Churches held a historic gathering here, resulting in the current name for the peak. The summit was once heralded as the "Dreamland of the Northwest," and was the site of the Council Crest Amusement Park, complete with a roller coaster, hot air balloon rides, a Japanese tea garden, a scenic railway, and an observatory. The park closed in 1929, a casualty of the Great Depression.

Bike Shop

Bike Gallery: 1001 SW 10th Ave., Portland, OR 97205; (503) 222-3821; bikegallery.com

Nowadays, Council Crest is a much more sparse area with no amenities, but the scenery just can't be beat. Some of the most classic Portland postcard views come from here: On a clear day you can see five snow-capped peaks, 3,000 square miles of land, and rivers that connect them. To the west, trees blanket the landscape, towering over the busy city underneath. From the crest the suburb looks lush and forested, when really what lies below are strip malls and busy roads.

After spending some time soaking in the vistas, it's time to coast downhill on a jaunt past some of the most outstanding houses of Portland, miraculously tucked into the hillsides and cliff faces that comprise this sloping region

Council Crest affords postcard views of Mount Hood and the city to the east. PHOTO BY AYLEEN CROTTY

of the Southwest Hills. The route sneaks into Audrey Lane, a charming tiny street. This is an impossibly winding route on terraced roads with more stunning views. You'll come out in downtown Portland and wind your way back up as you return to Washington Park.

From the city core, this route takes you on steep paved trail through Washington Park to bypass the traffic you would otherwise encounter. Share this path respectfully with hikers. You'll soon come out on the roads of Washington Park, where your climb back up to the beginning resumes. Along the way this route passes the International Rose Test Garden, a free, city-maintained garden with 7,000 rose plants of approximately 550 different varieties—the oldest of its kind in the world. During World War I, rose lovers feared unique hybrid varieties would be destroyed in warfare, and the concept for a safe haven outside the fighting zone was conceived of for Portland, already well known as the "City of Roses," where the plants flourish. Rose cultivators from all over Europe sent their varieties to Portland for safekeeping, and the garden has blossomed into an internationally recognized testing, research, and breeding ground for the beloved flower.

Just above the rose garden is the Portland Japanese Garden, a 5.5-acre traditional Japanese garden with five unique subgardens. The garden opened in 1967, and has been awarded the prestigious honor of being named the second best Japanese garden outside of Japan by the *Journal of Japanese Gardening*. There is an admission fee to enter the garden, but if you have the time it is a special experience.

From this point, you can opt to explore more of Washington Park or return to the start of the ride by continuing along SW Kingston Drive. It's a steady climb of just 1.0 mile past the Japanese garden to return to the gravel pullout where the ride started.

MILES AND DIRECTIONS

0.0   Turn left onto SW Kingston Drive.

0.5   Turn left onto SW Knights Boulevard.

1.0   Turn right onto SW Canyon Court.

1.7   Ride on the sidewalk pathway on the left side of the road, and cross left over the highway.

2.0   Turn left onto SW Hewett Boulevard.

3.7   Make a slight left onto SW Patton Road.

3.8   Turn right onto SW Talbot Road.

3.9   Make a slight left onto SW Talbot Terrace.

4.1   Make a sharp right onto SW Greenway Avenue.

4.4   Turn right onto SW Council Crest Drive and ride the loop around Council Crest. (*Option:* Dismount and walk to the crest of the hill for views or to take a rest. This will add 0.5 mile of walking.)

5.0   Turn left onto SW Greenway Avenue.

5.3   Turn right to continue on SW Greenway Avenue.

5.4   Turn right onto SW Talbot Road.

5.8   At SW Patton Road, jog left and head down the tiny SW Audrey Lane.

5.9   Turn right onto SW Montgomery Drive.

6.6   Turn left to stay on SW Montgomery Drive.

7.1   Turn sharply left onto SW Vista Avenue.

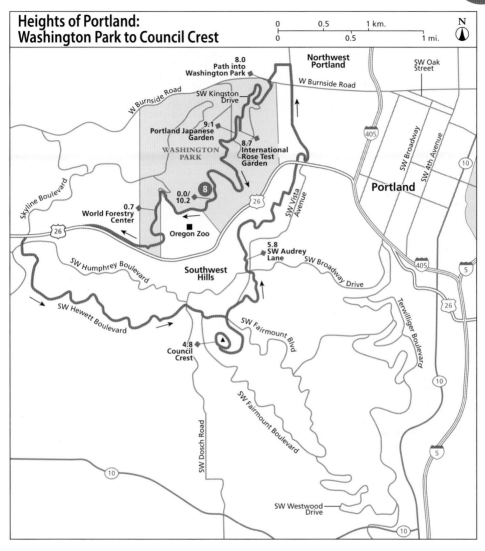

Heights of Portland: Washington Park to Council Crest

8

0   0.5   1 km.
0   0.5   1 mi.

N

8.0
Path into
Washington Park

Northwest Portland

SW Oak Street

W Burnside Road

W Burnside Road

SW Kingston Drive

SW Broadway

SW 4th Avenue

405

10

9.1
Portland Japanese Garden

8.7
International Rose Test Garden

WASHINGTON PARK

SW Vista Avenue

Portland

Skyline Boulevard

0.0/ 10.2

8

26

0.7
World Forestry Center

26

Oregon Zoo

5.8
SW Audrey Lane

SW Broadway Drive

405

26

5

SW Humphrey Boulevard

Southwest Hills

SW Hewett Boulevard

SW Fairmount Blvd

Terwilliger Boulevard

10

4.8
Council Crest

SW Dosch Road

SW Fairmount Boulevard

10

5

SW Westwood Drive

10

7.7   SW Vista becomes NW 23rd Avenue.

7.8   Turn left onto NW Flanders Street.

7.9   At NW Westover, jog left, then right, to continue on NW 24th Place.

7.9   Turn right onto NW 24th Place.

8.0   Cross W Burnside Avenue and continue onto the paved switchback trail as you wind uphill.

Grandiose homes are tucked into the steep, sloping hills of the West Hills, and can be seen by cyclists flying downhill from Council Crest. PHOTO BY AYLEEN CROTTY

8.3 Turn right onto SW Washington Way.

8.6 Turn right onto SW Rose Park Road. (**Option:** Enter the International Rose Test Garden.)

9.2 SW Rose Park Way becomes SW Kingston Drive.

10.2 Arrive back where the ride started.

RIDE INFORMATION

Local Events/Attractions

Washington Park Summer Festival: Washington Park hosts free summertime concerts and activities in the amphitheater of the rose garden. Performances begin at 6 p.m. and occur on various days of the week, mostly in Aug. Details at portlandoregon.gov/parks.

The Oregon Zoo: Located within Washington Park at 4001 SW Canyon Rd., Portland, OR 97221; (503) 226-1561; oregonzoo.org. Visit the zoo and see a variety of animals in their natural environments.

The World Forestry Center: Located within Washington Park, this nonprofit institution educates and informs people about the world's forests, trees, and environmental sustainability through a series of exhibits and events at its Discovery Museum. Check the website for specialty events, museum discount days, and other happenings. 4033 SW Canyon Rd., Portland, OR 97221; (503) 228-1367; worldforestry.org.

Restrooms

Restrooms are located at mile 8.7, near the International Rose Test Garden.

Eastbank Esplanade–
Tom McCall Waterfront Park Loop

Portland's Eastbank Esplanade is a short, urban ride that gives you a different per-spective of Portland's vibrant waterfront. This 1.7-mile-long promenade hugs the east bank of the Willamette River, which flows right through the heart of down-town. Located between the historic Hawthorne and Steel Bridges, this riverfront biking and walking path gives you an unobstructed view of Portland's skyline and boasts unique art sculptures that celebrate Portland's history. The Esplanade also ties the east and west sides of the city's waterfront district together with nice pathways that cross the Steel and Hawthorne Bridges. A walkway on the Steel Bridge allows you to cross the river to Tom McCall Waterfront Park, located on the west bank of the Willamette River, where you can visit Saturday Market, tour the Japanese American Historical Plaza and the Oregon Maritime Museum, and enjoy scenic views of the Willamette River.

Start: RiverEast parking area in Southeast Portland

Length: 2.9-mile loop

Approximate riding time: 1.5 to 2.5 hours with stops

Best bike: Mountain bike or road bike

Terrain and trail surface: Paved bike and pedestrian path that are shared with walkers and runners

Traffic and hazards: This route can be very crowded with walkers and runners on the weekends.

Things to see: Views of the Willamette River and downtown Portland; Portland's historic bridges; Oregon Museum of Science and Industry (OMSI); Oregon Maritime Museum; the Portland Saturday Market; Japanese American Historical Plaza; public art

Map: USGS Portland

Getting There: By car: From I-5 south in Portland, take exit 300B and get into the left lane. Follow the brown OMSI (Oregon Museum of Science and Industry) signs that take you to SE Belmont Avenue, where you'll head east. Turn right (south) onto 7th Avenue and drive to the intersection with SE Clay Street. Turn right (west) onto SE Clay Street and drive to the intersection with SE Water Avenue. Turn left (south) onto SE Water Avenue and proceed 0.3 mile to the RiverEast parking area on the right side of the road. You can park in visitor parking spaces for up to two hours. You can also park here on the weekends.

From I-5 north in Portland, take exit 300, signed for "I-84/The Dalles/Portland Airport." Get in the right lane and exit at the "OMSI/Central Eastside Industrial District" sign. Turn right (south) onto SE Water Avenue and proceed 0.3 mile to the RiverEast parking area on the right side of the road.

By public transportation: From SW Salmon and SW Taylor Streets in downtown Portland, board Bus 4 for Division to Gresham Transit Center. Get off at the Hawthorne Bridge. You can ride this route by heading north on the Eastbank Esplanade, which is accessed adjacent to the Hawthorne Bridge. GPS: N45 30.703' / W122 39.997'

THE RIDE

You'll begin this urban cycling adventure by riding north on the Eastbank Esplanade. This side promenade is lined with attractive benches and native plants and trees. You will soon pass the Hawthorne Bridge, which was designed to carry streetcars, wagons, and early motor vehicles.

After 0.4 mile, you'll pass under the Morrison Bridge and arrive at a unique bronze sculpture titled *The Echo Gate*. This is Portland's oldest bridge, and was built in 1887 as a toll bridge.

At 0.7 mile, turn left and ride down a metal ramp to a 1,200-foot-long floating walkway that takes you to the river's edge. This walkway is 17.5 feet wide and is anchored together with sixty-five concrete pylons—it's the longest floating walkway in the United States, and it rises when the water level is high.

At 1.2 miles, stay to the left and cross the Steel Bridge on the pedestrian/bike path. (Periodically this path is closed and you'll have to cross the Steel Bridge on the pedestrian/bike path located on the upper deck.) After crossing the bridge, turn left (south) and begin riding along Tom McCall Waterfront Park. The riverside edge of this park is built on top of part of the Portland

Cyclists can enjoy nice views of the Portland city skyline from the Eastbank Esplanade.
PHOTO BY LIZANN DUNEGAN

Harbor Wall. This harbor wall is the most expensive single piece of infrastructure built by the city of Portland. The mile-long wall extends from the Steel Bridge to the Hawthorne Bridge, and was built as a part of an urban renewal project in the 1920s. It replaced many of the rotting docks and old pier buildings that once stood here, and also introduced the first sewer system on the west side of the river.

At 1.5 miles, be sure to take a side trip on the stone path that leads to the Japanese American Historical Plaza, which features large stone sculptures with engravings.

At 1.7 miles, ride under the Burnside Bridge and then pass the Portland Saturday Market, which is worth visiting. You can find unique Oregon-made items and quench your appetite by visiting

Bike Shops

River City Bicycles: 706 SE Martin Luther King Jr. Blvd., Portland, OR 97214; (503) 233-5973; rivercity bicycles.com
Clever Cycles: 900 SE Hawthorne Blvd., Portland, OR 97214; (503) 334-1560; clevercycles.com

Best Bike Rides Portland, Oregon

The historic Steel Bridge was built in 1912. PHOTO BY LIZANN DUNEGAN

a variety of food carts that feature many different cuisines. The market is open on weekends from March through the end of December.

At 1.8 miles, ride past the Oregon Maritime Museum. This museum is housed in the last steam-powered, stern-wheel tugboat operating in the United States. This tugboat was originally put into service in 1947 and cost over $15 million to restore.

At 2.2 miles, you'll pass the Salmon Street Fountain on your right. During the summer months this fountain is filled with kids and adults cooling off.

Complete the loop by crossing the Hawthorne Bridge. This bridge is the most used bicycle and pedestrian bridge in Oregon. When you cross the bridge, cyclists need to stay to the left and pedestrians should stay to the right. After you cross the bridge, turn north on the Eastbank Esplanade and ride a short distance to your starting point.

MILES AND DIRECTIONS

0.0 Begin on the paved path from the RiverEast parking area that intersects with the Eastbank Esplanade paved pedestrian and bike path

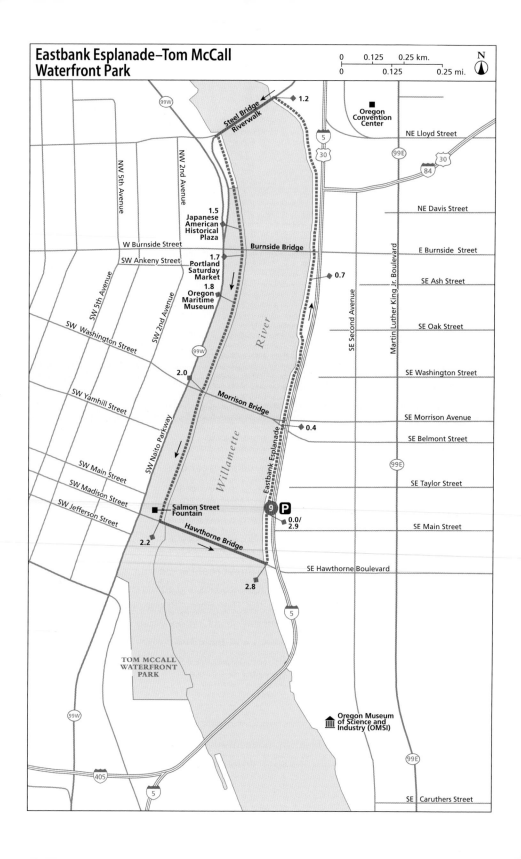

Eastbank Esplanade–Tom McCall
Waterfront Park

0   0.125   0.25 km.

0   0.125   0.25 mi.

N

99W

♦ 1.2

Steel Bridge
Riverwalk

■ Oregon
Convention
Center

NE Lloyd Street

NW 5th Avenue

NW 2nd Avenue

5

30

99E

30

84

NE Davis Street

1.5
Japanese
American
Historical
Plaza

W Burnside Street

Burnside Bridge

E Burnside Street

SW Ankeny Street

1.7
Portland
Saturday
Market

♦ 0.7

SE Ash Street

1.8
Oregon
Maritime
Museum

Martin Luther King Jr. Boulevard

SE Oak Street

SW 5th Avenue

SW 2nd Avenue

SW Washington Street

River

SE Second Avenue

99W

SE Washington Street

2.0

SW Yamhill Street

Morrison Bridge

SE Morrison Avenue

♦ 0.4

SE Belmont Street

SW Naito Parkway

Eastbank Esplanade

99E

Willamette

SW Main Street

SE Taylor Street

SW Madison Street

SW Jefferson Street

■ Salmon Street
Fountain

9 Ⓟ

SE Main Street

**0.0/
2.9**

Hawthorne Bridge

2.2

SE Hawthorne Boulevard

2.8

5

TOM McCALL
WATERFRONT
PARK

🏛 Oregon Museum
of Science and
Industry (OMSI)

99W

99E

405

5

SE Caruthers Street

parallel to the Willamette River. Turn right (north) on the Eastbank Esplanade.

0.1 Pass public drinking fountains on your left.

0.4 Ride under the Morrison Bridge and pass a bronze sculpture called The Echo Gate on your left.

0.7 Turn left at the "Southeast Ash Street" sign and walk down a metal ramp to a floating walkway.

1.2 Cross the Steel Bridge on the pedestrian/bike walkway. Turn left (south) after crossing the bridge.

1.5 Turn right onto a stone path and then ride through the Japanese American Historical Plaza. After viewing the rock engravings, continue riding south on the concrete walk that parallels the Willamette River and takes you through Waterfront Park.

1.7 Pass under the Burnside Bridge and pass by a public fountain and the plaza that hosts the Portland Saturday Market.

1.8 Pass the Oregon Maritime Museum on your left.

2.0 Ride under the Morrison Bridge.

2.2 Pass the Salmon Street Fountain on your right.

2.3 Pass a public restroom on the right. Ride under the Hawthorne Bridge. After going under the bridge, follow the paved path that curves to the right and intersects with the bikeway that heads east over the bridge. Use caution when crossing the bridge. Cyclists stay to the left and pedestrians stay to the right.

2.8 After crossing the bridge, turn right onto a paved path that spirals down to the Eastbank Esplanade.

This is an example of a Benson Bubbler—one of Portland's iconic drinking fountains. The fountains are found throughout Portland and offer fresh drinking water to anyone who passes by. PHOTO BY LIZANN DUNEGAN

2.9 At the bottom of the spiral path, turn left (north) on the Eastbank Esplanade and arrive back at the RiverEast parking area.

RIDE INFORMATION

Local Events/Attractions

Providence Bridge Pedal: 1631 NE Klickitat St., Portland, OR 97212; (503) 281-9198; blog.bridgepedal.com. This annual event (held in mid-Aug) is a noncompetitive bike ride crossing Portland's historic bridges: Morrison, Sellwood, Hawthorne, Ross Island, Marquam, Burnside, Broadway, Steel, St. Johns, and Fremont.

OMSI: 1945 SE Water Ave., Portland, OR 97214; (800) 955-6674; omsi.edu. This museum houses many interactive exhibits that feature science and math.

Portland Saturday Market: Located in Ankeny Plaza adjacent to the Burnside Bridge in Portland; (503) 222-6072; portlandsaturdaymarket.com. This fun outdoor market features handcrafted items and food carts that serve a variety of cuisines. The market is open on weekends Mar 2 through Dec 24 from 10 a.m. to 5 p.m. on Sat and from 11 a.m. to 4:30 p.m. on Sun.

Restrooms

There is a restroom at mile 2.3.

Tryon Creek State Natural Area and Portland Bridges Loop

This scenic city ride begins on the east side of the Willamette River on the East-bank Esplanade. This magnificent multiuse path features many interpretive plaques, art sculptures, and a floating boardwalk. You'll cross the Steel Bridge and pedal through popular Tom McCall Waterfront Park. After a short but intense passage through downtown Portland, you'll head up shady SW Terwilliger Boulevard. The route stays fun until you cross SW Barbur Boulevard and contend with a bit of automotive congestion. After about 1.0 mile, turn onto a tranquil multiuse path that meanders through Tryon Creek State Natural Area to its nature center.

Start: SE Caruthers cul-de-sac just west of SE 2nd Place

Length: 18.1-mile lollipop

Approximate riding time: 2 to 3.5 hours with stops

Best bike: Road bike

Terrain and trail surface: Paved multiuse path and paved city streets

Traffic and hazards: Take care when traveling among pedestrians on the multiuse paths along the Eastbank Esplanade and in Tom McCall Waterfront Park. Use caution when riding on city streets in downtown Portland, including SW Taylor Street, SW Broadway, SW Sixth Avenue and SW Madison Street. Use crosswalks when crossing the busy intersections at SW Terwilliger Boulevard and SW Boones Ferry Road.

Things to see: Downtown Portland; historic Portland bridges; Oregon Museum of Science and Industry (OMSI); the Willamette River; Tom McCall Waterfront Park; Portland Saturday Market; Tryon Creek State Natural Area and nature center

Maps: USGS Portland and Lake Oswego

Getting There: From I-5 south in Portland, take exit 300B and get into the left lane. Follow the brown OMSI (Oregon Museum of Science and

Industry) signs that take you to SE Belmont Avenue, where you'll head east. Turn right (south) onto SE 7th Avenue and drive to the intersection with SE Clay Street. Turn right (west) onto SE Clay Street and drive to the intersection with SE Water Avenue. Turn left (south) onto SE Water Avenue and proceed to OMSI. Once you reach OMSI, continue driving south on SE Water Avenue for another 0.3 mile to the intersection with SE Caruthers Street. Turn right onto SE Caruthers and park where SE Caruthers dead-ends at a cul-de-sac.

From I-5 north in Portland, take exit 300 toward I-84/The Dalles/ Portland airport. Get into the right lane and exit at a sign for the OMSI/Central Eastside Industrial District. Turn right (south) onto SE Water Street. Proceed 0.7 mile (you'll pass OMSI after 0.4 mile) to the intersection with SE Caruthers Street. Turn right onto SE Caruthers Street and park where SE Caruthers dead-ends at a cul-de-sac. GPS: N45 30.353' / W122 39.852'

THE RIDE

The loop portion of this route begins in Southeast Portland and heads north along the banks of the Willamette River on the Eastbank Esplanade, an exceptional multiuse path. Along the way you can stop and read interpretive signs that give you an inside look at Willamette River history and development. The Willamette River begins in the Cascade Mountains and flows north past Eugene, Corvallis, Albany, and Salem. It then continues northward, past Oregon City and Portland, to where it joins the Columbia River at the southern tip of Sauvie Island (about 10 miles north of Portland off US 30). Lewis and Clark first canoed past the entrance to the Willamette in the fall of 1805, and again in the spring of 1806. At that time the Willamette was a pristine watershed teeming with salmon and bordered by green meadowlands, marshes, and thick stands of fir and cedar.

Portland was incorporated in 1851, and the government decreed that settlers were entitled to one square mile of free land. It wasn't long before timber was cut, houses were built, and warehouses sprang up to store and receive cargo from ships traveling up the Columbia River from Astoria. By 1859, most of the Native Americans who once enjoyed the bounty of this rich river valley were displaced by white settlers. As the city grew, the marshes and ponds were filled to build rail lines and rail yards. In addition, a 25-foot channel was dredged in the Willamette River from Portland to where it meets the Columbia River to allow ships to pass more easily into the Portland Harbor.

By the 1920s the river became so polluted it was not suitable for fishing, swimming, or boating. The once bountiful salmon runs plummeted. Beginning in the 1970s new laws were adopted to clean up the Willamette River, and in the mid-1980s the city began working to solve the problem of frequent sewer overflows that occurred when excess storm water and untreated waste flowed into the river during heavy rainfall. Despite these efforts, in 2000, the Portland Harbor was designated as a Superfund site because of its extreme pollution, with contaminants such as lead, arsenic, benzene, mercury, and pesticides entering the river from agricultural runoff and industrial wastes. After hard work on the part of Willamette Riverkeeper and other organizations to restore this habitat and clean up the river, the Willamette River was finally declared safe for swimming by the Environmental Protection Agency in 2014. Though swimming is not yet common along the river, early adopters

The Eastbank Esplanade is very popular with Portland cyclists. PHOTO BY LIZANN DUNEGAN

Tryon Creek State Natural Area and Portland Bridges Loop

The historic Hawthorne Bridge was opened in 1910, and is host to the most cycling traffic in Oregon. PHOTO BY LIZANN DUNEGAN

have begun to host regular swimming events, and on hot days the Eastbank Esplanade is dotted with a few suited revelers. Organizations such as the Human Access Project are working to raise awareness about the river's much improved quality while advocating for recreational access points and urban beaches.

As you ride north you'll have an unobstructed view of Portland's skyline and its many historical bridges. At 0.2 mile you'll pass the Oregon Museum of Science and Industry. Established in 1944, this world-class science museum is a popular Portland attraction. It teaches visitors about the wonder of science through hands-on demonstrations, interactive exhibits, and science labs. It also features an OMNIMAX Theater—a five-story, domed screen with viewers seated in the middle of the movie action. Farther on, cross the Steel Bridge on the special lower deck, a pathway designed to make the river crossing easy for pedestrians and cyclists. The Steel Bridge opened in 1912 to carry trains, trucks, and horse-drawn vehicles across the Willamette. It remains one of the best-known features of the waterfront, and carries freight train traffic, the MAX light-rail, cars, buses, cyclists, and pedestrians. It is also the only bridge in the world that lifts with upper and lower decks rising simultaneously.

After crossing the river, swing south and cruise through Tom McCall Waterfront Park. This stretch of the path can be very crowded, so use your bell or voice to alert other trail users when you are approaching, and give pedestrians and runners the right of way. When you are on this section of the route, you may want to stop at the Portland Saturday Market (open on weekends March through the end of December), located adjacent to the Burnside Bridge. Check out the array of handcrafted items and sample delicious ethnic foods.

After riding through Tom McCall Waterfront Park for about a mile, you'll reach the Salmon Street Fountain. In the summer months adults and kids alike enjoy cooling off in this circular fountain.

Bike Shops

River City Bicycles: 706 SE Martin Luther King Jr. Blvd., Portland, OR 97214; (503) 233-5973; rivercity bicycles.com

Go By Bike (closed on weekends): 3303 SW Bond Ave., Portland, OR 97239; (971) 271-9270; goby bikepdx.com

The route continues south through downtown Portland, then hooks up with SW Terwilliger Boulevard after 4.4 miles. This winding road boasts an excellent bike lane that travels through Portland's West Hills and Burlingame District until it reaches Tryon Creek State Natural Area. It is worth taking a break from the saddle here to check out the nature center and to hike on some of the forested trails that surround the park.

From the park backtrack to downtown Portland, then head east across the Hawthorne Bridge on expansive bike lanes. After crossing the bridge turn south onto the bike-and-pedestrian path that leads back to your starting point.

MILES AND DIRECTIONS

0.0 Start riding west on SE Caruthers Street until it dead-ends at the start of the multiuse Eastbank Esplanade. Turn right (north) onto the Eastbank Esplanade, which parallels the Willamette River.

0.2 Pass the Oregon Museum of Science and Industry (OMSI) on the right.

1.2 Turn left at the "Ash Street" sign, then ride down a ramp and follow the path as it continues north. You are now riding on a floating ramp.

1.7 Cross the Steel Bridge.

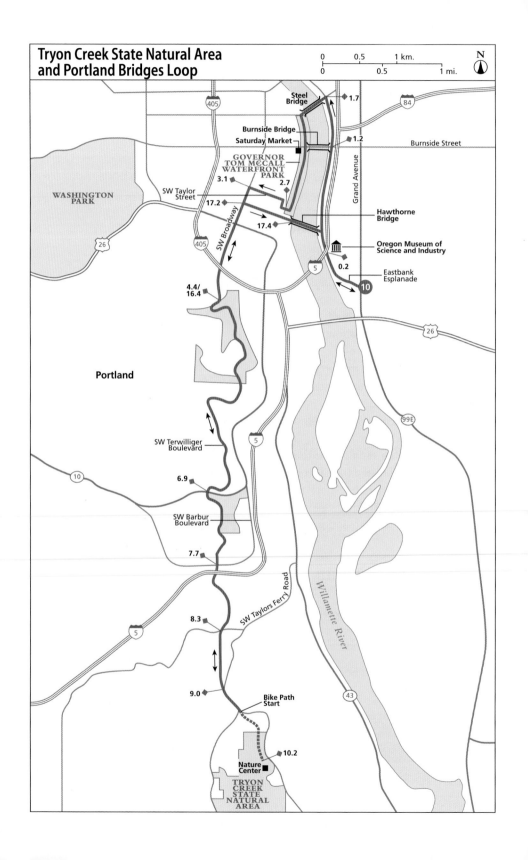

1.9 After crossing the Steel Bridge, turn left (south) and follow the paved path as it takes you through Tom McCall Waterfront Park.

2.7 Pass the Salmon Street Fountain on your right. Turn right here, then take another right when you reach SW Front Avenue. Walk your bike 1 block along SW Front Avenue.

2.8 Use the crosswalk to cross SW Front Avenue. After crossing, continue riding west on SW Taylor Street.

3.1 Turn left onto SW Broadway.

3.9 At the stoplight head left toward "Barbur Blvd./Ross Island Bridge/ Hospitals."

4.0 At the stoplight turn right where a sign indicates "6th Ave./Terwilliger Blvd./OHSU/VA hospitals."

4.1 Cross SW Sherman Street and continue to the right on SW Sixth Avenue (SW Broadway turns into SW Sixth Avenue).

4.4 At the stoplight turn left onto SW Terwilliger Boulevard.

6.9 At the stoplight cross Capitol Highway and continue riding straight on SW Terwilliger Boulevard.

7.7 At the stoplight cross SW Barbur Boulevard and continue riding straight on SW Terwilliger Boulevard.

8.3 At the stoplight cross SW Taylors Ferry Road and continue riding straight on SW Terwilliger Boulevard.

9.0 The road forks here, with SW Terwilliger Road heading left and SW Boones Ferry Road going right. Stay to the right on SW Boones Ferry Road and immediately catch a series of crosswalks to the other side of SW Boones Ferry Road. Begin riding on a paved bike path that heads into the forest.

10.0 Arrive at a junction. Head right and continue riding on the bike path.

10.1 Arrive at a junction with the entrance road to Tryon Creek State Natural Area. Check for traffic, cross the entrance road, and veer right toward the nature center.

10.2 Arrive at the nature center. (**Option:** Lock up your bike and explore the center and the trails in the park. Restrooms and water are available here. When you are finished exploring, head north on the bike path back toward downtown Portland.)

10.3 Arrive at a junction. Turn left (north). Cross the entrance road to Tryon Creek State Natural Area and continue riding north on the bike path.

11.4 The bike path ends. Cross two crosswalks and continue riding north on SW Terwilliger Boulevard.

16.2 At the stoplight turn right and continue riding on SW Terwilliger Boulevard.

16.4 Cross SW Sheridan Street and continue riding straight on SW Sixth Avenue (SW Terwilliger Boulevard turns into SW Sixth Avenue).

17.2 Turn right onto SW Madison Street.

17.4 Cross the Hawthorne Bridge over the Willamette River.

17.9 Turn right onto the bike ramp that heads south along the Willamette River.

18.1 Arrive at SE Caruthers Street on your left, where the ride started.

RIDE INFORMATION

Local Events/Attractions
Oregon Museum of Science and Industry (OMSI): 1945 SE Water Ave., Portland, OR 97214; (800) 955-6674; omsi.edu. Visit a world-class science museum that teaches kids about science with interactive exhibits and hands-on demonstrations. Call for admission rates and hours.

Providence Bridge Pedal: 1631 NE Klickitat St., Portland, OR 97212; (503) 281-9198; blog.bridgepedal.com. This annual event (held in mid-Aug) is a noncompetitive bike ride crossing Portland's historic bridges: Morrison, Sellwood, Hawthorne, Ross Island, Marquam, Burnside, Broadway, Steel, St. Johns, and Fremont.

Tryon Creek State Natural Area: 11321 SW Terwilliger Blvd., Portland, OR 97219; (503) 636-4398; oregonstateparks.org.

Restrooms
Public restrooms are located along Naito Parkway at SW Taylor; at mile 2.4; and at the nature center at Tryon Creek State Natural Area at mile 10.2.

Family Friendly Fountain Tour

Nothing says summertime like splashing around in an interactive water feature designed especially for kids' enjoyment, and Portland has plenty of them. This fun, flat ride takes you to five different play fountains for children of all ages. The route is an out-and-back ride, so on your return trip you can vote for your favorite fountain and stop for a second time. Most of this ride is on smoothly paved off-the-road paths or low-traffic roads, making it easy to tow a child trailer behind.

Start: Elizabeth Caruthers Park

Length: 7.6 miles out and back

Approximate riding time: 1 to 1.5 hours of riding plus ample time for fountain play

Best bike: Road, mountain, or hybrid bike

Terrain and trail surface: Smooth pavement

Traffic and hazards: A 0.5-mile stretch along a slow-moving city street leads to the Director Park fountain, and can be skipped without altering your route.

Things to see: Portland's waterfront; an aerial tram; Director Park; Salmon Street Springs; Jamison Square; Portland Saturday Market; South Waterfront Farmers Market; Caruthers Park Fountain; Bill Naito Legacy Fountain

Maps: USGS Portland; Metro Bike There! map

Getting There: By car: From downtown Portland, take Naito Parkway south to SW Moody Avenue. Follow SW Moody Avenue for 1.0 mile to Elizabeth Caruthers Park (3508 SW Moody Ave.) and look for parking. There is ample on-street parking with paid spaces, but the maximum time allowed is three hours. If you think you will be longer, park in a nearby parking garage. The ride begins from the Caruthers Park Fountain on the northwest corner of Elizabeth Caruthers Park.

By public transportation: Take the number 35 bus for "Macadam/ Greeley to Oregon City TC" south. Disembark at SW Moody Avenue and SW Gaines Street, then walk 300 feet to the park. The ride begins from the Caruthers Park Fountain on the northwest corner of Elizabeth Caruthers Park. GPS: N45 29.849' / W122 40.280'

THE RIDE

Suit up the kiddos, pack some snacks, and head out for this splish-splash party on wheels that begins at the Caruthers Park Fountain in the south waterfront area. This water feature is geared toward little ones, with gently spurting water on a concrete surface. Watch the space-age Portland Aerial Tram soar high above, a unique feature of Portland's public transportation system that carries passengers to Oregon Health & Science University (OHSU) and Hospital way up on what's known as "Pill Hill." Grab a snack at the Farmers Market if you're there on a Thursday between 2 p.m. and 7 p.m.

When your group is ready to move on, hop on the bike and cruise along the Moody bike path. You'll pass by food carts and a huge "Go by Bike" bike parking arena at the base of the aerial tram. This free parking lot sees an average of 220 bikes a day as commuters avoid the steep climb to OHSU by taking a much more leisurely ride on the tram.

Your next stop is the iconic Salmon Street Springs (mile 1.2) on the Portland waterfront. This prized fountain was dedicated in 1988 and is featured prominently in many photos of Portland. The fountain's three distinct water patterns are the Bollards, Misters, and the very dramatic Wedding Cake. Portland Parks & Recreation, which oversees the fountain, notes it recycles up to 4,924 gallons of water per minute through its 185 jets. At first the gorgeous fountain seems rather calm, but it quickly builds into a dramatically high cascade of water (the Wedding Cake), making for an exciting wall of water that kids love to try to run under. Kids (and the occasional adult) challenge themselves to stand under the merciless water until they can no longer endure the intensity. It's hard to stay dry at this entertaining play area.

A new adventure awaits your swim team at Teachers Fountain, located at Director Park (mile 2.1). This

Bike Shops

Go By Bike (bike repair and rentals; closed on weekends): 3303 SW Bond Ave., Portland, OR 97239; (971) 271-9270; gobybikepdx.com

Cycle Portland: 117 NW 2nd Ave., Portland, OR 97209; (844) 739-2453; portlandbicycletours.com

The "Wedding Cake" pattern, one of the three designs created by the Salmon Street Springs fountain's 185 water jets. PHOTO BY AYLEEN CROTTY

urban oasis features plaza seating and a huge, shallow wading pool in the heart of the city. Small spurts of water provide additional entertainment, and a wide wall around the pool keeps kids contained on the plaza. You'll ride a short 0.5 mile along SW Taylor Avenue to get there, your only uphill climb of the day. The street is very crowded with cars, but the traffic is slow-moving, making it a fine route for cycling. If you don't prefer to ride in traffic, you could walk along the sidewalk. (**Note:** It is illegal to ride a bike on the sidewalk in downtown Portland.) A huge food cart arena is located just 2 blocks away, at SW Taylor Street and SW 9th Avenue, if you want to grab an easy, tasty snack or lunch.

From Director Park, it's just a short 1.0-mile ride to the next destination—the Bill Naito Legacy Fountain (mile 3.1), marking a return to the waterfront path. If you're there on a Saturday or Sunday, stop by the Portland Saturday

Market for treats and to peruse the creative array of locally made crafts. When the market is not in session, the plaza transforms into an additional water feature that's mellow and perfect for the younger set.

Cruise along the waterfront path, past (but not across) the monolithic Steel Bridge, and pedal out onto NW Naito Parkway, a broad street with a generously wide bike lane. Weave your way into Northwest Portland to visit Jameson Square (mile 4.3), which features a wall of cascading waterfalls set against stunning rock. The water feature was originally designed simply as a way to keep skateboarders off the rocks, but it quickly became a popular urban pool, and is now a favorite swimming hole for kids. There are plenty of places to hang out on the rocks and cool your feet while you watch the kids play. The fountain starts off very low, allowing ample playtime for toddlers before

Water cascades over the rocks at the Jameson Square Fountain, much to the delight of children of all ages. PHOTO BY AYLEEN CROTTY the water increases and eventually beings its exciting cascade down the rock, a thrill for the older kids. This expansive play area has an abundance of platforms to stand on and rocks to climb, making it a particular favorite for older kids. There are several cafes and an ice cream parlor surrounding the park if you want to take a break.

MILES AND DIRECTIONS

0.0 From the Caruthers Park Fountain, turn right onto SW Moody Avenue and follow the bike path that parallels SW Moody.

0.8 Turn left toward the Waterfront Park Trail.

1.2 Arrive at Salmon Street Springs.

1.4 After enjoying the fountain, continue on the Waterfront Park Trail.

1.6 Cross the park and head toward the intersection of SW Naito Parkway (the big road that parallels the river) and SW Taylor Street. Carefully cross SW Naito Parkway with the streetlight and continue up SW Taylor Street.

2.1 Arrive at Director Park. From the fountain, head back downhill toward the river by turning right on SW Yamhill Street.

2.5 Cross SW Naito Parkway and cross the park to get back onto the Waterfront Park Trail. Continue north (left) on the trail.

3.0 Arrive at the Bill Naito Legacy Fountain. As you're facing the river, turn left to continue on the trail.

3.3 Continue past and under (but not across) the Steel Bridge.

3.4 Use the slight curb cut to make your way out onto SW Naito Parkway, then ride in the broad bike lane.

4.0 Carefully turn left onto NW 9th Avenue.

4.2 Turn right onto NW Kearney Street.

4.3 Arrive at Jameson Square. After enjoying the park, retrace the same route back to the starting point.

6.1 Unless you want to head back to Director Park, continue on the Waterfront Park Trail. (***Note:*** The mileage of this route does not include a return to Director Park.)

7.6 Arrive back at Elizabeth Caruthers Park.

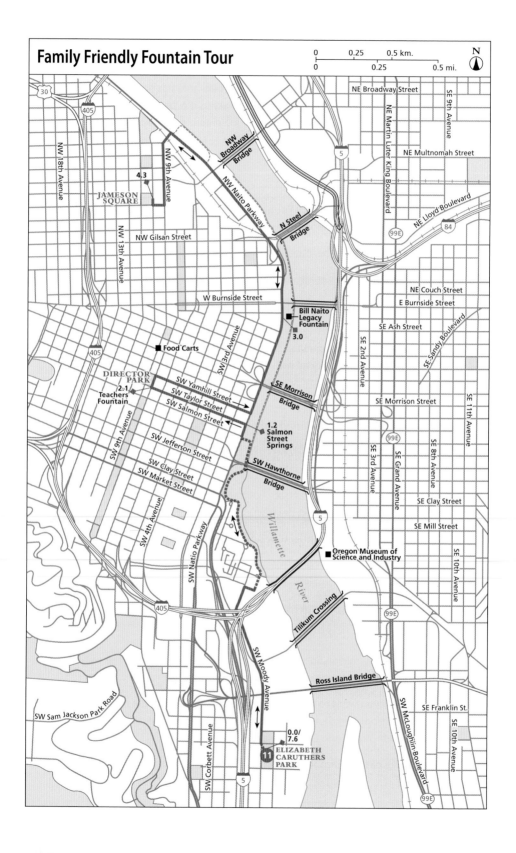

Family Friendly Fountain Tour

| 0 | 0.25 | 0.5 km. |
| 0 | 0.25 | 0.5 mi. |

N

NE Broadway Street

SE 9th Avenue

30

405

NW 18th Avenue

NW Broadway Bridge

NW 9th Avenue

NW Naito Parkway

NE Martin Luter King Boulevard

NE Multnomah Street

NE Lloyd Boulevard

5

84

99E

4.3

JAMESON SQUARE

NW 13th Avenue

NW Gilsan Street

N Steel Bridge

W Burnside Street

NE Couch Street

E Burnside Street

SE Ash Street

SE Sandy Boulevard

Food Carts

NW 3rd Avenue

Bill Naito Legacy Fountain

3.0

SE 2nd Avenue

DIRECTOR PARK

2.1 Teachers Fountain

SW Yamhill Street

SW Taylor Street

SW Salmon Street

SE Morrison Bridge

SE Morrison Street

SE 11th Avenue

SW 9th Avenue

SW Jefferson Street

1.2 Salmon Street Springs

99E

SE 8th Avenue

SW Clay Street

SW Market Street

SW Hawthorne Bridge

SE 3rd Avenue

SE Grand Avenue

SE Clay Street

SW 4th Avenue

SW Natio Parkway

Willamette

5

SE Mill Street

River

Oregon Museum of Science and Industry

SE 10th Avenue

405

Tilikum Crossing

99E

SW Sam Jackson Park Road

SW Corbett Avenue

SW Moody Avenue

Ross Island Bridge

SW McLoughlin Boulevard

SE Franklin St.

SE 10th Avenue

0.0/ 7.6

11 ELIZABETH CARUTHERS PARK

5

99E

RIDE INFORMATION

Local Events/Attractions

South Waterfront Farmers Market: Held Thurs from June 5 to Oct 30 from 2 to 7 p.m.; 3508 SW Moody Ave.; southwaterfrontfarmersmarket.com.

Portland Saturday Market: Held every Sat and Sun year-round; 2 SW Naito Parkway; portlandsaturdaymarket.com.

Director Park Events: Search the Portland Parks & Recreation website for an updated listing of the many free community events happening at the park, especially in the summertime.

Restrooms

Restrooms are located at the start/finish in Elizabeth Caruthers Park; at mile 1.4 on the SW Naito Parkway along the waterfront; at mile 2.1 (Director Park); and at mile 4.3 (Jameson Square).

Tilikum Crossing: The People's Bridge

The Tilikum Crossing is the newest Willamette River bridge, notable because it was created only for trains, buses, pedestrians, and cyclists; auto traffic is not permitted. The bridge structure is lovely, with nighttime lights that change in color patterns that reflect the height of the river water. The car-free bridge is much quieter than the other bridges in Portland, making it a lovely spot to stop and take in the Willamette River views. Tilikum is a word in the Native American Chinook language meaning "people." The bridge is also known as The People's Bridge. This route takes you on a relaxed spin from Southeast Portland and across the bridge on a mixture of low-traffic streets and off-the-road paved paths that were constructed specifically to help cyclists safely reach the Tilikum Crossing. You'll also ride an elevator and use a bridge over train tracks, a crossing also constructed to help nonmotorized traffic flow toward the Tilikum Crossing.

Start: Northwest corner of Kenilworth Park

Length: 6.3-mile lollipop

Approximate riding time: 1 to 2 hours, including time to stop along the way

Best bike: Road or hybrid bike

Terrain and trail surface: Smooth pavement

Traffic and hazards: A mix of low and moderate traffic routes.

Things to see: Hazelnut groves; Willamette River; birds; tree farms; active farming

Maps: USGS Portland; Metro Bike There! map

Getting There: By car: From downtown Portland, take the Ross Island Bridge (US 26) east over the Willamette River. Take 99E South and exit at Holgate Boulevard. Follow through the stoplight and back across OR 99E to SE Holgate Boulevard, then continue on SE Holgate. Turn left onto SE 32th Avenue; Kenilworth Park will be on your right-hand side.

There is ample street parking across from the park. Begin your ride at the northwest corner of Kenilworth Park.

By public transportation: From downtown Portland, board the number 17 "Holgate/Broadway" bus. Get off at SE Holgate Boulevard and SE 32nd Avenue. Walk 770 feet north to Kenilworth Park. GPS: N45 29.518' / W122 37.957'

THE RIDE

Like the region's abundant salmon swimming downriver to reach the ocean, so this route guides packs of commuting cyclists on their quest for downtown Portland and the West Hills beyond on a daily basis. Though this area of the city, tucked into industrial Southeast Portland, is laden with traffic obstacles

This playful mural is one of the many cool features you'll see along the Tilikum Way.
PHOTO BY AYLEEN CROTTY

Tilikum Crossing: The People's Bridge

79

like congested knots of busy intersections and an active rail line, the Tilikum Way, as this route is known, boasts modern active transportation features that make it an extremely safe and fun route to ride, with clear signage and road crossings designed with cyclists in mind.

Begin your adventure at Kenilworth Park, a neighborhood park with limited amenities. For the first stretch of the ride, you'll wind along mellow city streets with barely any traffic. When Lafayette Street dead ends (mile 1.0), the choice is yours: Take the elevator up to the bridge over the train tracks or carry your bike up the stairs for extra points.

It's a short bridge, and you'll come right back down on the other side to continue your expedition through the Brooklyn neighborhood. At SE Powell Boulevard (mile 1.9) use the pedestrian bridge to safely cross over the busy

A bike counter records traffic on this striking bridge. PHOTO BY AYLEEN CROTTY

road. Soon after you'll connect up with Tilikum Way, the off-the-road road path network that helps connect people to the Tilikum Crossing.

As you approach the bridge, take note of a few cool features. Markings on the pavement designate the left side of the walkway for cyclists and the right side for pedestrians—extremely helpful on weekends when the bridge is crowded. You'll also see a traffic counter that records the number of cyclists that have traveled across the bridge that day, and for all time. Traffic flows into the city on the north side of the bridge and back out of the city on the south side.

After crossing the bridge, you will arrive at the MAX light rail station, a nice spot to take a break and watch the bridge traffic. This is your turnaround point. Return back over the bridge to continue on the route.

Bike Shops

Seven Corners: 3218 SE 21st Ave., Portland, OR 97202; (503) 230-0317; 7-corners.com
Bikes for Humanity: 3354 SE Powell Blvd., Portland, OR 97202; (503) 496-6941; b4hpdx.org

On the return trip you'll travel the entirety of Tilikum Way, where tidbits of poetry line the sidewalk. Stop to read the messages as you pedal along this wide, off-the-road pathway. When Tilikum Way ends, you'll emerge into the Hosford–Abernathy neighborhood. Closer to Division Street, this is a bustling neighborhood packed with dozens of independent shops, extensive services, a busy main road, and delicious restaurants. On this ride, however, you'll travel the mellow southern edge of the fray as you slowly wind back to Kenilworth Park, where the ride started.

MILES AND DIRECTIONS

0.0 From Kenilworth Park, head north on SE 32st Avenue.

0.1 Turn left onto SE Gladstone Street.

0.6 Turn right onto SE 22nd Avenue.

0.8 Turn left onto SE Lafayette Street.

1.0 Board the elevator or take the stairs up to the bridge over the railroad tracks, then come back down on the other side.

1.1 Continue on SE Rhine Street.

1.4 Turn left onto SE 11th Avenue.

1.5 Turn right onto SE Rhone Avenue.

Tilikum Crossing: The People's Bridge

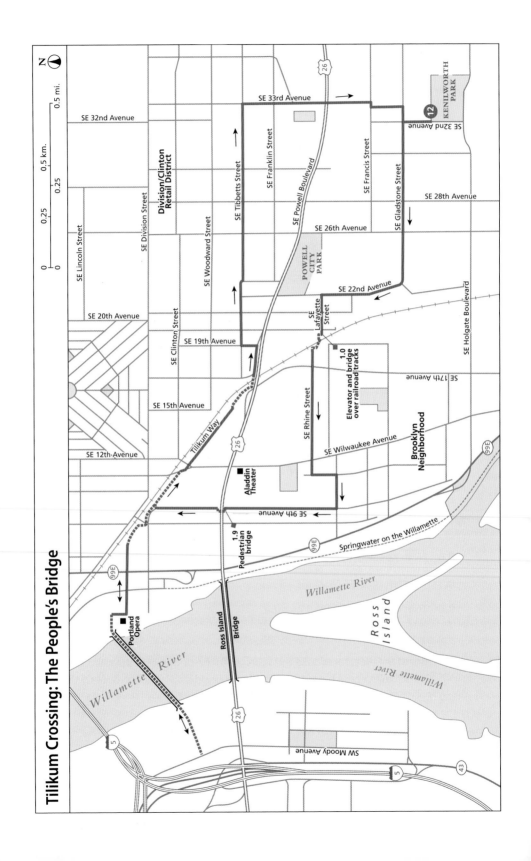

1.6 Turn right onto SE 9th Avenue.

1.9 At SE Powell Boulevard, take the pedestrian walkway to safely cross over this busy road.

2.0 Continue on SE 9th Avenue.

2.2 Turn left onto the wide sidewalk; this is Tilikum Way.

2.4 Continue onto SE Caruthers Street.

2.6 Turn right onto SE 2nd Place up toward the Tilikum Crossing.

2.7 Turn left onto Tilikum Crossing.

3.2 At the MAX light rail station, cross the Tilikum bridge to return.

3.6 Turn right onto SE 4th Avenue.

3.7 Turn left onto SE Caruthers Street and continue onto the wide sidewalk for Tilikum Way.

3.9 At SE 9th Avenue, continue straight on Tilikum Way.

4.6 Follow the signage to SE Portland (not Brooklyn). You will dip down under the railroad tracks along busy SE Powell Boulevard, but on a separated path.

4.8 Emerge from the tunnel and the path ends. Turn left onto SE 19th Avenue.

5.0 Turn right onto SE Tibbetts Street.

5.7 Turn right onto SE 33rd Avenue.

6.2 Turn right onto SE Gladstone Street, then take an immediate left onto SE 32nd Avenue.

6.3 Return to the southwest corner of Kenilworth Park, where the ride started.

RIDE INFORMATION

Local Events/Attractions
Oregon Museum of Science and Industry: This museum features an abundance of exciting interactive exhibits for kids. The museum is located at 1945 SE Water Ave., Portland, OR 97214; (503) 797-4000; omsi.edu.

Portland Opera: This revered opera house is located at the base of the Tilikum Crossing on the east side. The location is 211 SE Caruthers St., Portland, OR 97214; (503) 241-1802; portlandopera.org.

Aladdin Theater: Originally opened as a vaudeville house in 1927, this historic theater showcases a variety of performances and concerts nearly nightly. It is located at 3017 SE Milwaukie Ave., Portland, OR 97202; (503) 234-9694; aladdin-theater.com.

Restrooms
There are no designated public restrooms for this ride.

Springwater Corridor: Southeast Foster Road to Downtown Boring

This fun ride takes you on a tour of Springwater Corridor multiuse path through Southeast Portland and Gresham, then out to the more rural landscapes of Boring. Along the way the trail winds along Johnson Creek, where you'll have several opportunities to stop and view birds and other wildlife.

Start: Southeast Foster Road in Southeast Portland, off I-205

Length: 24.4 miles out and back

Approximate riding time: 3 to 4 hours

Best bike: Road bike

Terrain and trail surface: Paved multiuse trail

Traffic and hazards: This route can be very crowded with walkers and runners on the weekends. There are some busy road crossings where you need to use caution.

Things to see: Views of Mount Hood; Powell Butte Nature Park; Schweitzer Restoration Area; downtown Gresham; views of Johnson Creek and wildlife; downtown Boring

Map: USGS Gresham

Getting There: By car: From I-205 in Southeast Portland, take the Foster Road exit. Travel eastbound on Foster Road for 0.5 mile. Turn right into a trailhead parking area.

By public transportation: From SW Madison Street and SW 4th Street in downtown Portland, board bus 14 for Hawthorne, and get off on SE Foster Road and SE 94th Avenue (I-205 overpass). Ride 0.5 mile east on SE Foster Road to the trailhead parking area on the right side of the road. GPS: N45 28.562' / W122 33.320'

THE RIDE

This ride starts on SE Foster Road in Southeast Portland. You will ride east on the smooth, paved Springwater Corridor multiuse trail. The Springwater Corridor is very popular with cyclists, runners, and walkers. As you head east you will have nice views of majestic Mount Hood in the distance. This multiuse trail offers many opportunities to stop and view wildlife and nature as it parallels and then crosses Johnson Creek many different times.

The Springwater Corridor Trail follows the route of Springwater Division Line (also known as the Cazadero Line, Bellrose Line, and Portland Traction Company Line), which provided rail service in 1903. The rail line was jointly owned by the Portland Railway Light and Power Company and Portland General Electric. The rail line carried passengers and hauled farm produce to local markets. By 1910, the line had about 161 miles of rail and provided a vital source of transportation and commerce for many Southeast Portland communities, including Pleasant Valley, Powellhurst–Gilbert, Lents, Errol Heights, Woodstock, Eastmoreland, Sellwood, and Waverly Heights.

At 2.3 miles, you will have an opportunity for a side trip to visit Powell Butte Nature Park, which features many dirt hiking and mountain biking trails. If you are riding a road bike, you may want to lock it up and go hike the trails in the park.

At 3.2 miles, you'll arrive at the Schweitzer Restoration Area viewpoint. This viewpoint is named after the Schweitzer family, which lived on much of this property for more than fifty years. They raised cattle, chickens, and dairy cows, and grew strawberries. When the Springwater Corridor rail line was built it disrupted Johnson Creek's water flow from parts of

Cyclists can enjoy creek views from the Schweitzer Restoration Area viewpoint. PHOTO BY LIZANN DUNEGAN

Tandem riders taking a break at Gresham Main City Park. PHOTO BY LIZANN DUNEGAN

the floodplain, causing the creek to rise more quickly. In the 1930s, the Works Progress Administration (WPA) rerouted the creek in an unsuccessful effort to prevent flooding. When building the Schweitzer Restoration Area in 2007, the Portland Bureau of Environmental Services goal was to restore Johnson Creek to its original natural state by improving water quality and wildlife habitat and reducing flood damage. A new creek channel was built, and logs and boulders with root wads were added to stabilize the banks. In addition, gravel beds and pools were built to encourage fish and amphibians to feed and breed in this area. The logs and snags also provide a place for birds to rest and build nests. Another highlight of this viewpoint is the colorful mosaic tiles of different animals that are present in the walkway, which were created by artist Lynn Takata.

At 4.5 miles you'll arrive at Linneman Station, and you will also intersect with the signed "Gresham–Fairview Trail" on the left. Linneman Station has restrooms, water, and picnic tables if you want to take a break.

At 6.6 miles you'll arrive at Gresham Main City Park on your left. If you want to take a side trip to downtown Gresham, turn left at this junction and ride about 1.5 miles to reach downtown. Downtown Gresham has many fun shops and restaurants, and is a good place to go exploring. Downtown Gresham also features the Gresham History Museum, which provides many exhibits that explore Gresham's history and growth.

Over the next 5.6 miles you'll follow the smooth paved trail until you reach your turnaround point at Boring Station Trailhead Park in Boring. This park has restrooms, water, and picnic tables. After taking a break, turn around and ride the same route back to your starting point. If you want to taste some delicious organic coffee, stop by Country Coffee at 28320 SE OR 212) in downtown Boring. (**Option:** If you are riding a mountain bike or a bike that does well on gravel, you have the option of crossing OR 212 and continuing on the Cazadero State Park Trail for an additional 3.0 miles. For more information, see the Cazadero State Park Trail route description.)

Bike Shop

Gresham Bicycle Center: 567 NE 8th St., Gresham, OR 97030; (503) 661-2453; greshambike.com

MILES AND DIRECTIONS

0.0 From the parking area on SE Foster Road, turn left (west) and ride about 400 feet to a stoplight and crosswalk. Cross SE Foster Road and start riding east on the paved Springwater Corridor Trail.

0.4 Cross SE 111th Avenue and continue riding east on the Springwater Corridor Trail.

1.0 Cross SE 122nd Avenue and continue riding east on the Springwater Corridor Trail.

1.7 Cross SE 136th Avenue. After crossing the road, there is a country store located on your right, on SE 136th Avenue, if you want to stop for snacks and drinks.

2.3 Pass the signed turnoff to Powell Butte Nature Park on your left.

3.2 Take a break and enjoy the views of the Schweitzer Restoration Area on your right. An interpretive sign and viewing area allow you to look for local wildlife and take in views of Johnson Creek. After enjoying the views, continue riding east on the Springwater Corridor Trail.

3.8 Cross SE Jenne Road and continue riding on the Springwater Corridor Trail.

Springwater Corridor: Southeast Foster Road to Downtown Boring

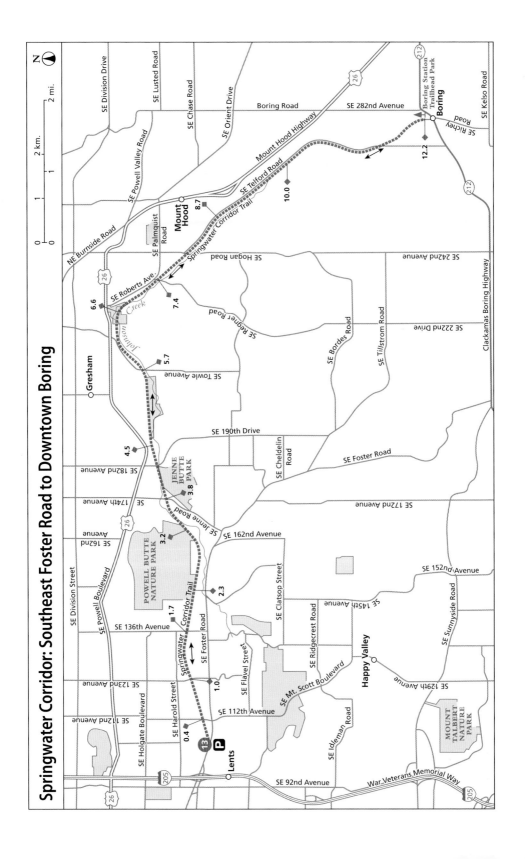

4.5 Arrive at Linneman Station on the left. Linneman Station has restrooms, water, and provides picnic tables if you want to take a break.

5.7 Cross SE Towle Avenue and continue riding east on the Springwater Corridor Trail.

6.6 Arrive at Gresham Main City Park on your left. If you want to take a side trip to downtown Gresham, turn left at this junction.

7.4 Cross SE Regner Road and continue riding east on the Springwater Corridor Trail.

8.7 Cross SE Palmblad Road and continue riding east on the Springwater Corridor Trail.

10.0 Cross SE Rugg Road and continue riding east on the Springwater Corridor Trail.

12.2 Arrive at Boring Station Trailhead Park in Boring—the paved trail ends here. This is your turnaround point. This park has restrooms, water, and picnic tables. After taking a break, turn around and ride the same route back to your starting point.

24.4 Arrive back at the SE Foster Road trailhead where the ride started.

RIDE INFORMATION

Local Events/Attractions
Gresham History Museum: 410 N Main Ave., Gresham, OR 97030; (503) 661-0347; greshamhistoricalsociety.org.

Restrooms
Restrooms are located at mile 4.5 (Linneman Station); at mile 6.6 (Gresham Main City Park); and at mile 12.2 (Boring Station Trailhead Park).

Springwater Corridor: Sellwood–Hawthorne Loop

This 19.3-mile ride takes you along the Springwater Corridor multiuse trail and through Southeast Portland neighborhoods. On this route you have many opportunities to stop and explore, including the Tideman Johnson Natural Area, Oaks Bottom Wildlife Refuge, and the historic Sellwood and Hawthorne districts.

Start: SE Foster Road in Southeast Portland, off I-205

Length: 19.3-mile loop

Approximate riding time: 3 to 4 hours with stops

Best bike: Road bike

Terrain and trail surface: Paved path shared with walkers and runners. Some sections of paved road.

Traffic and hazards: This route can be very crowded with walkers and runners on the weekends. There are some busy road crossings where you need to use caution.

Things to see: Tideman Johnson Natural Area; Sellwood historic neighborhood; views of the Willamette River and downtown Portland; Portland's historic bridges; Oaks Bottom Wildlife Refuge; Oaks Bottoms Amusement Park; Oregon Museum of Science and Industry (OMSI); historic Hawthorne and Ladd's Edition neighborhoods

Map: USGS Portland

Getting There: By car: From I-205 in Southeast Portland, take the SE Foster Road exit. Travel eastbound on SE Foster Road for 0.5 mile. Turn right into the trailhead parking area.

By public transportation: From SW Madison Street and SW 4th Street in downtown Portland, board bus 14 for Hawthorne and get off on SE Foster Road and SE 94th Avenue (I-205 overpass). Ride 0.5 mile east on SE Foster Road to the trailhead parking area on the right side of the road. You can also start this route from downtown Portland by crossing the Hawthorne Bridge and following the ride directions from SE Hawthorne Boulevard. GPS: N45 28.566' / W122 33.323'

THE RIDE

This ride takes you along the flat, smooth, paved Springwater Corridor rail-trail in Southeast Portland. The Springwater Corridor rail-trail takes you through residential neighborhoods, past wetlands and natural areas, as well as through some industrial districts. The trail crisscrosses Johnson Creek multiple times as it flows toward the Willamette River, and provides you with opportunities to view different types of wildlife in an urban setting.

The Springwater Corridor is a very popular multiuse trail for cyclists, walkers, and runners.
PHOTO BY LIZANN DUNEGAN

At 3.9 miles you'll arrive at the Tideman Johnson Natural Area. It is recommended to stop here and explore this 7.69-acre natural area. This land was given to the city of Portland in 1942 by the Johnson family. A short hiking trail winds through the natural area, offering you opportunities to see great blue herons, ducks, and geese feeding in the creek.

At 5.2 miles the paved Springwater Corridor bike path ends, and you will ride on quiet city streets through the historic community of Sellwood. Sellwood is filled with antique shops, coffeehouses, brewpubs, and other unique shops and restaurants that are worth exploring.

At 6.2 miles you will hook up with the paved Springwater Corridor Trail. Follow this path as it heads north and parallels the Willamette River. There are many places along the way to enjoy nice views of the river.

The Willamette River is a well-known Portland landmark and divides the east and west sides of Portland. PHOTO BY LIZANN DUNEGAN

At 7.6 miles, pass the entrance to Oaks Bottom Wildlife Refuge. The 141-acre refuge was established in 1988 as Portland's first wildlife refuge. The preserve is host to more than 140 species of reptiles, birds, amphibians, and mammals. It is worth stopping here and exploring the refuge.

At 9.8 miles you'll pass OMSI (Oregon Museum of Science and Industry), which is worth visiting. This museum has many interesting science exhibits that change throughout the year.

The route continues along the Willamette River for the next 2.5 miles, then you will turn east and start riding on SE Hawthorne Avenue through the Hawthorne District. This popular southeast neighborhood district has a hipster vibe and is filled with unique shops and restaurants. A fun place to stop is the Bagdad Theater, where you can drink local microbrews and eat great pizza while you watch a movie.

Bike Shop

Joe Bike: 2039 SE Cesar Chavez Blvd., Portland, OR 97214; (503) 954-2039; joe-bike.com

A bright summer bloom appears in a Southeast neighborhood garden. PHOTO BY LIZANN DUNEGAN

At 11.2 miles, turn onto SE Harrison Street and pass Palio Dessert and Espresso House on the right (1996 SE Ladd St.; 503-232-9412; www.palio-in-ladds.com). This coffeehouse is a great place to stop and take a break.

At 12.5 miles, use caution when you cross SE Cesar Chavez Boulevard (SE 39th Avenue). Although the road sign says it is a one way for cars, cyclists are allowed to continue straight on SE Lincoln Street.

Over the next 1.3 miles, you'll pedal through quiet Southeast Portland residential streets until you reach Mount Tabor Park. Ride through the park, and then ride through the Montavilla neighborhood until you reach the I-205 bike path at 16.0 miles. You'll ride south on the I-205 bike path to the intersection with SE Foster Road, and then turn east to ride 0.7 mile on SE Foster Road back to your starting point.

MILES AND DIRECTIONS

0.0 From the parking area, turn left (west) and ride on the sidewalk until you see the paved Springwater Corridor Trail on your left. Turn left and begin following the paved path.

0.6 Arrive at an intersection with the paved I-205 bike path. Continue straight toward the signed "Tideman Johnson Natural Area."

0.7 Continue straight and cross SE 92nd Avenue toward Sellwood.

2.4 Continue straight across SE Johnson Creek Boulevard. There is a bike signal. You can activate the signal by standing in the green rectangle.

3.9 Pass a viewing platform for the Tideman Johnson Natural Area. (**Option:** Just beyond the viewing platform, you can turn left on the path to explore the Tideman Johnson Natural Area.)

Springwater Corridor: Sellwood–Hawthorne Loop

5.1 Turn right on the paved path where a sign indicates "Springwater Corridor Trail."

5.2 The paved path ends. Continue straight on SE 19th Avenue.

5.4 Turn left onto SE Umatilla Street.

5.5 Continue straight and cross SE 17th Avenue.

5.8 Continue straight and cross SE 13th Avenue.

6.2 Use caution when crossing railroad tracks. After crossing the tracks, turn right and continue riding on the paved Springwater Corridor path.

6.4 Continue straight and cross SE Spokane Street.

6.9 Pass Oaks Bottom Amusement Park on the left.

7.6 Pass the entrance to Oaks Bottom Wildlife Refuge on the right.

9.4 The paved path ends. Continue straight and ride in the bike lane on SE Water Avenue.

9.8 Pass the Oregon Museum of Science and Industry (OMSI) on the left.

10.0 At the junction with SE Clay Street, turn left and ride on the paved path until it intersects with the Eastbank Esplanade. Turn right onto the Eastbank Esplanade.

10.1 Turn right on the paved path that spirals upward and intersects with the paved bike path that parallels SE Hawthorne Boulevard. Follow signs to "Southeast Portland."

10.8 Cross SE 12th Street, then turn right onto SE Ladd Road and follow the signs to Mount Tabor Park.

11.2 Ride the Ladd's Circle roundabout and go right on SE Harrison Street. The Palio Dessert and Espresso House is on the right. Continue to follow bike signs to Mount Tabor Park.

12.5 Cross SE Cesar Chavez Boulevard (SE 39th Avenue). Although the road sign says this is a one-way street for cars, cyclists are allowed to continue straight on SE Lincoln Street. If you need any bike supplies you can stop in at Joe Bike.

13.6 Continue straight and cross SE 60th Avenue.

13.8 Turn left and enter Mount Tabor Park. Follow the main entrance road as it continues uphill.

14.1 At the road junction, turn right. (*Option:* If you go left, you can pedal to the summit of Mount Tabor.)

14.4 Continue straight and cross SE 72nd Avenue. Continue riding on SE Harrison Street.

14.6 Turn left onto SE 76th Avenue.

15.0 Turn right onto SE Yamhill Street.

15.4 Continue straight and cross SE 82nd Avenue.

16.0 SE Yamhill Street dead ends into the I-205 bike path. Turn right (south) onto the paved I-205 bike path.

16.8 Continue straight and cross SE Division Street.

17.9 Continue straight and cross SE Holgate Boulevard.

18.5 At the junction, turn right toward signed "SE Foster Road," and follow the paved bike path as it descends to SE Foster Road.

18.6 The paved path ends. Go left and cross SE Foster Road using the crosswalks. Start riding in the bike lane on SE Foster Road by turning left (east).

19.3 Arrive back at the parking area.

RIDE INFORMATION

Local Events/Attractions

Providence Bridge Pedal: 1631 NE Klickitat St., Portland, OR 97212; (503) 281-9198; blog.bridgepedal.com. This annual event (held in mid-Aug) is a noncompetitive bike ride crossing Portland's historic bridges: Morrison, Sellwood, Hawthorne, Ross Island, Marquam, Burnside, Broadway, Steel, St. Johns, and Fremont.

Oregon Museum of Science and Industry: 1945 SE Water Ave., Portland, OR 97212; (800) 955-6674; omsi.edu. This fun museum has many interactive science and math exhibits that change throughout the year.

Restrooms

A restroom is located at mile 3.7.

Mount Tabor Park

Mount Tabor Park is in the heart of Southeast Portland and features a three-million-year-old volcano and stunning views of Portland's skyline. The park is a great place to enjoy a fun ride after work or, if you are only visiting for a short time, this ride gives you a mini workout with plenty of views of the city, opportunities to enjoy nature, and view some of Portland's historic reservoirs.

Start: The main parking area off East Tabor Drive adjacent the Mount Tabor Visitor Center.

Length: 4.6 miles in a series of loops

Approximate riding time: 1 hour with stops

Best bike: Mountain bike or road bike

Terrain and trail surface: Paved roads shared with hikers, runners, skateboarders, and cars

Traffic and hazards: Roads in the park can get busy on the weekends. On Wed, cars are not allowed in the park, making it a good day to ride.

Things to see: Historic Portland reservoirs; bird-watching; summer concerts; road cycle racing

Map: USGS Mount Tabor

Getting There: By car: From downtown Portland, head 5.5 miles east on I-84 toward The Dalles. Take exit 5 for NE 82nd Avenue. At the end of the off-ramp, turn right and go 1 block to a stoplight at the intersection of NE 82nd Avenue. Turn left (south) on NE 82nd Avenue and travel 1.1 miles to the intersection with SE Yamhill Street. Turn right and proceed 0.2 mile west to the intersection with SE 76th Street. Turn right, and then take an immediate left onto SE Yamhill Street, and continue heading west for 0.3 mile. Turn left on SE 69th Avenue, go 1 block, and turn right on E Tabor Drive at the base of Mount Tabor Park. (***Note:*** E Tabor Drive is unmarked.) Continue 0.1 mile to the stop sign and continue straight. The parking area on the right side of the road just past the stop sign.

By public transportation: From downtown Portland at the intersection of SW 5th Street and SW Salmon Street, board the number 15 bus. The bus will drop you off at the intersection of SE 69th Street and SE Yamhill Street. Follow the driving directions from SE 69th Street to proceed to the ride start. GPS: N45 30.620' / W122 35.647'

THE RIDE

Located in Portland's Southeast District, 190-acre Mount Tabor Park offers cyclists an opportunity to have a fun ride in the city. The park is located on an

Riders race in the Mount Tabor Circuit racing series, held on Wednesday nights during June and July.
PHOTO BY LIZANN DUNEGAN

extinct three-million-year-old volcano, and from its 643-foot summit you can enjoy stunning views of Portland's skyline and sneak peeks of Mount Hood. Mount Tabor is a Plio-Pleistocene cinder cone and is part of the Boring lava fields, which are made up of multiple cinder cones.

Plympton Kelly, an early Portland resident, named Mount Tabor after a mountain in Palestine. In the early 1900s this park was in a semirural area dominated by fruit orchards. Luckily, the city recognized the area as a place to preserve, and the Portland Parks & Recreation department began purchasing land for the park in 1909.

This scenic city park is covered with a canopy of shady Douglas fir, Japanese flowering cherry, European beech, ginkgo, coastal redwood, Norway maple, Oregon myrtle, big-leaf maple, Pacific wax-myrtle, western red cedar, elkhorn cedar, blue spruce, Sitka spruce, giant sequoia, and Pacific dogwood.

A cyclist rides around Harvey Scott Summit Circle on the summit of Mount Tabor Park.
PHOTO BY LIZANN DUNEGAN

The park is also host to abundant wildlife and birdlife. You can learn more about the park's native plants and animals at the visitor center, which is adjacent to the parking lot at the start of this ride.

On Wednesday nights in June and July, you can watch a circuit cycling race series that is hosted by the Oregon Bicycle Racing Association. The course follows a 1.3-mile hilly loop around Historic Reservoir #5, and offers challenges for seasoned racers as well as novice riders.

This ride starts at a paved parking area adjacent to the park's visitor center and Crater Amphitheater, which hosts concerts during the summer months. There are restrooms available here. Start by pedaling uphill about 0.5 mile to the 643-foot summit of Mount Tabor. Once you reach the summit, you have the opportunity to view a statue of Harvey W. Scott, one of Portland's prominent citizens. He was editor and part owner of the *Oregonian* newspaper from

Cyclists can enjoy views of Historic Reservoir #5 and the downtown Portland skyline.
PHOTO BY LIZANN DUNEGAN

Mount Tabor Park

1866–1872. To continue, you will pedal around the paved Harvey Scott Summit Circle, where you will have opportunities to soak in vast views of Portland's skyline. Restrooms and a drinking fountain are available on the summit circle.

After you complete the summit circle, cruise downhill and head around the west side of the park. At 1.9 miles, pass restrooms on your right. At 2.0 miles, you will ride by Historic Reservoir #5, which was built in 1911 and is one of three historic open reservoirs in the park. The 14 million gallons of water that flow daily from reservoir #5 to Historic Reservoir #6 generate hydroelectric power that is used to power the lights in the park, as well as park equipment. After you view the reservoir, continue riding steeply uphill on an unmarked paved road.

After 2.4 miles, pass the parking area and starting point, and begin another loop around the park following East Tabor Drive. At 3.3 miles, ride past the leash-free dog park, where you can view many happy canines playing. At 3.8 miles, you have the opportunity to view Historic Reservoir Gatehouse #1, which is located on the southern edge of the park. This reservoir was built in 1894. The reservoirs no longer hold water and are now empty.

Continue riding on Reservoir Loop Road, which offers many spectacular views of Portland's downtown skyline. You'll end the ride with a quick downhill cruise on North Tabor Drive to your starting point.

MILES AND DIRECTIONS

0.0 From the parking area, turn left on East Mount Tabor Drive and proceed about 20 feet to a stop sign. At the stop sign, turn right on North Tabor Drive and start pedaling uphill toward the Mount Tabor summit.

0.2 Arrive at a four-way road junction. Continue to left on Mount Tabor Summit Drive. You will pass a small parking area on the right and you will need to go around a white metal gate (cars are not allowed on the summit). Continue pedaling uphill toward the summit.

0.5 Reach an intersection with the Harvey Scott Summit Circle. On the left is a statue of Harvey W. Scott. Turn right and start riding on the paved summit circle.

0.7 A drinking fountain is available on the right. Up ahead you'll pass a restroom on the right.

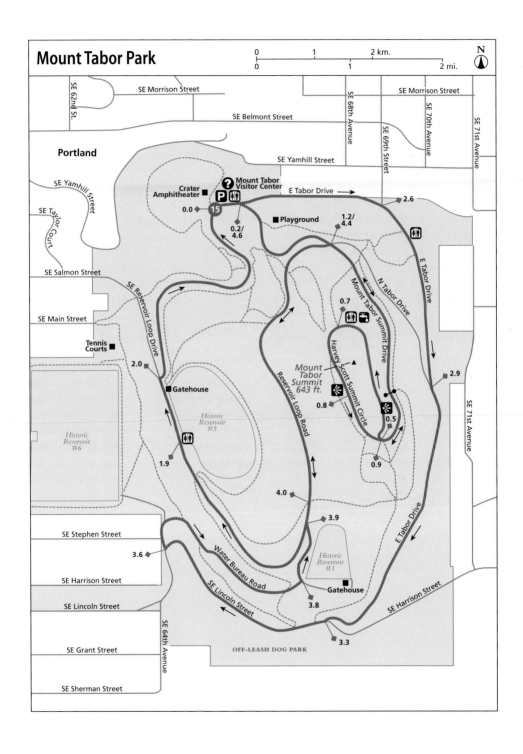

Mount Tabor Park

0   1   2 km.

0   1   2 mi.

N

SE 62nd St.

SE Morrison Street

SE Belmont Street

SE 68th Avenue

SE Morrison Street

SE 70th Avenue

SE 71st Avenue

SE 69th Street

SE Yamhill Street

Portland

SE Yamhill Street

SE Taylor Court

Mount Tabor Visitor Center

Crater Amphitheater

P

E Tabor Drive

0.0

15

2.6

0.2/4.6

Playground

1.2/4.4

E Tabor Drive

SE Salmon Street

SE Reservoir Loop Drive

0.7

Mount Tabor Summit Drive

N Tabor Drive

SE Main Street

Tennis Courts

2.0

Gatehouse

Historic Reservoir #5

Historic Reservoir #6

1.9

Reservoir Loop Road

Mount Tabor Summit 643 ft.

Harvey Scott Summit Circle

0.8

0.5

2.9

SE 71st Avenue

0.9

4.0

3.9

SE Stephen Street

3.6

Water Bureau Road

Historic Reservoir #1

E Tabor Drive

SE Harrison Street

SE Harrison Street

SE Lincoln Street

Gatehouse

SE Lincoln Street

3.8

SE 64th Avenue

SE Grant Street

3.3

SE Sherman Street

OFF-LEASH DOG PARK

A cyclist heads to the summit of Mount Tabor Park. PHOTO BY LIZANN DUNEGAN

0.8 Stop to enjoy a stunning view of Portland's downtown skyline. Benches are available if you want to stop and take a break.

0.9 Complete the summit circle. Stay to the right and start cruising downhill.

1.2 At the road junction, go around a white metal gate. Turn left on Reservoir Loop Road.

1.6 A drinking fountain is available on the right.

1.9 Restrooms are available on the right.

2.0 Pass Historic Reservoir #5, built in 1911, on the right. Continue about 25 yards and go through a black metal gate. At a Y intersection turn right and start riding uphill on an unmarked paved road.

2.4 Pass the parking area (and your starting point) on the left. Continue to a stop sign. Continue straight (left) on East Tabor Drive.

2.6 At the intersection with SE 69th Street, continue straight (right) on East Tabor Drive.

2.9 At the intersection with North Tabor Drive, continue to the left and pedal downhill on East Tabor Drive.

3.3 Continue straight (right) on SE Lincoln Street. The leash-free dog park is on the left.

3.6 Turn right onto a paved pathway and ride through a black metal gate marked "Lincoln Street and Reservoir Loop Road." Ride 50 feet and take a very sharp right run on Water Bureau Road. You will begin a steep, uphill climb.

3.8 Pass the Historic Reservoir Gatehouse #1 on the right.

3.9 At the T intersection, turn left on Reservoir Loop Road.

4.0 Pass a drinking fountain on the left.

4.4 Go around a white gate and turn left on North Tabor Drive.

4.6 At the stop sign, turn left on East Tabor Drive. Ride about 25 feet and turn right into the parking area where the ride started.

RIDE INFORMATION

Local Events/Attractions
Mount Tabor Series: This racing series is held in June and July on Wednesday nights. It is organized by the Oregon Bicycle Racing Association; (503) 278-5550; obra.org.

The Grotto: 8840 NE Skidmore St., Portland, OR 97220; (503) 254-7371; the grotto.org. You can tour beautiful gardens and see unique statues in this hidden, Catholic sanctuary.

Academy Theater: 7818 SE Stark St., Portland, OR 97215; (503) 252-0500; academytheaterpdx.com. You can watch a movie, eat pizza, and drink microbrews at this fun local theater.

Restrooms
There are restrooms adjacent to the parking area at the start of the ride and at mile 0.75.

After you complete your ride, be sure to check out the Caldera Public House (6031 SE Stark St., Portland, OR 97215; 503-233-8242; calderapublichouse.com). The restaurant has delicious salads, burgers, microbrews, and also features specialty cocktails. Or visit Montavilla Brew Works (7805 SE Stark St., Portland, OR 97215; 503-954-3440; montavillabrew.com), which serves delicious microbrews and snacks.

Mount Tabor Park–Rocky Butte

This ride takes you to the scenic summits of two volcanic buttes in Southeast Portland. You start the ride in Mount Tabor Park and ride to the summit to enjoy views of the Southeast District and downtown Portland. From there, you descend and ride through quiet neighborhood streets to Joseph Wood Hill Park and the summit of Rocky Butte. From this viewpoint, you have spectacular views of the Columbia River, Mount Hood, and Mount Saint Helens, and the vast cityscape of east Portland. You can also enjoy views of downtown Portland.

Start: The main parking area off East Tabor Drive adjacent to the Mount Tabor Visitor Center

Length: 12.3 miles out and back, including summit loops

Approximate riding time: 1 to 2 hours with stops

Best bike: Mountain bike or road bike

Terrain and trail surface: Paved roads shared with walkers and cars. Watch for skateboarders in Mount Tabor Park.

Traffic and hazards: The roads in Mount Tabor Park can get busy on the weekends. On Wed, cars are not allowed in Mount Tabor Park, making it a good day to ride.

Things to see: Historic Portland reservoirs; bird-watching; summer concerts; road cycle racing; viewpoints of Southeast and Northeast Portland; downtown Portland; views of Mount Hood and Mount Saint Helens

Maps: USGS Mount Tabor and Vancouver

Getting There: By car: From downtown Portland, head 5.5 miles east on I-84 toward The Dalles. Take exit 5 for NE 82nd Avenue. At the end of the off-ramp, turn right and go 1 block to a stoplight at the intersection with NE 82nd Avenue. Turn left (south) on NE 82nd Avenue and travel 1.1

miles to the intersection with SE Yamhill Street. Turn right and proceed 0.2 mile west to the intersection with SE 76th Avenue. Turn right, and then take an immediate left onto SE Yamhill Street and continue heading west for 0.3 mile. Turn left on SE 69th Avenue, go 1 block and turn right on E Tabor Drive, at the base of Mount Tabor Park. Continue 0.1 mile to the stop sign and continue straight. The parking area is on the right side of the road just past the stop sign. (**Note:** E Tabor Drive is unmarked.)

By public transportation: From downtown Portland at the intersection of SW 5th Street and SW Salmon Street, board the number 15 bus. The bus will drop you off at the intersection of SE 69th Avenue and SE Yamhill Street. Follow the driving directions from SE 69th Avenue to proceed to the ride start. GPS: N45 30.620' / W122 35.647'

THE RIDE

This ride starts at a paved parking area next to Mount Tabor Park's visitor center and Crater Amphitheater, which hosts concerts during the summer months. Restrooms are adjacent to the parking area.

This statue of Harvey W. Scott is at the summit of Mount Tabor Park.
PHOTO BY LIZANN DUNEGAN

Start by pedaling uphill about 0.5 mile to the 643-foot summit of Mount Tabor. Once you reach the summit, you have the opportunity to view a statue of Harvey W. Scott. Restrooms and a drinking fountain are available on the summit circle. You also can enjoy nice views of Southeast Portland and downtown.

After you complete the summit circle, enjoy a fun downhill cruise; after 1.6 miles you will exit the park. Descend on SE Yamhill Street to SE 76th Avenue. After 2.0 miles you will cross SE Washington Street and SE Stark Street, which lead into the heart of the popular Montavilla District.

This district has a variety of restaurants and shops that are fun to explore. The area was originally called the Mount Tabor Villa Addition when it was platted in 1889, but eventually the name was combined to become Montavilla. The area was originally filled with farms and

You'll enjoy nice views of the Columbia River from the summit of Rocky Butte. PHOTO BY LIZANN DUNEGAN

orchards. In the 1880s, much of the land was sold off to land speculators who started to build subdivisions. By 1890, Montavilla had its own post office, grocery stores, and livery shop. These days, from June through October, you can buy fresh, locally grown produce and other handmade items at the Montavilla Farmer's Market, which is open from 10 a.m. to 2 p.m. on Sunday. The market is located on the 7600 block of SE Stark Street.

Over the next 2.6 miles you will ride on flat terrain through quiet Southeast and Northeast neighborhood streets. You will ride by the vast expanse of Rose City Golf course, which was opened in 1923 and is the second oldest municipal golf course in Portland. At 4.2 miles, you will pass Hancock Park on the right. This shady park has benches and a large grassy lawn, and makes it is a good place to stop if you want to take a break.

At 4.6 miles, begin your ascent to the summit of Rocky Butte on NE Rocky Butte Road. Rocky Butte is one of four extinct volcanic cinder cones in the Portland area; the others are Mount Tabor, Kelly Butte, and Powell Butte. The climb is steep but the views from the summit are well worth all of your effort.

At 6.0 miles you will arrive at a green gate and a short gravel path that leads to the summit of Rocky Butte and the historic 2.38-acre Joseph Wood Hill

Ornate stone walls at the summit of Rocky Butte. PHOTO BY LIZANN DUNEGAN

Park. Dr. Joseph A. Hill established the private Hill Military Academy in 1901, and it was in operation until 1959. A path leads around the summit, which is bordered by a beautiful stone wall that features detailed arches, metal lamp posts, carved rock benches, and historic plaques. From the summit, on a clear day, you can enjoy a commanding view of the Columbia River, Mount Saint Helens, Mount Hood, and the vast cityscape of east Portland.

Rocky Butte also features a 17.2-acre natural area that is managed by the Portland Parks & Recreation, and is also popular with rock climbers who ascend its challenging routes.

Bike Shop
Oregon Bike Shop: 418 SE 81st Ave., Portland, OR 97215; (503) 575-1804; oregonbikeshop.com

After enjoying the views, walk your bike down the gravel path and continue straight from the green gate on a fun 1.2-mile descent on NE Rocky Butte Road. Over the next 5.0 miles, you will complete a small loop through Northeast Portland, and then ride back through the Montavilla District. Complete the route with a short, steep climb on SE Yamhill Street back to your starting point in Mount Tabor Park.

Best Bike Rides Portland, Oregon

MILES AND DIRECTIONS

0.0 From the parking area and visitor center in Mount Tabor Park, turn left on East Tabor Drive and proceed about 20 feet to a stop sign. At the stop sign, turn right on North Tabor Drive and start pedaling uphill toward the Mount Tabor summit.

0.2 Arrive at a parking area. Continue straight. At the end of the parking area, stay to the right and go around a white metal gate (cars are not allowed on the summit). Continue pedaling uphill toward the summit.

0.5 Reach an intersection with the Harvey Scott Summit Circle. On the left is a statue of Harvey W. Scott. Turn right and start riding around the paved summit circle.

0.6 A drinking fountain is available on the right.

0.7 Enjoy a stunning view of Portland's downtown skyline. Benches are available if you want to stop and take a break.

0.8 Complete the summit circle. Stay to the right and start cruising downhill on Tabor Summit Drive.

1.1 At the road junction, go around a white metal gate. Turn right on North Tabor Drive and keep descending.

1.3 Turn left onto East Tabor Drive.

1.5 Turn right onto SE 69th Avenue.

1.6 Turn right onto SE Yamhill Street.

1.9 Turn left on SE 76th Avenue.

2.0 At the stoplight, continue straight and cross SE Washington Street.

2.1 At the stoplight, turn left on SE Stark Street.

2.2 Turn right onto SE 74th Avenue.

2.4 At the stop sign, continue straight and cross E Burnside Street.

2.7 At the stoplight, continue straight and cross NE Glisan Street.

3.2 At the stoplight, turn left on NE Halsey Street, and then take a quick right onto NE 74th Avenue and continue riding on NE 74th Avenue.

3.5 Turn right on NE Tillamook Street.

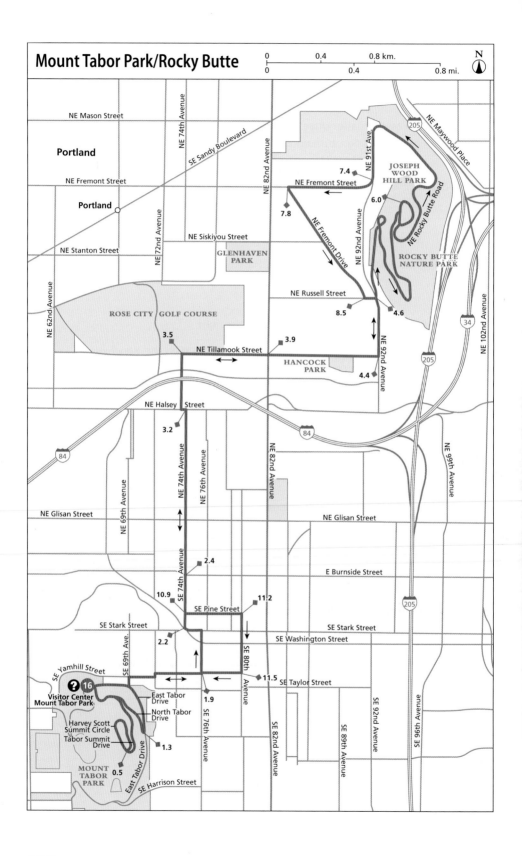

Mount Tabor Park/Rocky Butte

| 0 | 0.4 | 0.8 km. |
| 0 | 0.4 | 0.8 mi. |

N

NE Mason Street

Portland

NE Fremont Street

Portland

NE Siskiyou Street

NE Stanton Street

GLENHAVEN PARK

NE 74th Avenue

SE Sandy Boulevard

NE 82nd Avenue

NE 91st Ave.

JOSEPH WOOD HILL PARK

NE Maywood Place

205

7.4

6.0

NE Fremont Street

7.8

NE Fremont Drive

NE 92nd Avenue

NE Rocky Butte Road

ROCKY BUTTE NATURE PARK

NE 72nd Avenue

NE 62nd Avenue

ROSE CITY GOLF COURSE

NE Russell Street

8.5

4.6

NE 102nd Avenue

34

3.5

3.9

NE Tillamook Street

NE 92nd Avenue

HANCOCK PARK

4.4

205

NE Halsey Street

3.2

84

84

NE 69th Avenue

NE 74th Avenue

NE 76th Avenue

NE 82nd Avenue

NE 99th Avenue

NE Glisan Street

NE Glisan Street

E Burnside Street

2.4

10.9

SE 74th Avenue

11.2

SE Pine Street

205

2.2

SE Stark Street

SE Washington Street

SE Stark Street

SE 69th Ave.

SE 80th Avenue

SE Yamhill Street

11.5

SE Taylor Street

❓ 16

Visitor Center Mount Tabor Park

East Tabor Drive

North Tabor Drive

1.9

SE 76th Avenue

SE 82nd Avenue

SE 89th Avenue

SE 92nd Avenue

SE 96th Avenue

Harvey Scott Summit Circle

Tabor Summit Drive

1.3

MOUNT TABOR PARK

0.5

East Tabor Drive

SE Harrison Street

3.9 At the stoplight, continue straight and cross NE 82nd Avenue.

4.2 Pass Hancock Park on the right.

4.4 At the stop sign, turn left onto NE 92nd Avenue.

4.6 At the Y junction, turn right on NE Rocky Butte Road and start climbing to the summit of Rocky Butte.

5.0 Start riding through a short tunnel. Use caution in the tunnel because the road is narrow and there is no bike path.

6.0 At the T junction, turn right on the summit circle. Ride a short distance and you will arrive at a green gate on the left and the entrance

You can view an elaborate stone and metal plaque of Joseph Wood Hill on the summit of Rocky Butte. PHOTO BY LIZANN DUNEGAN

to Joseph Wood Hill Park. Walk your bike up a short gravel path to the summit circle.

6.1   Arrive at the summit of Rocky Butte. Walk around the summit circle on the gravel path and soak in the views of the Columbia River, Mount Saint Helens, Mount Hood, and east Portland. When you are ready to continue, descend the gravel path back to the green gate.

6.2   From the green gate, continue straight and begin descending on NE Rocky Butte Road.

7.4   At the Y junction, turn right on NE Fremont Street.

7.8   Go left on NE Fremont Drive.

8.5   At the stop sign, turn left on NE Russell Street.

8.6   Turn right on NE 92nd Avenue.

8.8   Turn right on NE Tillamook Street.

9.3   At the stoplight, continue straight and cross SE 82nd Ave.

9.7   Turn left on NE 74th Avenue.

10.0   Turn left on NE Halsey Street, and then take a quick right onto NE 74th Avenue.

10.5   At the stoplight, continue straight and cross NE Glisan Street.

10.7   At the stop sign, continue straight and cross E Burnside Street.

10.9   Turn left onto SE Pine Street.

11.2   Turn right onto SE 80th Avenue.

11.3   At the stop sign, continue straight on SE 80th Avenue and cross SE Stark Street. Continue on SE 80th Avenue for 1 block to the intersection with SE Washington Street. Cross SE Washington Street and continue riding on SE 80th Avenue.

11.5   Turn right on SE Yamhill Street.

11.7   Turn right on SE 76th Street, and then take a quick left on SE Yamhill Street and start climbing up the hill.

12.0   Turn left on SE 69th Street. Ride 1 block and then turn right on SE Harrison Street.

12.3 Arrive at the parking area and visitor center in Mount Tabor Park, where the ride started.

RIDE INFORMATION

Local Events/Attractions
Mount Tabor Series: This racing series is held in June and July on Wednesday nights. It is organized by the Oregon Bicycle Racing Association; (503) 278-5550; obra.org.

The Grotto: 8840 NE Skidmore St., Portland, OR 97220; (503) 254-7371; thegrotto.org. You can tour beautiful gardens and see unique statues in this hidden, Catholic sanctuary.

Academy Theater: 7818 SE Stark St., Portland, OR 97215; (503) 252-0500; academytheaterpdx.com. You can watch a movie, eat pizza, and drink microbrews at this fun local theater.

Restrooms
There are restrooms adjacent to the parking area at the start/finish of the ride, and at mile 0.7.

Southeast Portland is renowned for its colorful houses and bohemian vibe, which fully exudes the "Keep Portland Weird" mantra. This short loop takes you on a tour of some of the most "thoroughly Portland" locales in this funky area of the city. You'll journey along shady, low-traffic streets with plenty of opportunities to stop along the way for food, drink, and exploration.

Start: At the intersection of SE Floral Place and SE Ankeny Street

Length: 6.2-mile loop

Approximate riding time: 1 to 2 hours

Best bike: Road bike or hybrid

Terrain and trail surface: Smooth pavement; low traffic streets

Traffic and hazards: Low traffic city streets with a few busy street crossings

Things to see: Ladd's Addition; Laurelhurst Park; Sunnyside Piazza; Movie Madness Costume Museum; colorful houses; cycling "greenways" packed with cyclists

Maps: USGS Portland; Metro Bike There! map

Getting There: By car: From downtown Portland, take the Burnside Bridge over the Willamette River and continue for 2.4 miles on E Burnside Street. Turn right on SE Floral Place and look for on-street parking. Your ride begins from SE Ankeny Street at Floral.

By public transportation: Take the number 20 bus to "Gresham TC" and get off at E Burnside Street and SE Floral Place. Head 1 block south to SE Floral Place and SE Ankeny Street. GPS: N45 31.337' / W122 37.719'

THE RIDE

The ride begins at the gorgeous, sprawling Laurelhurst Park. Plan to spend some time here before or after your ride to stroll along the lovely winding paths, watch dogs romp in the off-leash dog play area, and gaze at the famous ducks paddling around Firwood Lake, the pond in the middle of the park.

You'll begin on low traffic streets as you wind through the Sunnyside neighborhood. Your first highlight is the famed Sunnyside Piazza (mile 0.4), a colorful painted intersection. This project is known as an "Intersection Repair," a method of making intersections safer and more welcoming by painting the pavement with a colorful design. Neighbors worked together to design this installation, which includes a book-lending library and a resting space on the corner. Projects like this define Portland's creative approach to calming traffic,

The colorful Sunnyside Piazza painted intersection helps calm traffic. PHOTO BY AYLEEN CROTTY

creating safer streets, and building community. Every few years the organization City Repair hosts lively volunteer parties to re-paint these intersections, and keep them vibrant for years to come.

For much of the beginning of your ride, you'll travel along SE Salmon Street, a popular bike route through the heart of Southeast Portland. You will then turn onto SE 11th Avenue, a bustling but fortunately short stretch. At mile 1.8 turn left onto SE Hawthorne Boulevard into the bike lane and take an immediate right onto the diagonal street, SE Ladd Avenue. You'll dip into the funky neighborhood of Ladd's Addition, where the streets run diagonal, intersecting five central hubs. It is tradition to take at least one additional spin around the main circle of Ladd's Addition, just for fun, before exiting on one of the spoke streets. Palio Dessert and Espresso House is quietly tucked into Ladd's Circle, a nice stopping point if you want to take a break and watch cyclists whizzing around the circle.

SE Clinton Street, a designated bikeway, will carry you through a broad stretch of Southeast Portland past funky small shops and cafes. Look for the creative ornamental bike designs that top the signposts and the bike frame mounted to a telephone pole. You'll pass the Clinton Street Theater, one of the oldest continually operating movie houses in the United States, where they've been regularly screening *The Rocky Horror Picture Show* since 1978.

Bike Shops

Seven Corners Cycles: 3218 SE 21st Ave., Portland, OR 97202; (503) 230-0317; 7-corners.com
Joe Bike: 2039 SE Cesar Chavez Blvd., Portland, OR 97214; (503) 954-2039; joe-bike.com

From SE Clinton Street, you'll saunter along quiet residential streets as you pass a sea of other cyclists, a sign of Portland's robust cycling culture. This area is one of the most colorful sections of the city. The lively homes are creatively painted every color imaginable. Many homes, large and small, are overtaken with spectacular gardens that seem to occupy every possible inch of land. Portland's mild, wet climate makes it easy to grow just about any plant, resulting in a multitude of lush floral gardens bursting with color.

When you get to SE Belmont Street (mile 5.1), take a break at Movie Madness to explore the Museum of Motion Picture History and what might be the world's largest collection of rare and out-of-print movie titles. Owner Mike Clark was vacationing in Las Vegas in 1995 when he discovered an antiques and oddities store selling Diane Keaton's dress from *The Godfather: Part II*. He knew this would be an interesting piece to display in his store and share with the movie fans of Portland. From there, the museum continued to grow. Today the collection spans a deep history of movies, with pieces from early Charlie Chaplin silent films, the shower scene knife from *Psycho*, Faye Dunaway's

5.6 Turn left onto SE 41st Avenue.

5.8 Turn left onto SE Ankeny Street and carefully cross SE Cesar Chavez Boulevard.

6.2 Arrive at SE Ankeny Street and Floral Place, where the ride started.

RIDE INFORMATION

Local Events/Attractions

Clinton Street Theater: The longest-running movie house west of the Mississippi River, this unique theater showcases events and movies not often available elsewhere. 2522 SE Clinton St., Portland, OR 97202; (503) 238-5588; cstpdx.com.

Division/Clinton Street Fair and Parade: Every July, the retail districts of Division and Clinton join forces for a gigantic celebration. See divisionclinton .com for details.

Restrooms

Restrooms are available at the start/finish in Laurelhurst Park.

Five "Quadrants" Ultimate Portland Loop

Want to know what Portland is truly like? This is the ride for you. The ride offers tours to some of the most popular retail and culture districts: the "Trendy Third" (boutiques), Hawthorne (the old hippie haven), Alberta Arts (an arts-centric area), and Mississippi Avenue (jam-packed with independent shops, restaurants, and bars). Between the bustle of these vibrant areas awaits a relaxed tour of the city, one that truly showcases Portland at its finest. There is plenty to see, do, and eat along the way. "Greenways" and other bike-friendly traffic-planning configurations make it easy to wind through the city on this flat, enjoyable route.

Start: At the Velo Cult Bike Shop at 1969 NE 42nd Ave.

Length: 20.2-mile loop

Approximate riding time: 2.5 to 3.5 hours of riding, plus 1 to 3 hours to stop and explore along the way

Best bike: Road bike or hybrid

Terrain and trail surface: Paved city streets

Traffic and hazards: None

Things to see: Portland's bustling retail districts: Alberta, Mississippi, Trendy Third, and Hawthorne — the historic hippie haven. Quiet tree-lined residential streets, home gardens bursting with color, funky shops, the Willamette River, the Ainsworth Linear Arboretum, a "sunken" rose garden, and colorful homes.

Maps: USGS Portland; Metro Bike There! map

Getting There: By car: From downtown Portland, take the Hawthorne Bridge east out of the city and turn north onto Martin Luther King Jr. Boulevard. Take I-84 east toward The Dalles. Take exit 2 for NE Cesar E. Chavez Boulevard. Turn right onto NE Hancock Street, then left onto NE 42nd Avenue, and continue until you arrive at Velo Cult Bike Shop, 1969 NE 42nd Ave. There is ample parking behind the shop. Most street parking is limited to a few hours unless you park farther north in the residential area. Head north on NE 42nd Avenue from Velo Cult to begin your ride.

By public transportation: Take the MAX Red, Green, or Blue Lines east to the Hollywood Transit Center. Walk down the stairs and through the parking lot, and you will be at the intersection of NE Halsey and NE 42nd Avenues. Take NE 42nd Avenue north for 0.3 mile until you arrive at Velo Cult Bike Shop. GPS: N45 32.395' / W122 37.198'

THE RIDE

This ride begins and ends at Velo Cult Bike Shop and tavern in Northeast Portland, the cultural hub for cycling in Portland. The shop is internationally known for its bicycle museum; most of the collection hangs from the ceiling and lines the walls. It has become tradition for cyclists on multiday tours to begin or end their journeys at Velo Cult, so it would be fitting to start this ride here. In addition to full bike shop services, Velo Cult also offers a sandwich menu, fine coffee, snacks, and a beer tap list featuring some of the rarest beers available in the region. Velo Cult also regularly hosts free live music and other events.

The northern end of the city is much higher than the southeast so there's no avoiding the challenge: You will head straight up the hill, right off the bat. You will travel in a counter-clockwise pattern, first along the meandering Alameda Ridge, a magnificent residential neighborhood that overlooks the city. As you pedal along the winding, shady streets, you'll pass gigantic homes with spectacular views.

Your first stop is the busy Alberta Arts District, where art galleries and creative shops abound. Alberta is home to the monthly Last Thursday event, where vendors overtake the sidewalks selling unique art, crafts, and food. This tour travels through the heart of this bustling district, where you can stop off at any time to explore on foot.

After dipping into the Vernon and King neighborhoods for a stretch, you'll come out on the edge of the Woodlawn neighborhood as you ride a few blocks of the Ainsworth Arboretum, a 2.0-mile linear arboretum planted in the median and along the sides of the road. This unique tree showcase features sixty species, many with exotic names (but selected for Portland's climate) including Kentucky coffee tree, Japanese pagoda-tree, Asian persimmon, and Persian ironwood.

Once you cross Martin Luther King Jr. Boulevard, you enter North Portland and pass the Peninsula Park Rose Garden (mile 4.9). Planted in 1912, it is one of Portland's most beautiful formal rose gardens, and the only sunken rose garden in Oregon. Stop to literally smell the roses or to take photos under the gazebo and by the baroque fountain.

No ultimate tour of Portland would be complete without a stop at Mock's Crest Park, commonly known as the Skidmore Bluffs (mile 6.1). This small swath of land in the Overlook neighborhood affords broad views as it overlooks a railroad yard, Swan Island, the West Hills, Forest Park, the Willamette River, and many bridges. It's a simple park with no amenities, but the views are spectacular, and the spot has become a popular hangout where people unfurl blankets and take in the impressive sunsets.

Before leaving North Portland, you'll travel through a stretch of the Mississippi Avenue retail district (mile 7.6), a region that's hopping with independent shops, cafes, restaurants, and bars. On-street bicycle parking abounds,

The famed Portland sign of the "Arlene Schnitzer Concert Hall" flanks SW Broadway Avenue in the heart of the city. PHOTO BY AYLEEN CROTTY

To understand the layout of Portland, it's essential to grasp the "Five Quadrants" orientation. Early Portland evolved to designate Burnside Avenue as the dividing line between North and South Portland, and the Willamette River as the dividing line between East and West Portland.

But a section of the land—North Portland—didn't quite fit into this layout because of the way the Willamette River takes a sharp turn before meeting up with the Columbia River to the north.

This area was physically separate and originally its own city, but eventually became absorbed into Portland.

For reasons largely unknown, the different areas of Portland, which were originally called "districts," became known as "quadrants," and the term remains to describe all five: Southwest, Southeast, Northwest, Northeast, and North Portland.

The city of Portland further designates regions by a neighborhood name, ranging in size from a mere 133 residents and 0.06 square miles (Healy Heights) to more than 20,000 residents and 3.3 square miles (Lents).

Most residents live outside the downtown core and fiercely align themselves with their specific neighborhood. To be able to walk out the front door and within minutes arrive at a park, breakfast joint, coffee shop, or bar is considered a central tenet of Portland living, and neighborhoods center around these amenities. When asked, "What part of town do you live in?" people respond with the name of their neighborhood. Portlanders flaunt their neighborhood pride with stickers and T-shirts.

You'll often hear people reference Hawthorne, Mississippi, and Alberta. Though not specifically neighborhoods, these retail districts—each one unique—add character and definition to their neighborhoods. Most commercial districts are named for the main street that runs through the bustling retail corridor.

so for the best sense of the neighborhood, lock up your bike and stroll this dense area on foot.

From North Portland, you'll cruise across the Willamette River on the Broadway Bridge and dip into Northwest Portland for a tour of the unique historic homes in what is commonly referred to as the "Alphabet District" (mile 11.2), where the streets run in alphabetical order (it's technically called Northwest District). You'll catch a glimpse of some of the oldest homes in Portland and the "Trendy Third," (mile 12.2) a popular high-end shopping district filled with unique boutiques.

The route also brings you past Powell's City of Books (mile 12.6)—the famous bookstore that contains 1.6 acres of retail floor space and occupies an entire city block. You could easily get lost inside Powell's for more than an hour, browsing the new and used books, so you might want to save this stop for a rainy day.

Now that you've seen a fair bit of the edges of the city, it's time to plunge into the heart of Portland by riding in the bike lane of SW Broadway Avenue through the city core. Though SW Broadway is a busy street with a steady climbing grade, the streetlights are timed for the pace of a cyclist, so cars do not move much faster than bikes. The bike lane extends the entire way. You'll pass Pioneer Courthouse Square, affectionately known as Portland's Living Room and home to many of the city's events, concerts, and activities, as well as a popular spot for a lunch break for the downtown office scene. Look for the elaborately dressed hotel attendants outside the Heathman Hotel, always standing at the ready in their festooned hats and ornate uniforms.

The route also takes you into the shady South Park Blocks, and past the Oregon Historical Society and the Portland Art Museum. Before leaving the Park Blocks, you'll skim the edge of Portland State University (mile 14.4). If you're there on a Saturday, stop at the gigantic Portland Farmer's Market, a wealth of produce, locally made edibles, live music, and cooking demonstrations.

Bike Shops

Velo Cult Bike Shop and tavern: 1969 NE 42nd Ave., Portland, OR 97213; (503) 922-2012; velocult.com
Gladys Bikes: 2905 NE Alberta St., Portland, OR 97211; (971) 373-8388; gladysbikes.com
Fat Tire Farm: 2714 NW Thurman St., Portland, OR 97210; (503) 222-3276; fattirefarm.com

Say goodbye to the Southwest quadrant; it's time to cross the river to Southeast, into the heart of Portland's bohemian past. The Hawthorne Bridge is your portal over the Willamette River, the most popular bridge for cyclists. A counter installed on the north side of the bridge records and boldly showcases as many as 9,000 bicycle trips across the bridge on any given (summer) day. Approximately 7 percent of commuters in Portland regularly travel by bicycle, the highest rate in the United States.

The route ambles through the uniquely designed Ladd's Addition neighborhood, where diagonal streets converge at five central hubs adorned with rose gardens. Nestled in the heart of Ladd's Addition is Palio Dessert and Espresso House (mile 16.4), a relaxing spot to sip a coffee as you watch the bicycle traffic drift by.

SE Harrison and Lincoln Streets, packed with cyclists but very few cars, provide a relaxing tour of the colorful homes of Southeast Portland, and will guide you toward the core of this historically hippie district, SE Hawthorne Boulevard (17.9). This area is known for liberal thinking, free-spirited

The historic Bagdad Theater in the heart of the Hawthorne District harkens back to Portland's baroque past. PHOTO BY AYLEEN CROTTY

tendencies and vibrant characters. Take some time to walk for a few blocks along the sidewalk and soak it all in. Before crossing SE Hawthorne Boulevard, check out the Bagdad Theater at the corner of SE 34th Avenue. Now a "brew-and-view" movie house owned by the popular local chain McMenamins, the theater once featured a large stage, a lavish fountain, Middle Eastern décor, and female ushers adorned in Arabian-themed attire.

The ride is drawing to a close, but first you'll return to Northeast Portland via the undulating streets of the grand Laurelhurst neighborhood (mile 19.3), which straddles Southeast and Northeast Portland and contains a multitude of vintage homes. You'll end back at the Velo Cult Bike Shop and tavern, an appropriate place to relax after a long urban tour.

MILES AND DIRECTIONS

0.0 Turn left out of the Velo Cult Bike Shop to head north on NE 42nd Avenue.

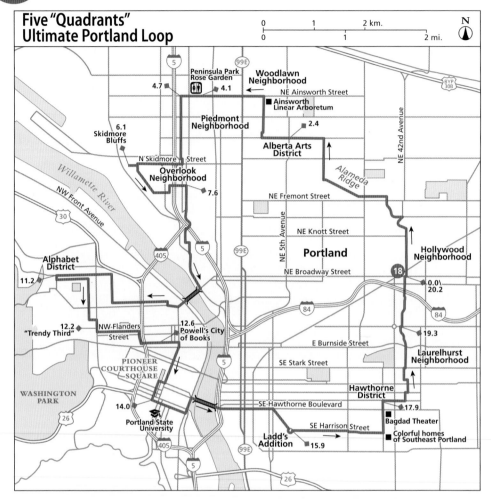

Five "Quadrants" Ultimate Portland Loop

- **0.5** Continue along NE 42nd Avenue as it becomes Wisteria Drive, then NE 41st Avenue.

- **0.7** Turn left onto NE Alameda Street. (**Note:** This is a tricky intersection because of the bend in the road and the fact that you are climbing.)

- **1.6** Continue straight onto NE Hamblet Street.

- **1.9** Turn right onto NE 24th Avenue.

- **2.4** Turn left onto NE Alberta Street.

- **3.2** Turn right onto NE 9th Avenue.

3.7 Turn left onto NE Ainsworth Street.

4.7 Turn left onto N Michigan Avenue.

5.5 Turn right onto N Skidmore Street.

6.1 Turn left onto N Overlook Boulevard, then turn right onto N Skidmore Terrace to reach Skidmore Bluffs park, at the end of the street.

6.2 Exit the park and return on N Skidmore Terrace.

6.3 Turn right onto N Overlook Boulevard.

6.5 Cross Interstate Avenue.

6.9 Turn left through the parking lot and head right toward the N Failing Street freeway overpass. Head up the ramp and over the freeway.

7.0 Continue on N Failing Street.

7.2 Turn right onto N Mississippi Avenue.

7.9 Turn left onto N Russell Street, at the bottom of the hill.

8.0 Turn right onto N Albina Avenue.

8.1 Turn left onto N Interstate Avenue.

8.4 Stay right and follow signs to the Broadway Bridge.

8.6 Turn right onto NW Broadway Bridge.

8.9 Take the first right after the bridge onto NW Lovejoy Street.

9.0 Turn right onto NW 9th Avenue, then left onto NW Marshall Street.

9.6 Turn right onto NW 20th Avenue.

10.0 Turn left NW Thurman Street.

10.8 Turn right onto NW 28th Avenue.

10.8 Turn left onto NW Savier Street.

11.2 Turn right onto NW 24th Avenue.

11.7 Turn left onto NW Irving Street.

11.8 Turn right onto NW 23rd Avenue.

12.6 Turn left onto NW Couch Street and pass Powell's City of Books.

13.2 Turn right onto SW Broadway.

13.6 Turn right onto SW Main Street.

13.7 Turn left onto SW Park Avenue.

14.0 Turn left onto SW Market Street.

14.4 Turn left onto SW Naito Parkway and go into Waterfront Park.

14.5 Take the sidewalk path up toward the Hawthorne Bridge.

14.7 Merge onto SW Hawthorne Bridge.

15.0 Continue onto SE Hawthorne Boulevard.

15.6 Turn right onto SE Ladd Avenue.

15.9 At the traffic circle, exit onto SE Harrison Street.

16.8 SE Harrison Street becomes SE Lincoln Street.

17.2 Turn left onto SE 37th Avenue.

17.6 Turn right onto SE Main Street.

17.9 Turn left onto SE 41st Avenue.

18.0 Turn right onto SE Taylor Street, then left onto SE 42nd Avenue.

18.1 Turn left onto SE Belmont Street, then right onto SE 42nd Avenue.

18.2 Turn left onto SE Morrison Street, then make a slight right onto SE 41st Avenue.

18.3 Turn right onto SE Stark Street.

18.4 Turn left onto SE 41st Avenue.

19.1 Continue onto NE 42nd Avenue.

19.3 Turn right onto NE Senate Street.

19.4 Head up the path to the pedestrian overpass and through the transit mall parking lot.

19.6 Continue onto NE 42nd Avenue.

19.7 Turn right onto NE Broadway Street.

19.7 Turn left onto NE 42nd Avenue.

20.2 Arrive back at Velo Cult, where the ride started.

RIDE INFORMATION

Local Events/Attractions

Filmed by Bike: Every May, the Filmed by Bike film festival showcases a collection of movies and awards the World's Best Bike Movies. The collection then travels the world, hosted by advocacy organizations, museums, and theaters internationally. The Portland festival is hosted at the historic Hollywood Theater every May. Contact the theater to host a bike movie night where you live: filmedbybike.org.

Music on Main Street: Free outdoor concerts are staged in July, Aug, and part of Sept outside the Arlene Schnitzer Concert Hall, SW Main Street at SW Broadway Avenue; portland5.com/events/music-main-street.

Portland Farmers Market at Portland State University: SW Park Avenue and SW Montgomery Street; portlandfarmersmarket.org. This is the area's largest farmers market, and regularly features live music, cooking demonstrations, and a phenomenal selection of produce and food vendors. The market is open year-round (various opening times), and closes promptly at 2 p.m.

Hollywood Farmers Market: Located on NE Hancock Street between NE 44th and 45th Avenues; hollywoodfarmersmarket.org. Every Saturday from Apr through Nov, and every other Saturday in the winter, this farmers' market is conveniently located just blocks from where this route starts and finishes.

Restrooms

Restrooms are located at the ride's start/finish at the Velo Cult Bike Shop and at mile 4.9 (Peninsula Park).

Northeast Portland Neighborhood Loop

This short route takes you through the quiet neighborhoods of Northeast Portland, including the historic Alameda District, which has century-old homes with beautiful architecture.

Start: Glenhaven Park parking area

Length: 6.2-mile loop

Approximate riding time: 1.5 to 2.5 hours

Best bike: Road bike

Terrain and trail surface: Paved city streets

Traffic and hazards: Busy road crossings on NE Sandy Boulevard and NE 57th Avenue

Things to see: Glenhaven Park; Wilshire Park; the historic Alameda District

Map: USGS Portland

Getting There: By car: From downtown Portland, head 5.5 miles east on I-84 toward The Dalles. Take exit 5 for NE 82nd Avenue. At the end of the off-ramp, turn north (right) and go 1 block to a stoplight at the intersection of NE 82nd Avenue. Turn right (north) and travel 0.7 mile to the intersection with NE Siskiyou Street. Turn left onto NE Siskiyou Street, and then take an immediate left into the Glenhaven Park parking area.

By public transportation: From SW 6th Avenue and SW Yamhill Street in downtown Portland, board TriMet bus 12 "Sandy Blvd to Parkrose TC." After getting off the bus, ride on NE 82nd Avenue for 0.6 mile to Glenhaven Park on the left. GPS: N45 32.652' / W122 34.742'

THE RIDE

This easy ride starts at Glenhaven Park in Northeast Portland. This shady, 15-acre park has picnic tables, restrooms, a skate park, a playground, a soccer field, a softball field, and tennis courts. You will cruise on quiet NE Siskiyou Street for the first 0.5 mile, and then turn north onto NE 72nd Street.

At 0.8 mile you should stop at admire the colorful mural on the side of the Missing Link Bike Shop, which depicts a neighborhood theme that incorporates cycling. You can pick up cycling supplies at this friendly bike shop as well.

At 1.0 mile, you'll turn west onto NE Skidmore Street and ride another mile through quiet Northeast neighborhoods.

At 2.8 miles, you may want to stop and check out popular Wilshire Park. This 14-acre park features picnic tables, restrooms, an off-leash dog park, a playground, a volleyball court, and soccer and softball fields.

Bike Shops

Bike Gallery: 5329 NE Sandy Blvd., Portland, OR 97213; (503) 281-9800; bikegallery.com

Missing Link Bike Shop: 7215 NE Sandy Blvd., Portland, OR 97213; (503) 740-3539; missinglinkpdx.com

A colorful mural depicts all types of cyclists riding through the Roseway neighborhood.
PHOTO BY LIZANN DUNEGAN

At 3.1 miles you'll turn onto NE Alameda Avenue, and over the next 2.0 miles you'll pedal through the Alameda neighborhood, which is filled with many beautiful historic homes and travels along Alameda Ridge. At 4.5 miles, use caution to cross busy NE Sandy Boulevard and NE 57th Avenue. Continue riding on NE Alameda Avenue to loop back to your starting point at Glenhaven Park at 6.2 miles.

MILES AND DIRECTIONS

0.0 From the parking area in Glenhaven Park, turn left onto NE Siskiyou Street.

0.5 Turn right on NE 72nd Avenue.

0.8 At the stoplight, cross NE Fremont Street and NE Sandy Boulevard and continue straight on NE 72nd Avenue. You will pass the Missing Link bike shop on the right. A very colorful mural is on the side of the building that is worth stopping for.

1.0 Turn left on NE Skidmore Street.

One of the many beautiful roses you will see blooming in early summer on this route.
PHOTO BY LIZANN DUNEGAN

Northeast Portland Neighborhood Loop

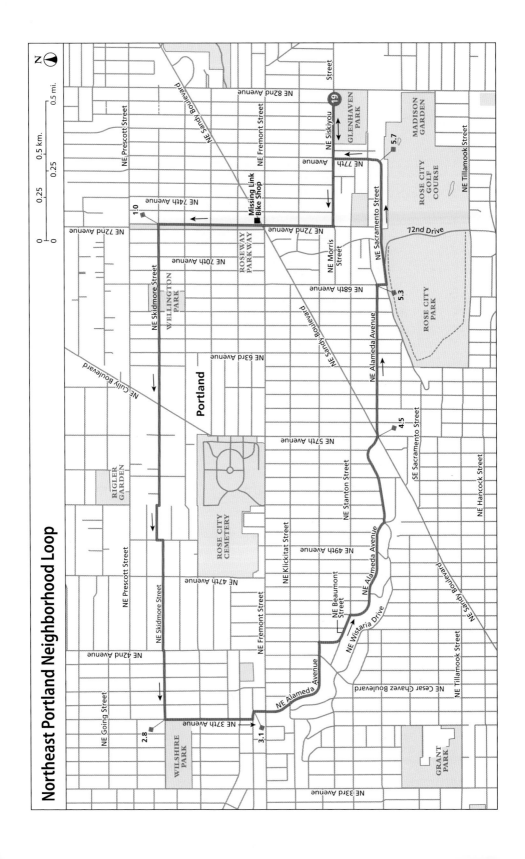

Bike signs like this one can be found throughout the Portland metro area. PHOTO BY LIZANN DUNEGAN

1.2 Cross NE 68th Avenue and then NE Skidmore Street dead ends. Continue on the paved bike path that goes through a grassy field adjacent to a school. When the paved path ends continue riding straight on NE Skidmore Street.

2.1 Turn left on NE 49th Avenue and then take a quick right onto NE Skidmore Street.

2.8 Turn left on NE 37th Avenue, and pass Wilshire Park on your right. Restrooms are available here.

3.1 Turn left on NE Alameda Avenue.

3.6 Arrive at a three-way intersection. Turn right and continue riding on NE Alameda Avenue.

4.5 Arrive at a very busy intersection. Cross NE Sandy Boulevard in the crosswalk, and then cross NE 57th Avenue in the crosswalk. Continue riding on NE Alameda Avenue.

5.3 Turn right on NE 68th Avenue. Ride 1 block, and then turn left on NE Sacramento Street.

5.7 Continue straight on NE 77th Avenue.

5.8 Turn right on NE Siskiyou Street.

6.2 Arrive back at the Glenhaven Park parking area and your starting point.

RIDE INFORMATION

Local Events/Attractions

Providence Bridge Pedal: 1631 NE Klickitat St., Portland, OR 97212; (503) 281-9198; blog.bridgepedal.com. This annual event (held in mid-Aug) is a noncompetitive bike ride crossing Portland's historic bridges: Morrison, Sellwood, Hawthorne, Ross Island, Marquam, Burnside, Broadway, Steel, St. Johns, and Fremont.

Restrooms

Restrooms at available at the start/finish at Glenhaven Park, and at mile 2.8 (Wilshire Park).

South of Portland

South of Portland, the land opens up to an array of landscapes and plenty of hills that cascade toward the Willamette River. We've included two extremely awesome rides in this section of the book, most notably the Petes Mountain–Canby Ferry route, a quintessential Portland ride. This section of the book is all about full-day bike adventure: Get ready to enjoy it!

The Trolley Trail provides serene off-the-road riding along a corridor that was long-ago a trolley line.
PHOTO BY AYLEEN CROTTY

Swimming and the Trolley Trail

This adventure meanders south of Portland on a route that has only newly become an excellent ride, thanks to the implementation of bicycle-friendly infrastructure. The ride is great year-round, but it's especially fantastic in the summertime when you can jump in the Clackamas River at the halfway point. You'll travel along a direct network of mostly off-the-road paved paths like the Trolley Trail, an old trolley line that has been converted into a trail. The loop ride weaves through five municipalities, including the little-known towns of Oatfield, Jennings Grove, and Oak Grove on the southern edge of Portland.

Start: At Cartlandia, at intersection of Springwater Trail and SE Harney Street

Length: 19.3-mile loop

Approximate riding time: 2 to 4 hours; add time for relaxation at the river

Best bike: Road or hybrid

Terrain and trail surface: Paved off-the-road paths and city streets

Traffic and hazards: Some busy roads with bike lanes; some busy crossings

Things to see: River views; wildlife; tiny towns; quaint neighborhoods

Maps: USGS Portland; Metro Bike There! map

Getting There: By car: From downtown Portland, take the Ross Island Bridge (US 26 east) to SE 82nd Avenue. Turn right onto SE 82nd Avenue and follow it for 2.3 miles to SE Harney Street. Turn right onto SE Harney Street, which will bring you to the back side of the Cartlandia Food Cart Pod. Find parking here. Your ride begins from the west side of the intersection of the Springwater Trail and SE Harney Street.

By public transportation: Take the "10 Toward 94 and Foster" bus to SE 82nd Avenue. Or take the MAX blue or red lines to SE 82nd Avenue.

From either of these routes, board the "72 to Clackamas TC" bus heading south. Get off at SE 82nd Avenue and Crystal Springs and walk one minute to the Springwater Trail. GPS: N45 32.395' / W122 37.198'

THE RIDE

This route starts from Cartlandia, an outdoor seating area that encompasses multiple food carts and a beer garden. It's a great spot for a pre-ride snack and post-ride revelry. From here you'll take an easy spin on the Springwater Trail, an off-the-road paved trail you'll follow for 1.0 mile before turning onto the I-205 bike path. One of these days, cyclists will be able to ride the I-205 bike path all the way to Gladstone, the ride's main destination, but until the entire path is completed, you'll need to ride on SE 82nd Drive, which has a wide bike path the entire way.

SE 82nd Drive brings you to the High Rocks City Park (mile 8.1). View the Clackamas River from the higher bank, or lock your bike and walk down to the water for a relaxing rest. The river is very calm here, and it's a popular swimming spot. To the west, the high rock face that gave the park its name is a popular diving spot, but the water below the high rocks can be dangerous and not diving is not recommended. From June through September the river is perfect for swimming.

Bike Shops

The Missing Link: 4635 SE Woodstock Blvd., Portland, OR 97206; (503) 206-8854; missinglinkpdx.com
Bike Gallery: 9347 SE 82nd Ave., Clackamas, OR; (503) 254-2663; bike gallery.com
First City Cycles: 916 Main St., Oregon City, OR 97045; (503) 344-4901; firstcitycycles.com

After your break, travel out of Gladstone along the Trolley Trail, a fantastic route that connects several small towns in this area. The land was originally owned by the Portland Traction Company, which operated a streetcar line that stretched between the cities of Milwaukie and Gladstone from 1893 to 1968. The streetcar line was abandoned for many years, and for decades the communities around it had dreams of developing it into the paved recreational path that it now is. This path takes you through quiet neighborhoods and on the backsides of houses as you wind your way back north to Portland.

Eventually the Trolley Trail peters out into a dirt walking path. Just before that happens (mile 13.2), the route turns onto SE Evergreen Street, then SE River Road to meet up with OR 99E, a busy road with a bike lane that you will only be on for 0.7 mile.

The Trolley Trail has ample features to help calm traffic and make for a safe ride through neighborhoods. PHOTO BY AYLEEN CROTTY

Exit OR 99E at Scott Street (mile 14.8), and wind toward the Springwater Corridor Trail. Turn right onto the Springwater, and it's an easy cruise back to the start of your ride. Along the way, you'll pass through the Johnson Creek Watershed area (16.7 miles) and Tideman Johnson City Park, a lovely stretch of the pathway that teems with wildlife. Take some time to stop along the path as it crosses the creek and look for ducks and other critters enjoying this restored habitat. Continue along the Springwater Trail back to Cartlandia, where the ride started.

MILES AND DIRECTIONS

0.0 From Cartlandia head east, away from the city, along the Springwater Corridor Trail.

0.9 Turn right onto the I-205 multiuse path.

4.7 Exit the multiuse path and continue onto SE 82nd Drive.

8.1 Arrive at Hard Rocks City Park. Cross the bridge or stay on the northern side, and find a spot to hang out on the river. When you are ready to leave, turn left onto E Clackamas Boulevard.

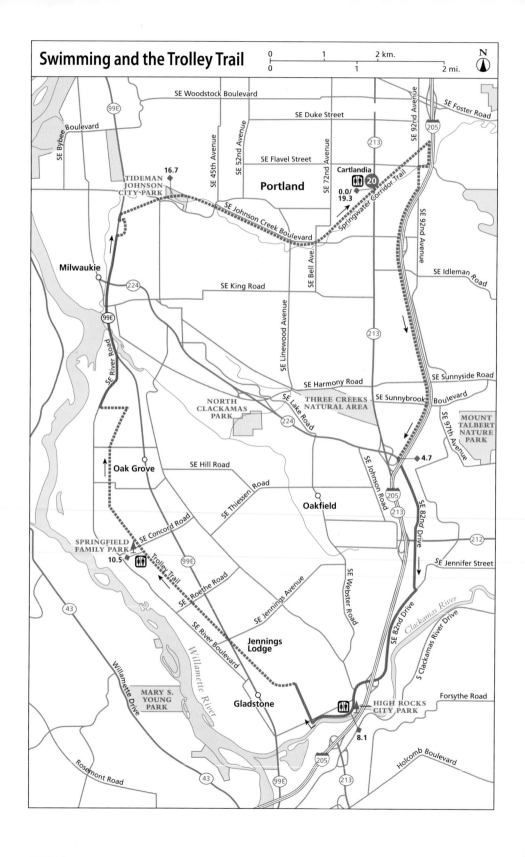

Swimming and the Trolley Trail

0		1		2 km.
0			1		2 mi.

N

SE Woodstock Boulevard

SE Foster Road

99E

Bybee Boulevard

SE Duke Street

SE 92nd Avenue

205

SE 45th Avenue

SE 52nd Avenue

SE Flavel Street

SE 72nd Avenue

213

16.7

TIDEMAN
JOHNSON
CITY PARK

Cartlandia

20

Portland

0.0/
19.3

SE Johnson Creek Boulevard

Springwater Corridor Trail

SE 92nd Avenue

Milwaukie

224

SE King Road

SE Idleman Road

99E

SE River Road

SE Linewood Avenue

SE Bell Ave.

SE Harmony Road

SE Sunnyside Road

213

NORTH
CLACKAMAS
PARK

THREE CREEKS
NATURAL AREA

SE Sunnybrook Boulevard

MOUNT
TALBERT
NATURE
PARK

224

SE Lake Road

SE 97th Avenue

Oak Grove

SE Hill Road

SE Johnson Road

4.7

SE Thiessen Road

Oakfield

205

213

SE 82nd Drive

SE Concord Road

212

SPRINGFIELD
FAMILY PARK

10.5

99E

SE Jennifer Street

Trolley Trail

SE Roethe Road

SE Jennings Avenue

SE Webster Road

SE 82nd Drive

Clackamas River

43

SE River Boulevard

S Clackamas River Drive

Jennings
Lodge

MARY S.
YOUNG
PARK

Willamette Drive

Willamette River

Gladstone

HIGH ROCKS
CITY PARK

Forsythe Road

8.1

43

Rosemont Road

99E

213

205

Holcomb Boulevard

8.3   Make a slight left onto Charles Ames Park Walk.

8.5   Return to E Clackamas Boulevard, then turn right onto SE Portland Avenue.

9.0   Turn left onto the Trolley Trail.

10.5   Pass Springfield Family Park, a nice spot to stop for a break.

12.0   Turn right onto SE Arista Drive/Trolley Trail.

12.7   Turn right to stay on the Trolley Trail.

13.2   Turn left onto SE Evergreen Street.

13.5   Turn right onto SE River Road.

14.2   Turn left onto SE McLoughlin Boulevard/OR 99E.

14.8   Turn right onto SE Scott Street.

14.9   Turn left onto SE Main Street.

15.9   Turn left onto SE Moores Street, then turn right onto the Springwater Corridor Trail.

19.3   Arrive back at Cartlandia, where the ride started.

RIDE INFORMATION

Local Events/Attractions

Woodstock Farmers Market: Open Sun from June through Oct at 4600 SE Woodstock Blvd. in Portland; (971) 208-5522; woodstockmarketpdx.com. You will find fresh produce, locally made goods, pastries, lunch options, and entertainment here.

Restrooms

Restrooms are located inside Cartlandia at the start/finish; at mile 8.1 (High Rocks City Park; and at mile 10.8 (Springfield Family Park).

Petes Mountain–Canby Ferry Loop

Hill climbers will delight in this gorgeous, challenging ride that is worth every single mile of the rewarding grind. Your adventure begins in the charming town of Oregon City, built on the steep slope above the Willamette River and Willamette Falls. So steep, in fact, that in 1915, the city erected a municipal elevator to transport citizens up a steep embankment, thereby connecting two disjointed sections of town. And yes, you'll have the opportunity to soar up the cliff-side in the elevator on this great ride. Over the course of 24.6 striking miles, you'll also climb over Petes Mountain and ride the Canby Ferry (bring some cash for a ticket) as you wind your way through rural farmland and quaint towns.

Start: At the intersection of 5th Avenue and South End Road

Length: 24.6-mile loop

Approximate riding time: 3 to 4 hours

Best bike: Road bike

Terrain and trail surface: Paved city streets

Traffic and hazards: A mix of quiet roads and short stretches of busy road without a bike lane or shoulder

Things to see: Canby Ferry; Oregon City Municipal Elevator; historic Oregon City; Willamette Falls; the Willamette River; horses and mansions; Petes Mountain

Maps: USGS Portland; Metro Bike There! map

Getting There: By car: From downtown Portland, take the Ross Island Bridge and exit onto OR 99E heading south. Once in Oregon City, turn left onto 2nd Avenue, and right onto South End Road. Just after Clinton Street, park in any of the pullouts on the right-hand side of the road, before Old Canemah Park. Your ride begins from the intersection of 5th Avenue and South End Road. Head up the hill on South End Road. GPS: N45 20.882' / W122 36.959'

THE RIDE

Oregon City is steeped in history and proud to celebrate it. In 1844, Oregon City became the first U.S. city west of the Rocky Mountains to incorporate. If you're a history buff and want to learn more, the Museum of the Oregon Territory, located along your ride, is worth a visit. Quaint shops and historic districts abound, so plan to spend some time exploring the city after your ride.

In Oregon City, most of the roads are extremely steep, and the first leg of this ride is no exception. It only gets steeper—and more scenic—from there. The initial stretch is a little hairy as you climb up South End Road, but most of the riding after that is much less traffic heavy.

Within a few minutes you'll be on the remote farm roads that flank this historic town. Pedal along Central Point Road with sweeping views of the

You'll have the opportunity to cross the Willamette River on the Canby Ferry, a fun, short ride.
PHOTO BY AYLEEN CROTTY

landscape and active farmland. Your legs will delight in a short break as you float along New Era Road, a mostly downhill, winding descent that begins your journey toward the Canby Ferry. You'll pass a horse farm, dip through forest roads, and wind through a neighborhood before arriving at the ferry.

The Canby Ferry is a short and direct crossing over the Willamette River that was first put into operation in 1914. There have been several ferry vessels since that time, and the current one can carry up to six cars and 49 people at once. The ferry is open from 6:45 a.m. to 9:15 p.m. every day, except a few national holidays and when the river is extremely high. See the ferry website (clackamas.us/roads/ferry.html) to confirm that it is running on a regular schedule, as there is no other bicycle crossing nearby. There is a cash fee to bring a bike on the ferry, and the ride takes just a few minutes. Before you head down the hill to board the ferry, downshift to your lowest gear (more spinning)—you're going to want this on the other side. Follow the signage and walk your bike onto the ferry. Once the ferry docks, first allow the cars to disembark, then begin the extremely steep climb out on the other side.

Bike Shops

First City Cycles: 916 Main St., Oregon City, OR 97045; (503) 344-4901; firstcitycycles.com
Classic Cycle: 812 Molalla Ave., Oregon City, OR 97045; (503) 557-1977; cycleoc.com
Cayuse Cycles: 1837 Willamette Falls Dr., West Linn, OR 97068; (503) 342-6168; cayusecycles.com

It has been a pleasant ride up until this point, and now your trek is about to get steep. The climb from the ferry was just a taste of what the rest of the journey holds. From the ferry, head immediately up and over Petes Mountain, one of the most classic road rides in the Portland area. You'll be joining an honored club of accomplished cyclists when you best this beast. Your Petes Mountain climb lasts only about 3 miles, but it's going to feel a lot longer than that, with a few stretches of 9-percent grade. Don't be fooled by the false summit at mile 13.9; the actual crest is at mile 14.7. The road is winding and dramatic, with large trees creating a shady canopy, striking vistas, huge luxury homes to admire, and very few cars.

No rest for the wicked on this ride: Once you coast down Petes Mountain, you'll ride through a short stretch of the town of West Linn before tucking into another steep climb: Wisteria Road (mile 18). This hidden gem of a road is unbelievably serene and quiet. It's quite possible you'll climb the entire 2.0-mile stretch of smooth pavement without seeing a single car. You'll pass homes that are both grandiose and unique—and even one that offers an on-the-honor-system fresh chicken egg stand. This might not be the wisest point in your journey to collect the fragile eggs, though!

The Oregon City Municipal Elevator connects two disjointed parts of this steeply sloped city. You'll catch a lift on the elevator near the end of this ride. PHOTO BY AYLEEN CROTTY

The Wisteria climb crests after turning right onto Rosemont Road (mile 19.6) and your rural exploration now comes to an end as you wind your way back into Oregon City. Turn right onto Salamo Road (mile 20.3) and enjoy a fast descent—you've certainly earned it! The route snakes through the manicured neighborhood of Barrington Heights, then pops out at Willamette Falls Road, where you'll cross over the Willamette River to Oregon City.

As you cross the Oregon City Bridge (mile 23.6), look straight ahead into the hillside. That looming white pillar is your destination: the Oregon City Municipal Elevator, a free, relaxing way to climb 130 feet. Bikes are welcome on the elevator.

Exit the elevator and turn right onto the path known as the McLoughlin Promenade. This path is part of a 7.8-acre linear park on the bluff above Oregon City, and provides spectacular views of the Willamette River, the dramatic Willamette Falls, and downtown Oregon City. Stop along the way to take pictures and enjoy the view; your ride is about to come to an end.

Now that you're rested from the elevator ride and the scenic stop along the bluff, you'll head up one more quick climb to round out the expedition, and remind you what the day was all about. When the path ends (mile 24.2), head through the parking lot and take a left on Tumwater Drive, past the Museum of the Oregon Territory, and turn left onto 2nd Street. Take a right onto South End Road and return to the start to conclude this awesome ride.

MILES AND DIRECTIONS

0.0 From its junction with 5th Avenue, head up the hill on South End Road.

1.4 Turn left onto S Partlow Road.

1.9 Turn right onto S Central Point Road.

4.3 Turn right onto S New Era Road.

6.3 Continue onto S Haines Road.

7.0 Turn right onto NE Territorial Road.

8.4 Turn right onto N Country Club Drive.

8.7 Turn left onto NE 22nd Avenue.

9.0 Turn right onto N Locust Street.

9.5 N Locust Street turns left and becomes NW 31st Avenue.

9.8 Turn right onto N Holly Street.

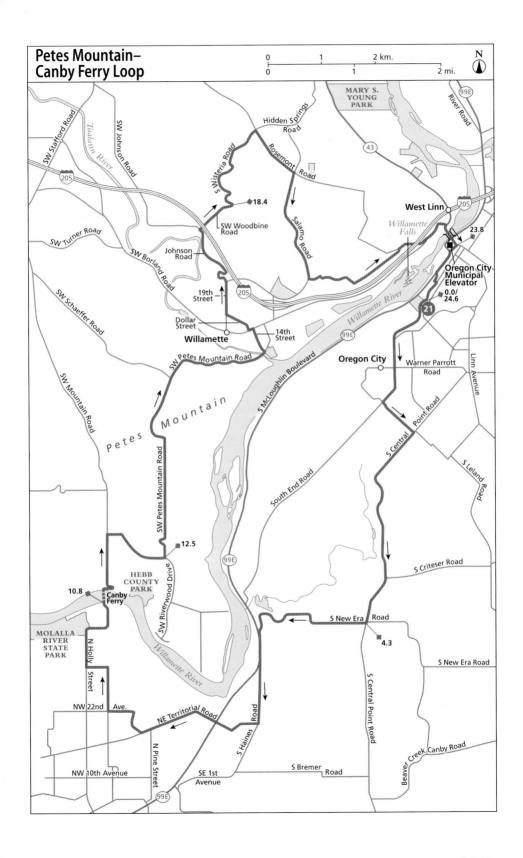

Petes Mountain–
Canby Ferry Loop

0   1   2 km.

0   1   2 mi.

N

MARY S.
YOUNG
PARK

River Road

99E

SW Stafford Road

Tualatin River

SW Johnson Road

Hidden Springs Road

Rosemont Road

43

205

205

SW Turner Road

S Wisteria Road

◆ 18.4

SW Woodbine Road

Salamo Road

West Linn

Willamette Falls

■ 23.8

SW Borland Road

Johnson Road

Oregon City
Municipal
Elevator

SW Schaeffer Road

19th Street

205

0.0/
24.6

Dollar Street

14th Street

Willamette

SW Petes Mountain Road

S McLoughlin Boulevard

Willamette River

99E

Oregon City

Warner Parrott Road

Linn Avenue

SW Mountain Road

Pete s Mountain

S Central Point Road

S Leland Road

SW Petes Mountain Road

South End Road

12.5 ■

99E

S Criteser Road

HEBB
COUNTY
PARK

SW Riverwood Drive

10.8

Canby
Ferry

MOLALLA
RIVER
STATE
PARK

S New Era Road

4.3 ■

S New Era Road

N Holly Street

Willamette River

S Central Point Road

S New Era Road

NW 22nd Ave.

NE Territorial Road

S Haines Road

Beaver Creek Canby Road

N Pine Street

NW 10th Avenue

SE 1st Avenue

S Bremer Road

99E

21

10.2   Continue onto NE 37th Avenue.

10.5   Slight left onto N Locust Street.

10.8   Board the Canby Ferry.

10.9   Continue straight onto SW Mountain Road.

11.7   Turn right onto SW Hoffman Road.

12.5   Turn left onto SW Petes Mountain Road.

15.9   Continue onto Tualatin Avenue.

16.0   Turn left onto 14th Street.

16.3   Turn left onto Willamette Falls Drive.

16.3   Turn right onto Dollar Street.

16.6   Turn right onto 19th Street.

17.3   Turn left onto S Johnson Road.

17.9   Turn right onto SW Woodbine Road.

18.4   Turn left onto S Wisteria Road.

19.6   Turn right onto Rosemont Road.

20.3   Turn right onto Salamo Road.

21.6   Turn left onto Barrington Drive.

21.7   Turn right onto Riverknoll Way.

22.1   Turn right onto Beacon Hill Drive.

22.2   Turn left onto Imperial Drive.

22.8   Turn right onto Sunset Avenue.

23.2   Continue onto Willamette Falls Drive.

23.5   Turn right onto OR 43 S/Willamette Drive and over the Oregon City Bridge.

23.8   Board the Oregon City Municipal Elevator.

23.8   Exit the elevator and turn right onto the path.

24.2   When the path ends, continue through the parking lot and turn left onto Tumwater Drive.

24.3   Turn left onto S 2nd Street.

24.3   Turn right onto South End Road.

24.6   Arrive back at the intersection of South End Road and SE 5th Street, where the ride started.

RIDE INFORMATION

Local Events and Attractions

Movies in the Park: Movies are shown Friday evenings around dusk at Wesley Lynn Park, 12901 Frontier Pkwy., Oregon City; orcity.org/parksandrecreation.

Free Guided Historical Walks: Several events are held each year in summertime at various locations. Visit rosecityroamers.org for more information.

Family Fun Days and the Pioneer Family Festival: Usually held in the third weekend in May at Clackamette Park in Oregon City; pioneerfamilyfestival .com. Enjoy an annual event that celebrates the history and heritage of the Oregon City region.

Museum of the Oregon Territory: Open Tues through Sat from 10:30 a.m. to 4:30 p.m. A fee is charged (free for children under 5 and active members of the military and their families). The museum is located at 211 Tumwater Drive, Oregon City, OR 97045; (503) 655-5574; clackamashistory.org/museum -of-the-oregon-territory.html.

Oregon City Municipal Elevator: Open Mon through Sat from 7 a.m. to 7 p.m., and Sun from 11 a.m. to 7 p.m., with some extended hours in the summer. The elevator is closed on Memorial Day, Independence Day, Labor Day, Thanksgiving, and Christmas. See the elevator website for detailed information: orcity.org/publicworks/elevator-operating-hours.

Restrooms

There are no designated public restrooms for this ride.

Southeast of Portland

To the southeast of Portland, the landscape is wooded with ample trails and rivers that cascade from Mount Hood toward the city. The routes in this section of the book are a mix of wooded and open rides, short and long, on and off the road.

Though these rides begin from areas very close to the city, traffic to and from your destinations can sometimes be congested. But the drive alone is worth the journey, as you'll travel through a gorgeous region. This is an outdoor playground if you like the woods, so plan to spend some time exploring other activities in the region.

You can pick juicy blackberries along the Cazadero Trail during the summer months.
PHOTO BY LIZANN DUNEGAN

Cazadero State Park Trail

This doubletrack gravel road follows part of the old rail line through the Deep Creek Canyon and a shady second-growth forest. In the summer months you will have opportunities to cool off in the Deep Creek, and to pick wild blackberries.

Start: Cazadero State Park Trailhead in Boring

Length: 6.0 miles out and back

Approximate riding time: 2 to 3 hours with stops

Best bike: Mountain bike

Terrain and trail surface: Doubletrack gravel road that is shared with hikers, runners, and equestrians

Traffic and hazards: Some areas of the road have very loose gravel. Stop your bike and pull off to the side of the road if you encounter horseback riders.

Things to see: Views of the Deep Creek; wildlife and wildflowers; blackberry picking in July and Aug

Maps: Cazadero Trail map available here: www.traillink.com/trail/cazadero-trail.aspx

Getting There: By car: From I-205 in East Portland, take exit 12A. Follow OR 212/OR 224 east toward Clackamas/Estacada for 3.5 miles to a road junction. Stay to the left and continue on OR 212, following the signs to "Damascus/Mt. Hood." Continue for another 6.7 miles until you reach downtown Boring. Turn right onto SE Richey Road. Just after the Shell station on the corner, turn right into the gravel parking area and trailhead. GPS: N45 25.754' / W122 22.531'

THE RIDE

This ride begins in downtown Boring and travels through the Deep Creek Canyon along the former rail line of Oregon Water Power and Railway Company, which was completed in 1904. This electric rail line extended from the Sellwood neighborhood in Portland east to Gresham, and then to Boring and the Cazadero Dam site south of Estacada. The Cazadero Power Plan provided

The Cazadero State Park Trail is an easy mountain bike ride on which you will enjoy a lot of solitude.

PHOTO BY LIZANN DUNEGAN

The canopy of trees shades the Cazadero State Park Trail. PHOTO BY LIZANN DUNEGAN

electricity for this rail line, which was used for passenger service as well as for hauling freight. Service from Boring to Estacada ended in the 1930s, when the wood trestles along Deep Creek burned down. However, service continued from Sellwood to Boring

Bike Shop

Clackamas Cycle World:
11493 SE 82nd Ave., Happy Valley, OR 97086; (503) 653-5390; clackamascycleworld.com

Beautiful penstemon bloom along the route. PHOTO BY LIZANN DUNEGAN

until 1958, when line was sold to Union Pacific and Southern Pacific exclusively for freight.

There are future plans to extend this trail to Eagle Creek, Estacada, and the Faraday, Cazadero and Promontory Park areas, which will allow it to follow the Clackamas River corridor and connect Mount Hood to the Pacific Crest Trail.

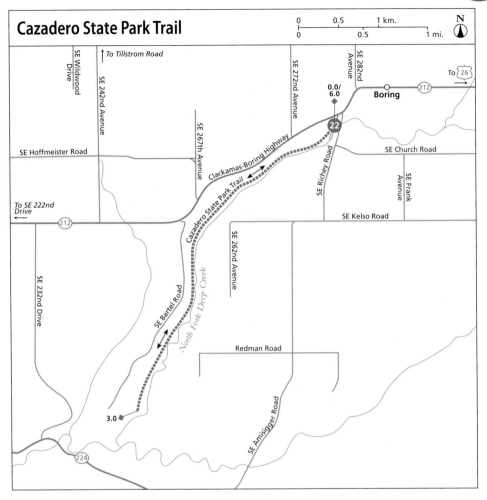

Cazadero State Park Trail

The doubletrack gravel road descends slightly for 3.0 miles as it winds through a second-growth forest and passes an occasional small farm. During the first mile there are opportunities to take side trails down to the bubbling Deep Creek. There is also wonderful blackberry picking during late July and August. In the spring and summer months you can enjoy the bright blooms of wildflowers.

The road ends after 3.0 miles and is lined by a wood rail fence. This is a good spot to take a break before you head back to your starting point.

MILES AND DIRECTIONS

0.0   Start riding on the doubletrack gravel road.

3.0   Arrive at the trail's end and turnaround point. Retrace the same route back to the trailhead.

6.0   Arrive back at the trailhead.

RIDE INFORMATION

Restrooms
There are no public restrooms on this ride.

Clackamas River Cruise

Faraday Road is a private road that parallels the Clackamas River. The road is owned by Portland General Electric, the utility company that operates the hydro power plant on the river. Only authorized motorized vehicles are allowed, but PGE has generously opened the route so cyclists, walkers, and runners can enjoy this lovely stretch along the river. The Clackamas River Cruise takes you along Faraday Road for a no-traffic, flat, relaxing ride. This is a perfect journey for new riders of all ages, but more experienced cyclists will appreciate the ride for the beauty and serenity. There is a boat launch at one end of the ride, and a fishing and picnic area at the other end. The nearby town of Estacada is a gateway to plenty of other recreational opportunities.

Start: Gate on Faraday Road

Length: 9.0 miles out and back

Approximate riding time: 1 hour of riding, plus additional time to relax and explore the area

Best bike: Road, hybrid, or mountain bike

Terrain and trail surface: Smooth pavement

Traffic and hazards: A mostly traffic-free route

Things to see: Dams and powerhouses; striking views down the canyon toward the peaks and mountains of the Mount Hood National Forest; abundant wildlife

Maps: USGS Portland; Metro Bike There! map

Getting There: By car: From downtown Portland, take the Hawthorne Bridge over the Willamette River and exit south onto OR 99E. Follow OR 99E for approximately 5 miles. Turn onto OR 224, toward Estacada, and continue for 28.3 miles until you reach the southern entrance to East Faraday Road, on your right-hand side. Park near the boat launch. The ride begins at the gate to the private section of Faraday Road. GPS: N45 14.404' / W122 15.565'

THE RIDE

As far back as 10,000 years ago, Native Americans settled into the basin around the Clackamas River, an 83-mile-long tributary of the Willamette River. The Clackamas begins its flow at Olallie Butte, a high peak between Mount Jefferson and Mount Hood on the southeastern outskirts of Portland, and eventually joins the Willamette River in Oregon City, south of Portland. This thundering river provides hydroelectric power for some of the Portland metro area. It is also an important resource for coho, Chinook, and steelhead salmon. Old-growth forest lines much of the river, providing habitat for several species of birds. This rich environment, combined with an abundance of recreational

Informational signs along Faraday Road celebrate the history of the hydropower facility and dams.
PHOTO BY AYLEEN CROTTY

Best Bike Rides Portland, Oregon

A view of the Faraday Forebay Dam and the fish ladder. PHOTO BY AYLEEN CROTTY

activities, landed the Clackamas River a spot on the National Wild and Scenic Rivers registry, a program that preserves the nation's important waterways.

The Faraday Forebay Dam along the Clackamas River was originally erected in 1907. Situated slightly upriver is the North Fork Dam, erected in 1958, a "thin arch" design that represents one of the tallest dams of this style at a towering 200 feet. For a 2-mile stretch along the river, one of the world's highest and longest fish ladders creates an accessible route so salmon and other fish can travel over the dam. Informational signage along Faraday Road provides opportunities to learn more about this large-scale hydropower project.

Faraday Road is hushed and relaxing. The road is well paved and traveled mostly by cyclists and walkers, though an authorized vehicle or two may pass at slow speeds. You'll see birds soaring overhead and glimpses of other wildlife flittering in the woods. The route takes you along the eastern edge of the Clackamas River to a bridge that crosses to the other side—the site of Faraday Forebay and the day-use fishing

Bike Shop

Sandy Bicycle: 17390 Smith Ave., Sandy, OR 97055; (503) 826-1070; sandybicycle.com

Clackamas River Cruise

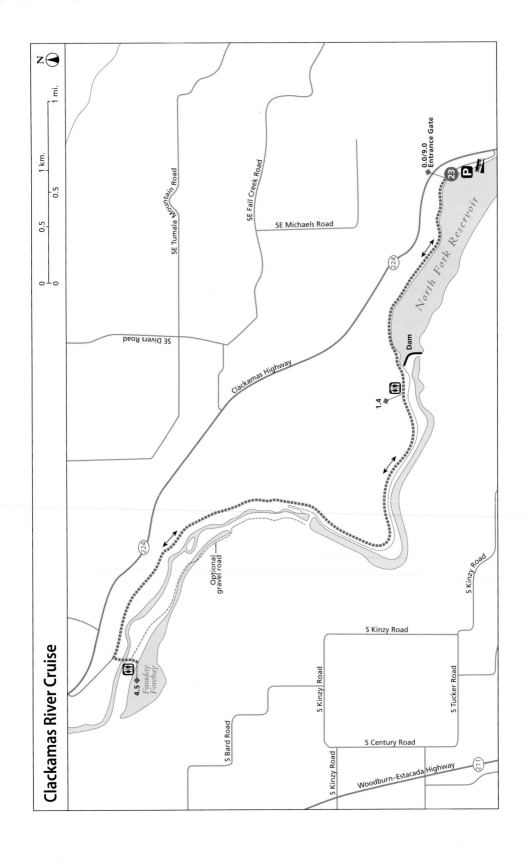

N

0   0.5   1 km.
0   0.5   1 mi.

SE Tumala Mountain Road

SE Fall Creek Road

SE Michaels Road

SE Divers Road

Clackamas Highway

224

North Fork Reservoir

Dam

1.4

0.0/9.0
Entrance Gate

23

P

224

Optional
gravel road

4.5
Faraday Forebay

S Kinzy Road

S Kinzy Road

S Kinzy Road

S Kinzy Road

S Bard Road

S Century Road

S Tucker Road

S Kinzy Road

Woodburn–Estacada Highway

211

area. The lake is well stocked with trout in the summer, and it's known to be a great spot for fishing from the bank.

From this side of the river, you can opt to ride an out-and-back loose gravel road for an additional 2.8 miles. This spur takes you on a more rugged expedition that sinks deeper into the natural landscape along the river, with the dense trees towering alongside the path.

After exploring the western side of the river, head back over the bridge, turn right, and follow Faraday Road back to the boat launch parking area where the ride started.

MILES AND DIRECTIONS

0.0 Start at the gate to the private section of Faraday Road.

4.4 Turn left, over the bridge, to Faraday Forebay. (**Option:** At this point, you can follow the gravel road to the left south for an additional 2.8 miles out and back.)

4.5 To return, cross back over the bridge and turn right onto Faraday Road.

9.0 Arrive back at the boat launch parking lot where the ride started.

RIDE INFORMATION

Local Events and Attractions

Float the Clackamas River: Milo McIver State Park is a popular launching point for casual (think inner tube) floats on the Clackamas River. You'll need to shuttle your vehicle, unless you use a guided service. Floats from the Upper Ramp to the Lower Ramp are approximately two hours. You can also drift all the way to Barton Park for a relaxing six-hour float. For more information, visit tinyurl.com/miloboatlaunch.

Blue Sky Whitewater Rafting Inc.: For guided service on the river; based out of Estacada. Call (503) 630-3163 for more information.

Restrooms

A restroom is at mile 4.4 on Faraday Forebay.

Sandy Ridge Mountain Bike Trail System

Nestled into the foothills of the Cascade Range near Mount Hood, this network of trails will delight intermediate and advanced mountain bikers. More than 15 miles of singletrack provide both flow trail-style riding and more technical options. This is the closest spot to Portland for extensive mountain biking, and it's a popular spot for Portland mountain bike enthusiasts who eagerly drive over after work to squeeze in a few weekday runs before the light runs out.

Start: In the parking lot at the map kiosk

Length: 5.4-mile figure eight (15 miles of trail available)

Approximate riding time: 2 to 4 hours

Best bike: Mountain bike

Terrain and trail surface: A mix of gravel and dirt single- and doubletrack

Traffic and hazards: Standard off-road riding obstacles such as roots, rocks, switchbacks, and berms

Things to see: Douglas fir, western hemlock, and western red cedar; wildlife; streams

Maps: Map kiosk at the trailhead

Getting There: By car: From downtown Portland, take the Ross Island Bridge and drive US 26 east for 32.0 miles to Sleepy Hollow Drive. Turn left onto Sleepy Hollow Drive soon after passing a large sign indicating a left turn for Marmot. (**Note:** This is the second turnoff for Sleepy Hollow.) Turn right on E Barlow Trail Road and drive over the Sandy River. After 1.0 mile on E Barlow Trail Road, the entrance will be on your left. Cars do not need a Northwest Forest Pass to park. The ride begins from the map kiosk in the parking lot. GPS: N45 22.835' / W122 01.788'

THE RIDE

The trails of the Sandy Ridge system vary in style and challenge with plenty of opportunity to craft your own thrilling day of riding. There are four levels of difficulty, and only two trails are suitable for beginners. If you are brand-new to mountain biking, spend time on the 0.75 mile Homestead Loop that encircles the parking lot. This flowy, flat loop is a great beginner trail, without major roots and rocks to navigate. From there, you can ride the pump track to Homestead Road (mostly closed to traffic, except for the occasional forest service vehicle) and take the first trail on your right (Laura's Line).

The more advanced trails all begin with a solid but manageable climb up the closed road to earn your turns. Depending on which trail you choose to ride first, the climb is 1.0 to 4.0 miles, and you'll split off to either the right or the left. The trails are well marked and range from 0.75 mile to 2.75 miles in length. They can be woven together in various patterns to create the ride of your choosing, but always ride in a downhill flow, and follow the directional signs to avoid collisions.

Advanced and skillful speed enthusiasts who like technical riding will love the Follow the Leader trail. With quick drops, extremely tight turns, rock overhangs, exposed slopes, and plenty of technical terrain, this trail is not for the faint of heart. The trail starts off in boulders and some broken-down boulder fields (known as scree fields) to get you warmed up, then drops 350 feet in 1.0 mile, with a lot of exposure and terrain changes.

If awesome views are what you crave, Quid Pro Flow is the way to go. It features big tables, rollers, and a few hips. All of the technical features can be simply ridden over, but those who like to jump will dig catching serious air on Quid Pro Flow.

Easy signage guides the way on the awesome trails of Sandy Ridge. PHOTO BY AYLEEN CROTTY

Sandy Ridge Mountain Bike Trail System

Pump track-style rollers kick off your ride with easy mounds and a wide trail. PHOTO BY AYLEEN CROTTY

Communication Breakdown is a popular trail that is rated less difficult but is still very technical, with features like rock gardens, rooty sections, baby heads, and steep, tight, climbing switchbacks. The first part of the trail is a bit of a climb through large sweeping berms, with a steady grade that's not too intense. At the green rock, stop to enjoy the views down across the valley. The descent on Communication Breakdown is well worth the climb—an almost continuous stream of berms that eventually intersects with the Quid Pro Flow trail.

Intermediate riders will delight in the 5.4-mile Flow Motion to Hide and Seek connection loop (mapped and described here). Flow Motion starts off with a quick climb and a mini rock garden before dumping you down 250 feet of elevation and through at least fifteen berms and switchbacks. Pop out onto Homestead Road, cross over, and join Hide and Seek Trail for a fast

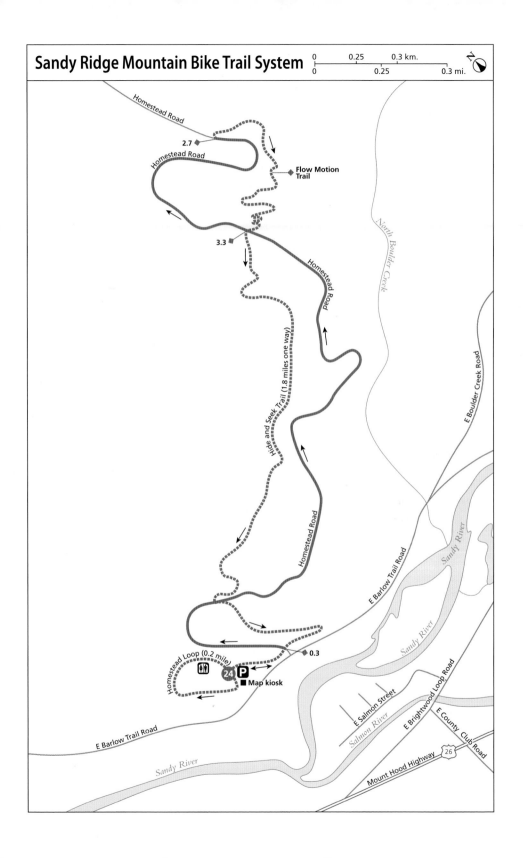

Sandy Ridge Mountain Bike Trail System

Homestead Road

Homestead Road

2.7

Homestead Road

Flow Motion Trail

3.3

Homestead Road

North Boulder Creek

Hide and Seek Trail (1.8 miles one way)

Homestead Road

E Boulder Creek Road

Sandy River

E Barlow Trail Road

Sandy River

0.3

Homestead Loop (0.2 mile)

24

Map kiosk

E Barlow Trail Road

E Salmon Street

Salmon River

E Brightwood Loop Road

E County Club Road

Mount Hood Highway

26

Sandy River

0   0.25   0.3 km.
0   0.25   0.3 mi.

N

descent. The trail squeezes through trees and cruises along switchbacks to wind back to the parking lot.

MILES AND DIRECTIONS

0.0 Start at the map kiosk and head straight onto the no-name trail that leads to Homestead Road.

0.3 Turn left onto Homestead Road to climb up to the Flow Motion Trail.

2.7 Turn right onto Flow Motion at the trailhead marker.

3.3 Arrive back at Homestead Road and cross the road onto the Hide and Seek Trail.

5.1 Return the map kiosk and cross the parking lot to the Homestead Loop Trail.

5.2 Head onto the Homestead Loop Trail for a victory loop.

5.4 Return to the map kiosk, where the ride started.

RIDE INFORMATION

Local Events and Attractions

Shuttle Day: The Portland-based trails advocacy organization Northwest Trail Alliance hosts an annual fundraising shuttle day—usually in Sept—where cyclists don't have to climb up Homestead Road to get to the trails. See nw-trail .org for details.

Jonsruds Viewpoint: This popular lookout features spectacular views of the Barlow Trail route over the mountain. The viewpoint is on Bluff Road, off US 26 in Sandy.

Restrooms

Restrooms are located at the start/finish in the parking lot.

East of Portland and the Columbia River Gorge

People often say "It's always sunny in Hood River," and that's mostly true. This region is known for abundant sunshine, even when it's dreary in Portland, making for an awesome opportunity to escape the Portland rain and hop on your bike. You'll be afforded the most striking mountain views and bright fluffy clouds, if not crystal-clear blue skies.

The Columbia River carves the great cliffs of the Columbia River Gorge National Scenic Area.
PHOTO BY LIZANN DUNEGAN

There is so much to see and do out here you could easily make a week of adventure out of a visit. The Columbia River Gorge is a canyon along the Columbia River and a designated National Scenic Area for good reason. I-84 is easily one of the most striking freeways in all of the United States, and the drive out is lovely. Windsurfers from all over the world flock to Hood River for its world-class winds and relatively calm waters, perfect conditions for catching some air. It's fun to head to the public beach in Hood River and watch the kiteboarders, windsurfers, and kayakers in action, with colorful sails and animated characters attempting sweet tricks and maneuvers.

The town of Hood River is a wonderful destination, with plenty of recreational activities nearby, nice accommodations like the historic Hood River Hotel, and several breweries and wineries. With an abundance of orchards and farms, you're sure to come home with a trunk full of peaches, pears, jams, and jellies.

Hood River Valley Loop

This loop takes you through the orchards and farms of the scenic Hood River Valley. Majestic Mount Hood, Mount Adams, and Mount St. Helens provide a stunning backdrop as you ride uphill from Tucker Park in Hood River to the quaint community of Parkdale. In Parkdale, you can explore the Hutson Museum and have lunch.

Start: Tucker Park in Hood River

Length: 31.3-mile loop

Approximate riding time: 2.5 to 3.5 hours with stops

Best bike: Road bike

Terrain and trail surface: Paved road

Traffic and hazards: The Hood River Highway has a 2-foot shoulder and moderate traffic. OR 35 has a 3-foot shoulder and moderate to heavy traffic. The rest of the roads on this route do not have shoulders, but have light traffic. There are several railroad crossings on this route. Use caution when crossing train tracks. This route can have ice and snow on it in the winter months.

Things to see: Fruit orchards; views of Mount Hood and the Hood River Valley

Maps: USGS Parkdale, Dog River, and Hood River

Getting There: From Portland, head east on I-84 and take exit 63 for Hood River. Turn south and drive uphill through town to State Street. Turn right (west) onto State Street and drive 0.8 mile to the junction with 13th Street. Turn left (south) onto 13th Street (this turns into 12th Street). Continue 3.0 miles on 12th Street to the intersection with Tucker Road. Turn left onto Tucker Road. Drive 2.4 miles to Tucker Park, located on the right side of the road. Turn right at the "Tucker Park" sign and park in the large shady parking area. GPS: N45 39.077' / W121 33.646'

THE RIDE

Located in the Columbia River Gorge, Hood River is a fantastic place to cycle. It's sunny for most of the year in Hood River, even on dreary Portland days, which makes for a pleasant near-by escape from the rain. This dynamic town has many low-traffic rural roads that begin on the outer limits of town and wind through the broad expanse of the Hood River Valley.

The rich volcanic soils and moist climate in the valley produce the perfect microclimate for many agricultural crops, including a variety of flowers, herbs, berries, apples, cherries, pears, and seasonal vegetables. Amazingly, this valley is one of the premier pear-growing districts in the world and produces 11 percent of the nation's supply of Bartlett pears and 30 percent of the country's

Riding through the Hood River Valley, you see many fruit orchards and the scenic backdrop of Mount Hood. PHOTO BY LIZANN DUNEGAN

Anjous, Bosc, and Comice pears. In addition to plant crops, the valley has many farms that raise cattle, llamas, alpacas, and horses, some of which you'll pass along the way.

This loop tour starts at the outskirts of Hood River in Tucker Park. From this quiet roadside stop, you'll pedal uphill on a fairly mild grade through pine-scented forest and pear and apple orchards for 12.4 miles until you reach the Hutson Museum. It is worth taking the time to explore this small Parkdale museum, which houses a special rock collection, arrows, spear points, mortars, and grinding tools, as well as historical artifacts from Parkdale's history. This location is also the ending point for the Mount Hood Railroad. The railroad originally began running in 1906, and carried lumber and agricultural crops from the Hood River Valley to Hood River. The line reopened in the early 1980s as a tourist train. You can take a four-hour scenic train ride from Hood River to Parkdale and back, as well as have dinner or brunch aboard the train. The train runs from June through December, and is another fun way to enjoy the spectacular beauty of the Hood River Valley.

Bike Shops

Dirty Fingers (bike shop and connected cafe): 1235 State St., Hood River, OR 97031; (541) 308-0420; dirtyfingersbikes.com
Discover Bicycles: 210 State St., Hood River, OR 97031; (541) 386-4820; discoverbicycles.com
Mountain View Cycles: 205 Oak St., Hood River, OR 97031; (541) 386-2453; mtviewcycles.com

Continue the tour by heading south from Parkdale on Clear Creek Road. On this section of the route, you'll continue uphill past more orchards and farms. Keep a sharp eye out for fruit markets during the summer months. Strawberries are ripe in June, cherries in July, apricots in late July, blueberries and peaches in August, pears from mid-August through September, and apples from mid-August through October.

After 15.6 miles you'll hook up with Cooper Spur Road and begin a fast downhill, with gorgeous views of the Columbia River Gorge and the glistening peaks of Mount Adams and Mount Saint Helens to the north. Finish the loop by heading downhill through the communities of Mount Hood and Odell to your starting point at Tucker Park.

MILES AND DIRECTIONS

0.0 Start by turning right onto the Hood River Highway from Tucker Park.

6.4 Arrive at a Y intersection. Stay left where a sign indicates "Parkdale 5 Miles."

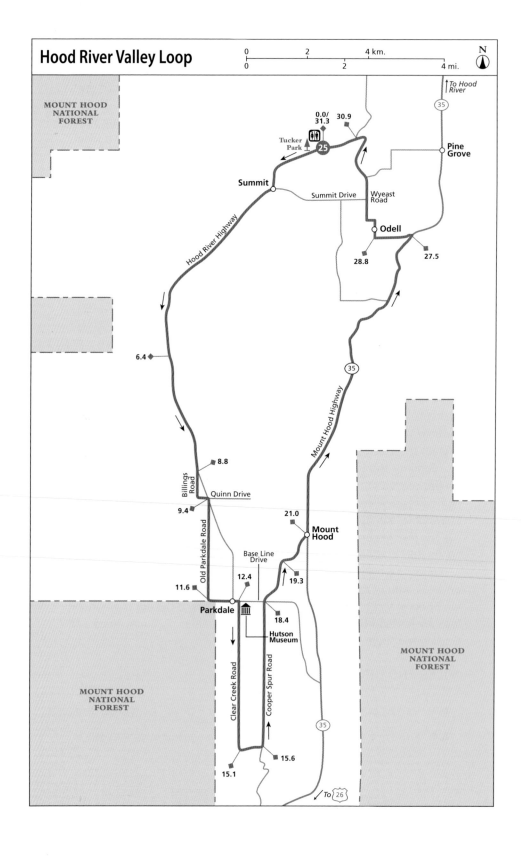

Hood River Valley Loop

0   2   4 km.

0   2   4 mi.

N

MOUNT HOOD
NATIONAL
FOREST

To Hood
River

35

0.0/
31.3

30.9

Tucker
Park

25

Pine
Grove

Summit

Summit Drive

Wyeast
Road

Odell

28.8

27.5

Hood River Highway

6.4

Mount Hood Highway

35

8.8

Billings
Road

Quinn Drive

9.4

21.0

Old Parkdale Road

Base Line
Drive

Mount
Hood

19.3

11.6

12.4

Parkdale

18.4

Hutson
Museum

MOUNT HOOD
NATIONAL
FOREST

Clear Creek Road

Cooper Spur Road

MOUNT HOOD
NATIONAL
FOREST

35

15.6

15.1

To 26

MOUNT HOOD
NATIONAL
FOREST

7.5 Cross the railroad tracks.

8.8 Turn right onto Alexander Drive. You'll have spectacular views looking south at Mount Hood.

8.9 At the stop sign turn left onto Billings Road. After 0.3 mile Billings Road turns into Quinn Drive.

9.4 At the stop sign turn right (south) onto the Hood River Highway. Ride 200 yards, then turn right onto Old Parkdale Road.

11.6 Turn left onto Base Line Drive.

12.3 At the stop sign continue straight and enter the small town of Parkdale.

12.4 Turn right onto Clear Creek Road. After you make this turn, pass the Hutson Museum on your left (restrooms and water are available here), and the Mount Hood Railroad.

15.1 Arrive at a Y intersection. Turn left. (Clear Creek Road turns into Evans Creek Drive.)

15.6 At the stop sign and T intersection, turn left onto Cooper Spur Road. Begin a fun downhill ride. You'll have great views of Mount Adams and Mount Saint Helens to the north.

18.4 At the stop sign and four-way intersection, turn left onto Base Line Drive.

19.3 At a four-way intersection, turn left on Cooper Spur Road toward Odell and Hood River. You'll start a fun downhill after this intersection.

21.0 Enter the small town of Mount Hood. At the stop sign turn left onto OR 35, toward Odell and Hood River. Begin a long, gradual downhill north toward Hood River.

27.5 Turn left onto the Odell Highway, where a sign indicates "Odell 1 Mile/Hood River 3.5 Miles."

28.4 Arrive in Odell.

28.8 Turn right onto unsigned Wyeast Road.

30.9 At the stop sign turn left onto unsigned Tucker Road.

31.3 Arrive at Tucker Park on the right, where the ride started.

RIDE INFORMATION

Local Events/Attractions

Apple Valley Country Store: 2363 Tucker Rd., Hood River, OR 97031; (541) 386-1971; applevalleystore.com. This friendly establishment serves mouth-watering slices of apple and berry pie, and huckleberry milkshakes. The store also offers a wide assortment of jams and jellies and other handmade gifts.

Mount Hood Scenic Railroad: 110 Railroad Ave., Hood River, OR 97031; (800) 872-4661; mthoodrr.com. You can experience the beauty of the scenic Hood River Valley on this fun train ride that starts in Hood River and travels to Parkdale.

Western Antique Aeroplane & Automobile Museum: 1600 Air Museum Rd., Hood River, OR 97031; (541) 308-1600; waaamuseum.org. This expansive museum features one of the largest collections of still-flying antique aero-planes and still-driving antique automobiles in the country. On the second Saturday of the month, volunteers fly the planes and drive the cars, quite a thrill to watch.

Restrooms

Restrooms are available about the start/finish at Tucker Park. There is also a restroom at mile 12.4 (Hutson Museum).

Historic Columbia River Highway State Trail: Hood River to The Dalles

This ride takes you on a scenic journey on the Historic Columbia River Highway through the magnificent Columbia River Gorge. It begins in historic Hood River and heads east toward Columbia Gorge Discovery Center in The Dalles. The first 4.6 miles are open to bikers and pedestrians only, and offer many viewpoints of the cliff-lined gorge, Mount St. Helens, and Mount Adams, as well as the opportunity to explore the Mosier Twin Tunnels. As you continue east you'll pass through the small town of Mosier. The route then travels uphill through cherry orchards to the Mema-loose Overlook and Rowena Crest Viewpoint. From the Rowena Crest Viewpoint, you'll have a sweeping descent down hairpin curves to a straightaway that takes you past Mayer State Park and through the small community of Rowena. Your turnaround point is at Columbia Gorge Discovery Center and Wasco County His-torical Museum in The Dalles. Be sure to start this route early in the day so you have time to explore the informative displays at this one-of-a-kind interpretive center.

Start: The Mark O. Hatfield West Trailhead

Length: 37.8 miles out and back

Approximate riding time: 6 to 8 hours with stops

Best bike: Road bike

Terrain and trail surface: Paved bike path shared with hikers and runners; paved road

Traffic and hazards: You'll share the first (and last) 4.6 miles of this route only with pedestrians, riding on a wide, smooth, paved path. The remainder of the route continues east on the Historic Columbia River Highway, and you'll share the roadway with motorists. The Historic Columbia River Highway is a very narrow, twisty road, and you'll have to constantly be on the lookout for cars. Be especially cautious when you are riding downhill from the Rowena Crest Viewpoint on the hairpin curves, which have many blind corners.

Things to see: Views of the Columbia River and Columbia River Gorge; Historic Columbia River Highway; historic Twin Tunnels; the Columbia Gorge Discovery Center

Map: USGS Bonneville Dam

Getting There: From the intersection of I-205 and I-84 in Portland, drive 54.0 miles east on I-84 toward Hood River and The Dalles. Turn off the highway at exit 64, where a sign indicates "Hood River Highway 35/ White Salmon/Government Camp." At the end of the off-ramp, turn right (south) toward Hood River. Drive 0.3 mile to a stop sign and a four-way intersection. Turn left (east) onto the Historic Columbia River Highway. You'll also see a sign indicating "Historic State Park Trail." Drive 1.3 miles on the Historic Columbia River Highway until you reach a parking area, visitor center, and the trailhead on the left side of the road. There is a day-use permit (small fee) to park at the visitor center. You can obtain the permit from the self-pay station in the parking lot or inside the visitor center. The visitor center also sells an annual pass that is good for all Oregon state parks. GPS: N45 42.205' / W121 29.188'

THE RIDE

On this classic route you'll explore the east end of the Columbia River Gorge, which is well known for its wide open plateaus, wildflower meadows, agricultural valleys, cloud-capped cliffs, and endless opportunities for outdoor fun. This ride takes you on a tour of a restored section of the Historic Columbia River Highway, which was originally completed in 1922 and ran east from Portland to The Dalles. This first major paved roadway in Oregon was the accomplishment of lawyer and visionary Samuel C. Hill and the talented engineer Samuel Lancaster. This duo and a dedicated team of skilled tradesmen defied the odds of nature and built a highway that complemented the landscape and offered motorists a unique look at the magnificent Columbia River Gorge. Samuel Hill once said about the highway, "We will cash in, year after year, on our crop of scenic beauty, without depleting it in any way."

When I-84 was built in the 1950s, many sections of the historic highway were abandoned. However, when the original Columbia River Highway was recognized as a National Historic Landmark in May 2000, there was a resurgence of interest in restoring unused sections for everyone to enjoy. In July 2000, a 4.6-mile section of the highway was opened as a hiker/biker-only trail between Hood River and Mosier. This impressive $5.6 million restoration project included

The Columbia River Gorge is filled with evidence of its volcanic past. PHOTO BY LIZANN DUNEGAN

paving the original highway route, building landslide-protective retaining walls, and reopening the Mosier Twin Tunnels, which were filled with rock in the mid-1950s. These impressive tunnels were originally designed by Conde B. McCullough, a famous Oregon bridge engineer, and you'll have the opportunity to ride through them and gaze at the cliff-lined gorge through arched viewing portals. These tunnels act as a gateway between two different ecosystems: the wetter, western side of the gorge and the dryer, eastern Columbia Basin Plateau.

After the hiker/biker trail ends at the Mosier Trailhead, you'll cruise down Rock Creek Road into downtown Mosier. From this point forward you'll share the road with motorists. As you continue east you'll start ascending, riding through hillsides covered with cherry orchards, where cherries ripen in July. Watch for "U-Pick" signs.

After cruising on this scenic stretch of road for just more than 8.0 miles, you'll arrive at the Memaloose Overlook, where you can view Memaloose Island—the location of a traditional Native American burial site. As you continue riding east, you'll climb to a spectacular roadside viewpoint at Rowena Crest. From this cliff-top vantage point, you'll see the wheat-covered hills of the Columbia Basin Plateau to the east, catch views of Mount St. Helens and

Fun curves drop below Rowena Crest. PHOTO BY LIZANN DUNEGAN

Mount Adams to the north, and soak in more wondrous views of the Columbia River Gorge. The Rowena Crest Viewpoint sits on the Rowena Plateau, which is literally bursting with a profusion of wildflowers during the spring months (peak blooming season is April and May).

If you want to take a break from riding, be sure to hike through the Tom McCall Preserve, which has some of the highest concentrations of wildflowers in this area. Varieties you may spot are the bright yellow balsamroot, the bluish-purple blooms of broadleaf lupine, white yarrow, wild parsley, penstemon, and wild lilies. If you decide to hike here, be sure to keep your eye out for poison oak! You can access a hiking trail to these bountiful wildflower meadowlands just opposite the entrance road to the Rowena Crest Viewpoint parking area.

Continuing east, the highway corkscrews down the cliff face and takes you past Mayer State Park (with restroom facilities), and then through the small town of Rowena. The change in landscape is quite dramatic, different from the wetter, heavier vegetation in the western part of the gorge. Nature's architecture here is characterized by black basalt cliffs, dramatic bluffs, grassy plateaus, and deeply carved canyons.

Bike Shops

Dirty Fingers (bike shop and connected cafe): 1235 State St., Hood River, OR 97031; (541) 308-0420; dirty fingersbikes.com
Discover Bicycles: 210 State St., Hood River, OR 97031; (541) 386-4820; discoverbicycles.com
Mountain View Cycles: 205 Oak St., Hood River, OR 97031; (541) 386-2453; mtviewcycles.com

Just short of 19 miles in, you'll arrive at your turnaround point at the Columbia Gorge Discovery Center and Wasco County Historical Museum. Be sure to take time to explore this interpretive center and museum, which describes the geological formation of the gorge and the fascinating history of the people who lived here. This complex also has a living history park, where you can see reenactments of life on the Oregon Trail, the experiences of Lewis and Clark, and much more.

MILES AND DIRECTIONS

0.0 Start by riding east on the paved trail adjacent to the visitor center, where a sign indicates "Mark. O. Hatfield West Trailhead." The visitor center has restrooms, water, and a phone.

2.7 Pass a viewpoint on your left.

3.5 Enter the Mosier Twin Tunnels.

Historic Columbia River Highway State Trail: Hood River to The Dalles

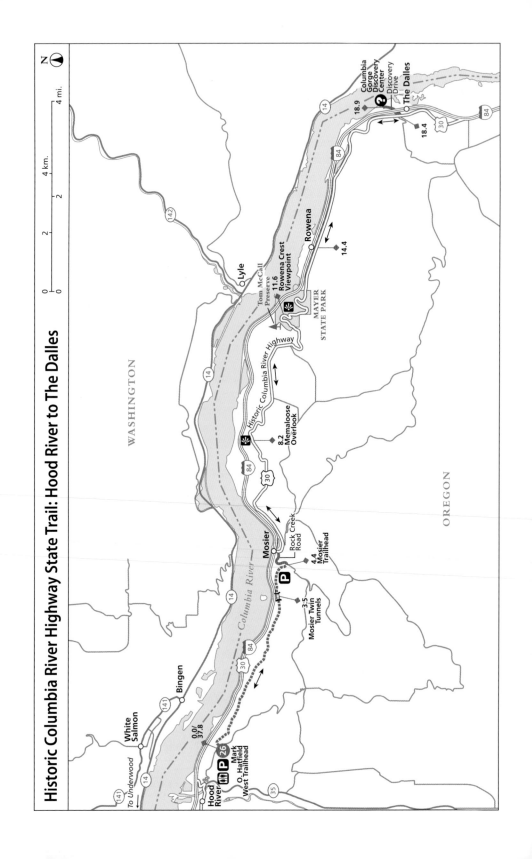

3.7 Exit the Mosier Twin Tunnels.

4.4 At the T intersection and stop sign, turn left onto Rock Creek Road. You have the option here of turning right and riding 0.2 mile uphill to the East Mosier Trailhead, which has water, restrooms, and a phone.

5.3 Arrive at a T intersection. Turn left (east) onto the Historic Columbia River Highway and continue pedaling through the small town of Mosier. As you ride through Mosier, be on the lookout for the Route 30 Ice Cream Store (on the right side of the highway in the center of town), where you can eat delicious ice cream and view vintage Porsche cars.

6.6 Ride through a long section filled with cherry orchards. The cherries are ripe in July, and there are many U-Pick stops along this route.

8.2 Pass the Memaloose Overlook on your left.

11.6 Arrive at the Rowena Crest Viewpoint on your right, where you can soak in fantastic views of the gorge. You'll also pass by the Tom McCall Preserve (on the left), which offers many hiking opportunities.

14.2 Pass the turnoff to Mayer State Park on your left. There are restrooms at this state park.

14.4 Ride through the small town of Rowena.

18.4 Turn left onto Discovery Drive at the "Columbia Gorge Discovery Center/Wasco County Historical Museum" sign.

18.9 Arrive at the Columbia Gorge Discovery Center and the Wasco County Historical Museum. Be sure to check out the displays and interpretive trails before you turn around and head back on the same route.

37.8 Arrive back at the Mark O. Hatfield West Trailhead.

RIDE INFORMATION

Local Events/Attractions
Columbia Gorge Discovery Center: 5000 Discovery Dr., The Dalles, OR 97058; (541) 296-8600; gorgediscovery.org.

Restrooms
There are restrooms at the start/finish (Mark O. Hatfield West Trailhead); at mile 4.6 (Mosier East Trailhead); and at mile 18.9 (Columbia Gorge Discovery Center).

Historic Columbia River Highway State Trail:
Cascade Locks to Moffett Creek Bridge

This ride follows the paved, multiuse Historic Columbia River Highway State Trail in the beautiful Columbia River Gorge, and features gorgeous views of the Columbia River, the Columbia River Gorge, Bonneville Dam, and Beacon Rock. You will also have the opportunity to explore the Cascade Hatchery and view the historic Moffett Creek Bridge.

Start: Cascade Locks Trailhead in Cascade Locks

Length: 11.6 miles out and back (with a longer option)

Approximate riding time: 2 to 3 hours with stops

Best bike: Road bike

Terrain and trail surface: Paved multiuse path shared with walkers and runners

Traffic and hazards: Be careful on the section where you have to climb stairs with your bike, and use caution when going through the bike tunnel

Things to see: Views of the Columbia River and Columbia River Gorge and Bonneville Dam; Beacon Rock; blackberry picking (July and August); Cascade Hatchery

Map: USGS Bonneville Dam

Getting There: By car: From Portland, follow I-84 east for approximately 44 miles, and take exit 44 for "Cascade Locks/Stevenson." After exiting, follow the main road 0.2 mile through Cascade Locks until you reach the signed "Cascade Locks Trailhead—Historic Columbia River Highway State Trail" on the left side of the road. GPS: N 45 38.048' / W 121 56.900'

THE RIDE

This route follows a section of the Columbia River Highway State Trail in the scenic Columbia River Gorge, and offers many gorgeous views of the Columbia River as well as of the Bonneville Dam.

You will start the ride in the small town of Cascade Locks, which is situated on the banks of the Columbia River. Start riding west on the paved path as it winds through a shady big-leaf maple woodland carpeted with sword

Jan Woldford negotiates the stairs with her bike. PHOTO BY LIZANN DUNEGAN

fern. During July and August you have opportunities to pick ripe blackberries. At 1.1 miles ride through a bike tunnel. Use caution because the tunnel is very dark.

At the 2.4-mile mark, a nice highlight of the ride is to stop at the Cascade Hatchery, which is fed by Eagle Creek. This hatchery raises coho salmon, and you can view the young salmon in the numerous rearing ponds in the hatchery. Each rearing pond holds about 75,000 young salmon. The adult salmon start arriving at the hatchery site in the early fall. The hatchery staff collects about 4,700,000 eggs from the spawning adult salmon. The eggs are then incubated, and the young salmon are raised at the hatchery for about a year and fed a strict diet before they are released.

After touring the hatchery, follow the trail sign by continuing to the right and crossing the bridge in the bike lane (this road is one way for cars, but bikes can continue west in the bike lane).

At 3.1 miles, you will need to push (or carry) your bike up a series of very steep stairs; use the concrete bike wheel groove to make it easier. At 4.0 miles you'll pass the Toothrock Trailhead. Toothrock is a large basalt rock bluff that provided many challenges for road builders. In 1915, builders of the Historic Columbia River Highway constructed a viaduct that navigated 224 feet around Toothrock, and was supported by a series of 23-foot-wide reinforced concrete slabs.

Bike Shop

Gresham Bicycle Center: 567 NE 8th Bicycle St., Gresham, OR 97030; (503) 661-BIKE; greshambike.com

At 5.8 miles you'll arrive at the Moffett Creek Bridge, your turnaround point. This historic bridge was built in 1915, and at the time it was the longest flat-arch bridge in the country, and the longest three-hinged concrete span worldwide. The bridge spans 170 feet and only rises 17 feet in the middle. The large cast-iron hinges on the bridge allow it to flex when loaded with weight. (**Option:** If you want to explore this scenic route more, you have the option of continuing another 1.6 miles to the John B. Yeon State Park/Elowah Falls trailhead.)

MILES AND DIRECTIONS

0.0   Start riding on the paved bike path.

1.1   Arrive at a bike tunnel. Use caution riding through the tunnel.

2.4   Pass the Cascade Hatchery on the left. Take a side trip to tour the hatchery. After touring the hatchery, follow the trail sign and

Historic Columbia River Highway State Trail: Cascade Locks to Moffett Creek Bridge

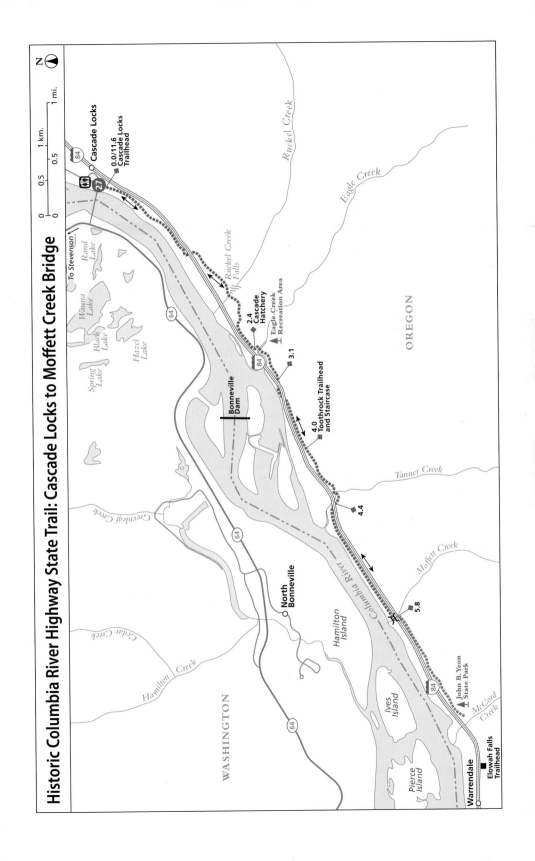

continue to the right, crossing the bridge in the bike lane (this road is one way for cars, but bikes can continue west in the bike lane).

3.0 Turn left and continue on the paved path.

3.1 Walk your bike up a series of concrete stairs. A groove is available on the side of the stairs if you want to push your bike as you climb the stairs.

4.0 Pass the Toothrock Trailhead on the left.

4.4 Cross the highway and continue straight on the bike path.

5.8 Arrive at the Moffett Creek Bridge and your turnaround point. You have the option of continuing another 1.6 miles on the paved bike path to John B. Yeon State Park/Elowah Falls Trailhead.

11.6 Arrive back Cascade Locks, where the ride started.

RIDE INFORMATION

Local Events/Attractions

Thunder Island Brewing: This craft brewery is situated directly on the Columbia River, offering gorgeous views as you relax in the outdoor seating area. The brewery is a popular stopping point for hikers on the Pacific Crest Trail and cyclists touring in the region. A photo wall celebrates patrons who arrive on foot or by bike. Located at 515 SW Portage Rd., Cascade Locks, OR 97014; (971) 231-4599; thunderislandbrewing.com.

Columbia Gorge Sternwheeler: Experience history, legend, and riverboat hospitality on a triple-decker paddle wheeler while you enjoy 360-degree views. The stern-wheeler offers narrated sightseeing excursions of the Columbia River Gorge National Scenic Area. Located in Marine Park in Cascade Locks; (503) 224-3900; sternwheeler.com.

Bonneville Lock and Dam: This hydropower production site also supports fish and wildlife protection and recreational activities. Visitors can experience the operation of two hydroelectric powerhouses, watch migrating fish traveling upstream at the underwater viewing rooms next to the fish ladders, and check out a salmon and sturgeon fish hatchery. Located at exit 40 on I-84; (541) 374-4564; nwp.usace.army.mil/Locations/ColumbiaRiver/Bonneville.aspx.

Restrooms

Restrooms are present at the Cascade Locks Trailhead.

easyCLIMB at Cascade Locks

easyCLIMB is a network of trails that snakes through a lightly wooded area of oak and grass savanna on the Columbia River. The trails were developed to help riders become more comfortable with mountain biking. About 2.0 miles of looped trails can be endlessly repeated, and there are just enough obstacles to help you hone your skills. New riders will love this opportunity to become more adept at riding singletrack, and experienced riders will enjoy the flowy trails and stunning Columbia River views. The name easyCLIMB stands for Cascade Locks International Mountain Biking Trail—there is actually very little climbing.

Start: At the parking lot trail map kiosk

Length: 3.5 miles of looping trails

Approximate riding time: 1 to 2 hours, plus additional time to relax and explore the area

Best bike: Mountain bike

Terrain and trail surface: A mix of gravel doubletrack and dirt singletrack

Traffic and hazards: Off-road riding

Things to see: Impressive Columbia River views; a boat launch; a swimming area; oak and grass savanna; large eagles and other birds

Maps: Trail map kiosk at the trailhead

Getting There: From downtown Portland, take I-84 east to Cascade Locks. Take exit 44 for Cascade Locks. Follow the Cascade Locks Highway/US 30/Wa Na Pa Street for 3.0 miles to Industrial Park Way. Head under I-84 and continue on Industrial Park Way until you reach the tree line and the trail map kiosk. Start your ride from the trail map kiosk. GPS: N45 41.182' / W121 51.281'

THE RIDE

The trails of easyCLIMB are interconnected, so you can choose your own plan of trail attack. Spend some time studying the trail map at the kiosk to decide where you want to ride. For a more challenging ride, head in a counterclockwise direction.

There is a pump skills track located on the edge of the parking lot before you enter the trails system. This is a great spot for warming up and getting more familiar with the handling skills required for mountain biking.

Once you enter the trail system, you'll encounter a mix of terrain. Occasional obstacles provide thrilling opportunities to hone your skills, but they are all avoidable if you'd prefer a gentler ride.

The trail skirts along Government Cove, a scenic, tucked-in spot on the Columbia River.
PHOTO BY AYLEEN CROTTY

Mountain bikers stop to take in striking views of the Columbia River near the boat launch at easyCLIMB. PHOTO BY AYLEEN CROTTY

The best way to experience easyCLIMB is to ride the pump track to warm up, then head onto the big eastern loop before working your way back up to the central area, and then on to the western loops. You'll be winding along tight turns on easy trails, a perfect introduction to mountain biking with the gorgeous backdrop of the Columbia River. After going through the suggested loop, you may opt to return to your favorite sections of the trail network for more shredding.

> **Bike Shop**
>
> **Dirty Fingers** (bike shop and connected cafe): 1235 State St., Hood River, OR 97031; (541) 308-0420; dirtyfingersbikes.com

MILES AND DIRECTIONS

0.0 Start from the trail map kiosk and loop around the practice loop on your right to get warmed up.

0.1 Return to the map kiosk and head straight onto the trail.

easyCLIMB at Cascade Locks

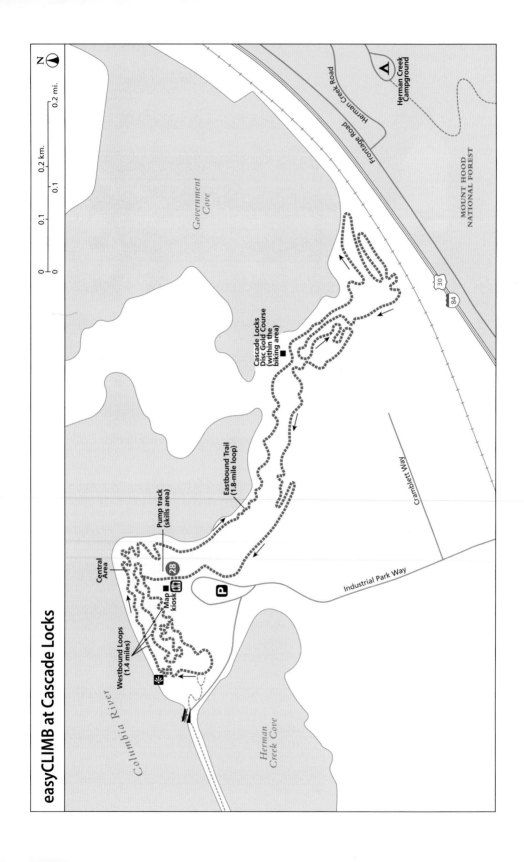

N

0   0.1   0.2 km.
0   0.1   0.2 mi.

Columbia River

Government Cove

Herman Creek Cove

Central Area

Westbound Loops (1.4 miles)

Map kiosk

Pump track (skills area)

28

P

Eastbound Trail (1.8-mile loop)

Cascade Locks Disc Gold Course (within the biking area)

Industrial Park Way

Cramblett Way

84

30

Frontage Road

Herman Creek Road

Herman Creek Campground

MOUNT HOOD NATIONAL FOREST

0.2 Turn right and head on the eastbound trail loop.

2.0 Return to the center section and continue toward the westbound loops.

3.4 Arrive at the center section and turn right.

3.5 Arrive back at the map kiosk, where your ride began. (**Option:** The loops are very short, so if you are eager to ride more it's easy to hop back on the trail for a few more.)

RIDE INFORMATION

Local Events/Attractions

Thunder Island Brewing: This craft brewery is situated directly on the Columbia River, offering gorgeous views as you relax in the outdoor seating area. The brewery is a popular stopping point for hikers on the Pacific Crest Trail and for cyclists touring in the region. A photo wall celebrates patrons who arrive on foot or by bike. Located at 515 SW Portage Rd., Cascade Locks, OR 97014; (971) 231-4599; thunderislandbrewing.com.

Columbia Gorge Sternwheeler: Experience history, legend, and riverboat hospitality on a triple-decker paddle wheeler while you enjoy 360-degree views. The stern-wheeler offers narrated sightseeing excursions of the Columbia River Gorge National Scenic Area. Located in Marine Park in Cascade Locks; (503) 224-3900; sternwheeler.com.

Bonneville Lock and Dam: This hydropower production site also supports fish and wildlife protection and recreational activities. Visitors can experience the operation of two hydroelectric powerhouses, watch migrating fish traveling upstream at the underwater viewing rooms next to the fish ladders, and check out a salmon and sturgeon fish hatchery. Located at exit 40 on I-84; (541) 374-4564; nwp.usace.army.mil/Locations/ColumbiaRiver/Bonneville.aspx.

Restrooms

Restrooms are located at the start/finish in the parking lot.

29

Columbia River Gorge Waterfall Tour

This tour travels on a restored section of the Historic Columbia River Highway, where you'll ride through one of the highest concentrations of waterfalls in North America. Other trip highlights include spectacular views of the Columbia River Gorge from Chanticleer Point, the opportunity to tour the historic Vista House, and chances to stop and hike at the state parks on this route.

Start: From Lewis and Clark State Park off the Historic Columbia River Highway

Length: 42.0 miles out and back

Approximate riding time: 5 to 7 hours including stops

Best bike: Road bike

Terrain and trail surface: Paved road

Traffic and hazards: This route follows the Historic Columbia River Highway, which has a 2-foot shoulder for almost 6.0 miles. After 8.8 miles the highway has no shoulder and blind curves as you descend to Crown Point State Park and the Vista House. You'll continue on a twisty descent (with no shoulder) for approximately 2.0 more miles. The route then continues east for another 10.0 miles to the turnaround at Ainsworth State Park. You can expect moderate to heavy car traffic on the highway on the weekends, and light to moderate traffic on weekdays. It is recommended that you travel on a weekday.

Things to see: Columbia River and Columbia River Gorge; waterfalls; the Historic Columbia River Highway; historic Multnomah Falls Lodge

Maps: USGS Washougal WA; Bridal Veil OR; Multnomah Falls OR

Getting There: By car: From the intersection of I-205 and I-84 in Portland, drive 9.0 miles east on I-84 to exit 18 for Lewis and Clark State Park. At the end of the off-ramp, turn left onto the Historic Columbia

River Highway. Continue 0.2 mile on the Historic Columbia River Highway, then turn left into the Lewis and Clark State Park parking area. GPS: N45 32.495' / W122 22.810'

THE RIDE

This ride starts at Lewis and Clark State Park and takes you east on a restored section of the Historic Columbia River Highway, where you'll visit multiple cascading waterfalls and numerous scenic state parks.

The construction of the Historic Columbia River Highway was thought to be one of the greatest engineering projects of its time. One of the original visionaries for the highway was Samuel C. Hill, also known as the father of the Columbia River Highway. Hill was a strong supporter of the "good roads" movement that was spawned from the development of the first commercially produced Model T Ford automobile. In 1900 Hill invited Samuel Lancaster, a well-respected road-building engineer, to the Northwest to discuss his vision for the Columbia River Highway. By 1913 Lancaster and his crew had built a series of impressive roads on Hill's 7,000-acre Maryhill Estate in Washington.

To help gain support for his vision for the Columbia River Highway, Hill invited members of the Oregon legislature to his estate to view the magnificent roadwork. Legislative members were so inspired by what they saw that they created the Oregon State Highway Commission to help oversee the development of the Columbia River Highway.

Samuel Lancaster was appointed supervising engineer for the project. Before survey work began in 1913, Lancaster commented, "Our first order of business was to find the beauty spots, or those points where the most beautiful things along the line might be seen in the best advantage and if possible to locate the road in such a way as to reach them." Work began in 1913 to build the highway, which would stretch from Astoria to The Dalles. In June 1922 the highway was finally completed, and consisted of eighteen bridges, three tunnels, seven viaducts, two footbridges, and 73.8 miles of roadway.

This tour starts by following the shores of the Sandy River and taking you past Dabney State Recreation Area at mile 3.0. This state park is a good place to go for a swim on a hot summer's day. Over the next 5.0 miles, the highway takes you past berry farms and orchards, and through the historic communities of Springdale and Corbett. If you are cycling in July and August, be on the lookout for "U-Pick" signs along this section of the highway.

At mile 8.4 you'll arrive at Portland Women's Forum State Scenic Viewpoint and Chanticleer Point. Here you have a gorgeous view of the dramatic

Vista House and Crown Point are famous landmarks in the Columbia River Gorge.
PHOTO BY LIZANN DUNEGAN

cliffs and forested ridges of Columbia River Gorge. This magnificent gorge was sculpted by catastrophic floods that occurred near the end of the ice age (19,000 to 12,000 years ago). These floods were created when the climate began to warm up, causing the 2,000-foot ice dams that held 3,000-square-mile Lake Missoula in Montana to break. The floods poured through eastern Washington, turned southwest across the Columbia Basin Plateau, and finally escaped through the Columbia River drainage, widening the valley floor and carving the cliffs you see today. As a result of these floods, the lower courses of many of the valley's tributary streams were cut off, creating an area with spectacular waterfalls.

From Portland Women's Forum State Scenic Viewpoint, pedal less than a mile downhill to Crown Point State Park and the historic Vista House (built in 1917). Restrooms are available here. From Crown Point sail downhill on a series of winding curves to Talbot State Park at 11.6 miles. This scenic picnic spot was donated to the state by Guy W. Talbot in 1929. Port Orford cedar, Douglas fir, alder, and big-leaf maple provide welcoming shade if you want to break from the saddle.

Scenic Multnomah Falls is one of the most well-known tourist destinations in Oregon and can be very crowded during the summer months. PHOTO BY LIZANN DUNEGAN

Latourell Falls, located in Guy W. Talbot State Park, is your next stop at 12.1 miles. From the parking area you can hike to view the 249-foot cascade.

Shepperd's Dell State Natural Area and falls is your next destination at the 13.3-mile mark. This 519-acre park was given to the state of Oregon by George G. Shepperd in remembrance of his wife. From the east end of the bridge, a short trail leads to a viewing area by the falls.

Shepperd's Dell Falls has its own unique, whimsical cascade.
PHOTO BY LIZANN DUNEGAN

Next you'll arrive at Bridal Veil Falls State Park and Bridal Veil Falls. You can view this two-tiered cascade by walking on the 0.6-mile out-and-back trail that begins behind the restrooms. You'll travel down a rocky dirt path into the creek canyon to a viewing area below the falls. Wild roses, lupine, and penstemon line the trail with their vivid colors. On a hot summer's day, you can cool off in the shallow pool at the base of the waterfall.

At 17.4 miles, Wahkeena Falls is your next waterfall destination. This spectacular, two-tiered cascade can be viewed from a paved trail accessed from the highway. Travel another 0.5 mile east and stop to view the amazing 642-foot cascade of Multnomah Falls. At this location you can also view Multnomah Falls Lodge, which was built in 1925. Inside the lodge is a restaurant, gift shop, visitor center, and public restrooms. If you are looking for a coffee fix, there is even an espresso stand here, where you can indulge yourself with a hot coffee drink. If you don't mind braving the crowds, you can hike a steep mile to the top of the falls on a paved trail. The cliff-top viewpoint is well worth the effort.

At 20.1 miles you'll pass a viewpoint of Oneonta Gorge on your right. Hidden a half-mile up this dramatic chasm is a 100-foot waterfall. On a hot summer's day, you can wade up the canyon to view the falls.

Bike Shop

Gresham Bike: 567 NE Eighth St., Gresham, OR 97030; (503) 661-2453; greshambike.com

Continue east another 0.5 mile to 176-foot Horsetail Falls. This fall swishes and swirls, mimicking the movement of a horse's tail. If you want to view two more wonderful falls, hike up the paved trail 0.2 mile, take a right, and arrive at Ponytail

Falls at 0.4 mile. The trail takes you behind the falls in an open circular cave. After 1.4 miles you'll arrive at a wooden bridge that affords outstanding views of 60-foot Oneonta Falls.

The turnaround point for this tour is at 21 miles, at Ainsworth State Park, which has a shady picnic area. If you want to spend more time exploring this area, you can camp at Ainsworth State Park campground, located another 0.4 mile east.

MILES AND DIRECTIONS

0.0 Start by turning left out of the Lewis and Clark State Park parking area onto the Historic Columbia River Highway. Water and restrooms are available here.

0.2 At the stop sign turn left where a sign indicates "Historic Highway/ Corbett/Dabney State Recreation Area."

0.6 Pass Tad's Chicken'n Dumplins restaurant on your right.

3.0 Pass Dabney State Recreation Area on your right. Water and restrooms are available here.

3.9 Enter the small community of Springdale.

4.5 At the Y intersection go right where a sign indicates "Historic Highway/Corbett/Multnomah Falls," and continue riding on the Historic Columbia River Highway.

6.5 Arrive in the small town of Corbett.

7.1 Pass Corbett Country Market on your left.

8.4 Arrive at Portland Women's Forum State Scenic Viewpoint and Chanticleer Point. Be sure check out the gorgeous view of the Columbia River Gorge and Crown Point, and to read the interpretive signs that describe the geology of the gorge.

8.8 Turn left where a sign indicates "Historic Highway/Vista House/ Multnomah Falls" and begin descending on a narrow, curvy, shoulderless road to Crown Point State Park and the Vista House.

9.5 Arrive at the parking area to Crown Point State Park and the Vista House. Be sure to take the time to view the historic 1917 Vista House. Restrooms and water are available here.

Columbia River Gorge Waterfall Tour

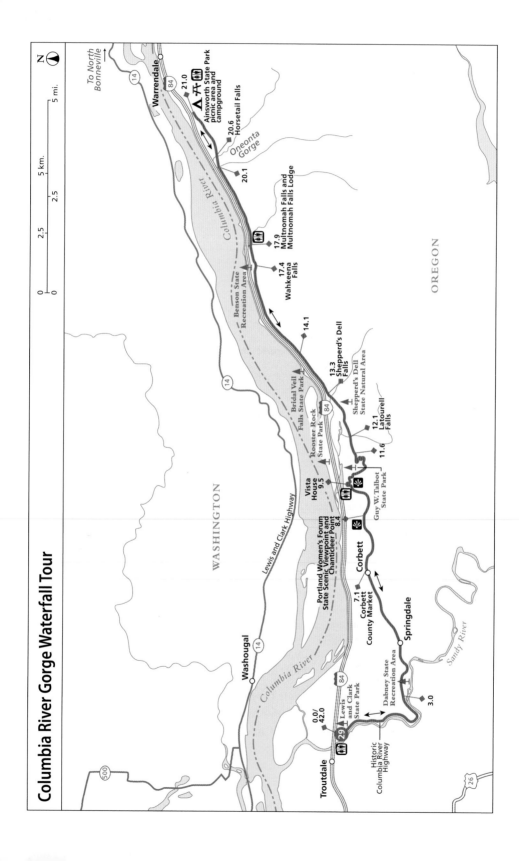

11.6 Pass the turnoff to Guy W. Talbot State Park on your left. Restrooms and water are available here.

12.1 Pass the Latourell Falls parking area and trailhead. (**Option:** You can take a short hike to view the falls.)

13.3 Arrive at Shepperd's Dell State Natural Area. (**Option:** Hike to the east end of the bridge to view Shepperd's Dell Falls.)

14.1 Bridal Veil Falls State Park is your next stop on the left. (**Option:** You can take a 0.6-mile round-trip hike to view Bridal Veil Falls. Picnic tables, restrooms, and water are available here.)

14.9 Angel's Rest Trailhead parking is on your left. (**Option:** You have the option here of hiking 4.4 miles out and back to a spectacular viewpoint at the top of Angel's Rest.)

17.4 Arrive at Wahkeena Falls on your right.

17.9 Arrive at Multnomah Falls and Multnomah Falls Lodge. Watch for vehicle and pedestrian traffic. A restaurant, gift shop, visitor center, restrooms, and water are located here.

20.1 Arrive at a viewpoint for Oneonta Gorge on your right.

20.6 Pass Horsetail Falls on your right. (**Option:** You can hike a 2.7-mile loop that takes you past Horsetail Falls, Ponytail Falls, and Oneonta Falls.)

21.0 Arrive at Ainsworth State Park. Picnic tables, restrooms, and water are available here. This is your turnaround point.

42.0 Arrive back at Lewis and Clark State Park.

RIDE INFORMATION

Local Events/Attractions

Harlow House Museum: 726 E Historic Columbia River Hwy., Troutdale, OR 97060; (503) 661-2164; troutdalehistory.org.

Rail Depot Museum: 473 E Historic Columbia River Hwy., Troutdale, OR 97060; (503) 661-2164; troutdalehistory.org.

Tad's Chicken'n Dumplins: 1325 E Historic Columbia River Hwy., Troutdale, OR 97060; (503) 666-5337; tadschicdump.com.

Wahkeena Falls is frequently photographed and admired by locals and visitors. PHOTO BY LIZANN DUNEGAN

Restrooms

Restrooms are located at the start/finish at the main parking lot at Lewis and Clark State Park; at mile 3.0 (Dabney State Recreation Area); at mile 9.5 (Crown Point State Park and the Vista House); at mile 11.6 (Guy W. Talbot State Park); at mile 14.1 (Bridal Veil Falls State Park); and at mile 17.9 (Multnomah Falls and Lodge).

Larch Mountain Cruise

This challenging ride takes you to the summit of 4,055-foot Larch Mountain, located in the Columbia River Gorge. On your way to the summit, you'll stop at two magnificent viewpoints—Portland Women's Forum State Scenic Viewpoint and Crown Point—that offer breathtaking views of the Columbia River Gorge. At Crown Point you'll also have the opportunity to look inside the historic Vista House, which was built in 1917. After exploring the Vista House, you'll pedal for 14.0 miles and gain 3,270 feet in elevation to the summit of Larch Mountain. At the summit you can take a 0.6-mile out-and-back hike to 4,055-foot Sherrard Point, where you can enjoy the views of Mount Saint Helens, Mount Rainier, Mount Hood, and Mount Jefferson.

Start: Dabney State Recreation Area in Troutdale

Length: 39.0-mile lollipop

Approximate riding time: 5 to 7 hours with stops

Best bike: Road bike

Terrain and trail surface: Rural paved roads that are flat and fast, with a variety of twists and turns and no shoulder

Traffic and hazards: This route follows the Historic Columbia River Highway, which has a 2-foot shoulder for almost 6 miles and moderate car traffic. After 5.7 miles the highway has no shoulder, and blind curves on the descent to Crown Point State Park and the Vista House. The 14.0-mile climb to the summit of Larch Mountain is difficult, and there is no shoulder. Wear bright clothing and bring extra layers for the fast, brisk descent from the summit. Use caution when descending because many spots on this road have rough surfaces that are hard to see, because the road is mostly shaded. Larch Mountain Road can also have moderate traffic on summer weekends. The return loop follows rural roads with mostly no shoulder and light to moderate traffic.

Things to see: Crown Point and the Vista House; the Historic Columbia River Highway; views of the Columbia River Gorge, Mount Hood, and Mount Saint Helens

Map: USGS Larch Mountain

Getting There: From the intersection of I-205 and I-84 in Portland, drive 9.0 miles east on I-84 to exit 18 for Lewis and Clark State Park. At the end of the off-ramp, turn left onto the Historic Columbia River Highway. Continue 0.5 mile to a stop sign and intersection. Turn left where a sign indicates "Historic Highway/Corbett/Dabney State Recreation Area." Proceed 2.7 miles on the Historic Columbia River Highway to the entrance to Dabney State Recreation Area on the right. The sign for the park is small and difficult to see. There is a small day-use fee. You can obtain a day-use pass at the self-pay station in the parking area. There are restrooms and water here. Larch Mountain Road is only open seasonally due to snowfall (typically the last part of May through Nov).

THE RIDE

This challenging tour to the summit of 4,055-foot Larch Mountain starts at Dabney State Recreation Site, which has restrooms and water. There is a small fee to park here. You can buy a permit from the automated pay station near the park entrance. Note that dogs are not allowed in this park.

Born on September 11, 1855, Richard T. Dabney moved to Portland in 1805 and bought fifty acres along the Sandy River, where he raised his family. He was a strong supporter of the Columbia River Highway and wanted to invest in resorts along the highway so others could enjoy its scenic beauty. After his death in 1916, his land was deeded to Multnomah County. The land was taken over by the state of Oregon in 1945 and turned into a state park.

This ride starts out innocently enough, by following a gentle grade on the Historic Columbia River Highway parallel to the shores of the Sandy River. Lewis and Clark gave the river this name in November 1805 because of its soft, quicksand bottom.

You'll arrive in the town of Springdale at just shy of 1.0 mile. This small, rural town was established in the 1880s by Danish immigrants. The town was named Springdale after the numerous natural springs in the area. The original commerce in Springdale was a mercantile and creamery. By the 1920s the town had expanded, with the newly built Columbia River Highway paving the way for more new commerce.

After you ride through Springdale, continue pedaling through scenic countryside filled with small farms and dotted with crops of blueberries and fruit trees. You'll arrive in Corbett after 3.5 miles. This community was named after Henry Winslow Corbett, a US senator and Portland businessman who settled in this area in the early 1900s. In the early part of this century, Corbett was a thriving timber and agricultural center. At the 4.0-mile mark, be sure to stop at the Corbett Country Market on your left to stock up on food and drinks before your ascent of Larch Mountain. There is no water at the summit of Larch Mountain.

At 5.3 miles you'll arrive at Portland Women's Forum State Scenic Viewpoint and Chanticleer Point. This scenic viewpoint has a grand view of the Vista House and Crown Point looking east, and more spectacular views of the cliff-lined gorge looking west toward Portland. Chanticleer Point was named after the Chanticleer Inn, which was built in 1912 by Mr. and Mrs. A. R. Morgan. When the Columbia River Highway opened in 1915, many flocked to the inn for its delicious food and gorgeous view. Unfortunately, the inn burned down in the 1930s and now only old photos depict its former grandeur.

At 6.5 miles you'll arrive at Crown Point State Park and the historic Vista House, built in 1917. This classic, domed structure perches on a 733-foot cliff overlooking Columbia River Gorge. It was the vision of Samuel Lancaster, the chief engineer of the original Columbia River Highway project. He wanted "an observatory from which the view both up and down the Columbia could be viewed in silent communion with the infinite." There are restrooms and water inside the Vista House, as well as displays that depict the history of this area.

As the westernmost high point in the Columbia River Gorge, Larch Mountain is a spectacular natural area. Douglas fir, silver fir, and noble fir grace its slopes, along with a thick understory of sword fern, licorice fern, and maidenhair fern. Ironically, no larch trees grow on Larch Mountain—these trees typically grow only on the eastern side of the Cascades. Loggers often mistakenly called the noble fir a larch, which leads to the misleading name.

When you arrive at the Larch Mountain summit picnic area, stash your bike behind some trees (or better yet, lock it up) and hike the 0.3-mile trail (one way) to the summit at 4,055-foot Sherrard Point. The rocky promontory of Sherrard Point rises sharply above a deep, extinct volcano. From the viewing area at the top, you can see (on a clear day) four prominent Cascade volcanoes: 8,363-foot Mount Saint Helens, 14,410-foot Mount Rainier, 11,235-foot Mount Hood, and 10,497-foot Mount Jefferson.

Bike Shop

Gresham Bicycle Center: 567 NE 8th St., Gresham, OR 97030; (503) 661-2453; greshambike.com

The historic Vista House was built in 1917. PHOTO BY LIZANN DUNEGAN

After you've spent some time enjoying the view, get ready for a fast, exhilarating downhill that is the great reward for all of your elevation gain. Be sure to throw on some extra layers for the very cool descent. Also, be cautious of traffic on this curvy, shady, and shoulderless road.

After you've traveled 10.6 miles, swing a left onto SE Louden Road. The rest of your return trip will be a fun romp on rural roads through the Sandy River foothills to your starting point at Dabney State Recreation Area.

MILES AND DIRECTIONS

0.0   Start by turning right out of the Dabney State Recreation Area entrance onto Historic Columbia River Highway. There is a 1- to 2-foot shoulder on this section of the road. Restrooms and water are available here.

0.8   Enter the small community of Springdale.

1.3   Pass the Springdale Historic Pub and Eatery on the right.

Best Bike Rides Portland, Oregon

1.4 At the Y intersection, go right where a sign indicates "Historic Highway/Corbett/Multnomah Falls," and continue riding on the Historic Columbia River Highway. At the next road junction, stay left.

3.5 Arrive in the small town of Corbett.

4.0 Pass Corbett Country Market on your left. You may want to stop and stock up on snacks and make sure you have enough to drink; there is no water at the summit of Larch Mountain.

5.3 Pass Portland Women's Forum State Scenic Viewpoint and Chanticleer Point on the left. Be sure to stop and check out the gorgeous view of the Columbia River Gorge and Crown Point, and to read the interpretive signs that describe the geology of the gorge.

5.7 Turn left where a sign indicates "Vista House/Multnomah Falls" and begin descending on a narrow, curvy road with no shoulder to Crown Point State Park and the Vista House.

6.5 Turn right and enter the parking area to Crown Point State Park and the Vista House. Inside the Vista House are water and restrooms and historic displays. There is a bike rack. After your visit, turn left out of the parking area and head back uphill.

7.2 At the intersection and stop sign, take a very sharp left onto Larch Mountain Road. Begin a very steep, difficult climb to the Larch Mountain summit parking and picnic area.

11.7 Enter the Larch Mountain Scenic Corridor.

15.5 Enter the Mount Hood National Forest.

20.9 Arrive at the Larch Mountain summit parking area. There are restrooms and picnic tables but no water. Hike the 0.3-mile (one way) trail to the viewpoint at the top of Sherrard Point. After you've enjoyed the view, head back down Larch Mountain Road.

31.5 Turn left onto SE Louden Road. This road is a mostly downhill cruise through picturesque foothills filled with farms and livestock.

35.1 At the T intersection and stop sign, turn left onto SE Littlepage Road.

35.3 At the stop sign turn right onto SE Hurlburt Road.

35.6 At the four-way intersection and stop sign, continue riding straight on SE Hurlburt Road.

Larch Mountain Cruise

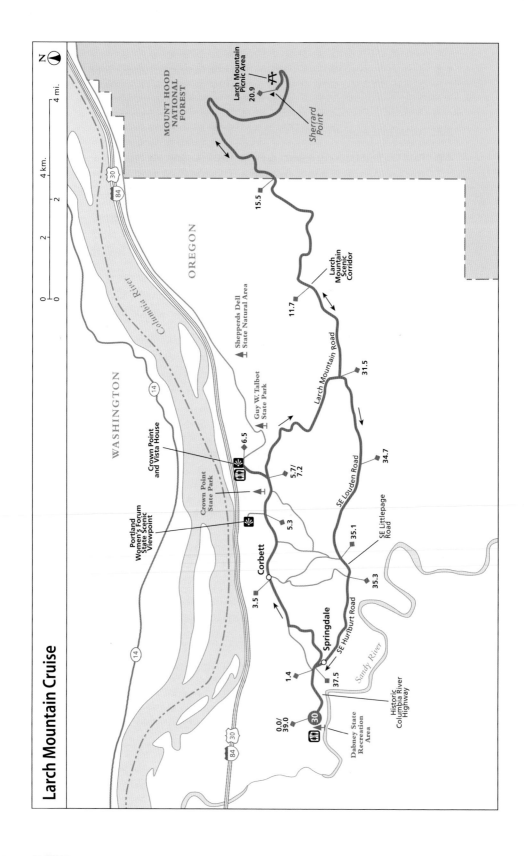

37.5 At the stop sign turn left onto the Historic Columbia River Highway, heading west toward Troutdale.

39.0 Turn left into Dabney State Recreation Area, where the ride started. The sign for this state park is difficult to see and this turnoff is easy to miss, so look closely.

RIDE INFORMATION

Local Events/Attractions

Harlow House Museum: 726 E Historic Columbia River Hwy., Troutdale, OR 97060; (503) 661-2164; troutdalehistory.org.

Rail Depot Museum: 473 E. Historic Columbia River Hwy., Troutdale, OR 97060; (503) 661-2164; troutdalehistory.org.

Restrooms

Restrooms are located at the start/finish at Dabney State Recreation Area; at mile 6.5 (Crown Point State Park and Vista House); and at mile 20.9 in the Larch Mountain summit parking area.

Gresham–Fairview Path

This ride takes you on a paved multiuse path through Gresham neighborhoods and business districts, and explores natural urban wetlands in the heart of the city. The trail connects with the expansive Springwater Corridor, an opportunity to lengthen your ride.

Start: Linneman Station in Gresham

Length: 7.2 miles out and back

Approximate riding time: 1 to 2 hours

Best bike: Road bike

Terrain and trail surface: Paved trail; paved street

Traffic and hazards: Use caution when crossing the MAX tracks and when crossing SE Stark Street, NE Glisan Street, and NE Holladay Street.

Things to see: Views of Mount Saint Helens; downtown Gresham; plant- and wildlife

Map: USGS Gresham

Getting There: By car: From I-84 eastbound in Gresham, take exit 13. Turn right onto NE 181st Avenue. Go 3.5 miles and turn left onto W Powell Boulevard. Continue to the junction with W Powell Loop, and turn right. Continue to the Linneman Station Trailhead parking area, located on the right side of the road. GPS: N45 29.298' / W122 28.198'

THE RIDE

The municipality of Gresham was incorporated in 1905, when it had a population of around 365. At that time, Gresham was predominantly a farming community and grew a variety of crops including grapes and cherries. In 1903, a trolley car service was opened and traveled for 36 miles east from Sellwood

Linneman Station was one of the stops for a trolley car service established in 1903.
PHOTO BY LIZANN DUNEGAN

and Mount Scott to Gresham, Boring, Estacada, and Cazadero. Linneman Station was one of the stops along this rail line, and is the starting point for this ride. The trailhead has restrooms, water, and picnic tables.

Start by turning east onto the popular Springwater Corridor multiuse trail. After 0.2 mile you will turn north onto the paved Gresham–Fairview Trail. At 0.5 mile you will cross over a bike- and pedestrian-only bridge, which crosses over busy W Powell Boulevard. On a clear day you will have nice views of Mount Saint Helens to the north.

After crossing the bridge the path passes Grant Butte on the left, and a small wetland where you will see some birdlife. In the spring months, trees planted along the paved path are in bloom and add splashes of color to the ride. In addition, there are many parklike open areas on this ride that make you feel like you aren't riding in the middle of the city.

After 2.2 miles, the paved path ends. Turn left onto NW Birdsdale Avenue and use caution

Bike Shops

Gresham Bicycle Center:
567 NE 8th St., Gresham, OR 97030; (503) 661-2453; greshambike.com

A cyclist enjoys a sunny spring day on the Gresham–Fairview Trail. PHOTO BY LIZANN DUNEGAN

when crossing the MAX tracks. Ride a short distance and turn left onto busy SE Burnside Street, and then turn right to continue riding on the Gresham–Fairview Trail. Continue riding for another 1.3 miles, through suburban neighborhoods and business districts, until the paved path ends at the intersection with NE Halsey Street. This is your turnaround point; ride back along the path to the trailhead.

MILES AND DIRECTIONS

0.0 From the Linneman Station Trailhead, turn left (east) onto the Springwater Corridor paved multiuse path.

0.2 Turn left on the signed Gresham–Fairview Trail.

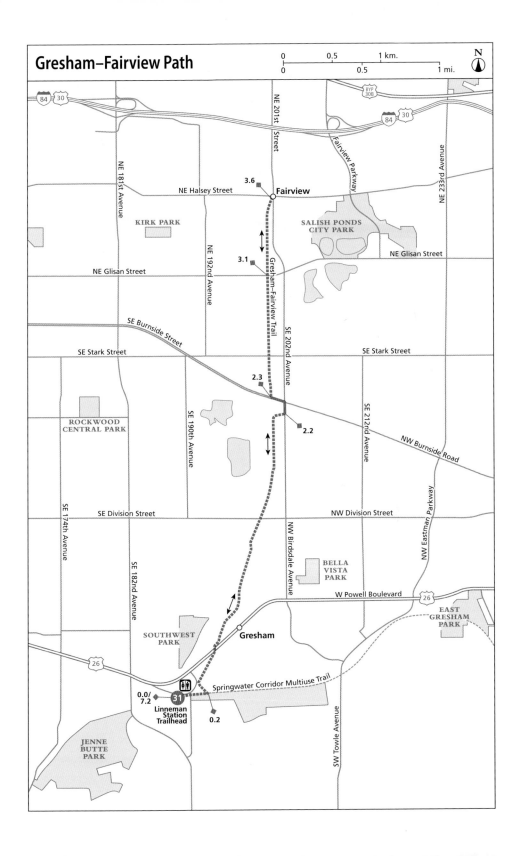

Gresham–Fairview Path

31

0.3 Turn right on the signed Gresham–Fairview Trail.

0.5 Cross a bike bridge and enjoy the nice views of Mount Saint Helens.

2.2 The paved path ends. Turn left onto NW Birdsdale Avenue and use caution when crossing the railroad tracks. Ride a short distance and turn left onto busy SE Burnside Street.

2.3 Turn right on the signed Gresham–Fairview paved multiuse path.

2.6 Cross SE Stark Street.

3.1 Cross NE Glisan Street.

3.4 Cross NE Holladay Street.

3.6 The paved path ends at NE Halsey Street. This is your turnaround point. Retrace the same route back to the starting point.

7.2 Arrive at the Linneman Station Trailhead, where the ride started. (***Options:*** From the route's end at NE Halsey Street, you can continue straight for 0.5 mile to the I-84 paved multiuse path. You also can turn right and continue 2.9 miles to Blue Lake Park, or continue 3.2 miles to intersect with the Historic Columbia River Highway.)

RIDE INFORMATION

Local Events/Attractions
Gresham Pioneer Museum: 410 N Main Ave., Gresham, OR 97080; (503) 661-0347; www.greshamhistoricalsociety.org.

Restrooms
Restrooms are located at the start/finish at Linneman Station.

North of Portland

The Columbia River edges the northern side of Portland, and just over the river is Vancouver, Washington. Though entirely its own city, Vancouver is very much a part of Portland and residents regularly go back and forth. There are many natural areas in the Vancouver region that are great for bike exploration, and the proximity over either of two bridges makes it easy to head to the other state for the day.

A gorgeous view of the tree-lined Lacamas Lake. PHOTO BY AYLEEN CROTTY

The routes in this section are great introductory rides, with off-the-road paths and short distances, making them perfect for new riders or young tikes. You'll be pleasantly surprised at the abundance of wildlife and lake views so close to the city.

Traffic to and from Vancouver on either of the bridges can be very congested during commute hours, so plan your adventure accordingly to avoid commuters leaving or returning to Vancouver.

Lacamas Lake Path

Take a mellow, flat cruise along Lacamas Lake, with a scenic tour around Round Lake, for a shady ride that is sure to please riders of all skill levels. The path is entirely off-the-road, with no road crossings except for a short stretch to get from Lacamas Lake to Round Lake. Most of the trail is either paved or very hardpack gravel, meaning it's easy to ride on. You'll take in lovely views of Lacamas Lake, a popular recreational lake, and waterfalls at Round Lake. This is a perfect trail for new young riders or those looking to improve their gravel riding comfort level. The trail has moderate use on the weekends and in the summertime, as it's also a popular hiking route for families and groups.

Start: Lacamas Heritage Trail parking lot at the intersection of NE Goodwin Road and NW Underwood Street in Camas, Washington

Length: 9.1-mile lollipop

Approximate riding time: 1.5 to 2.5 hours

Best bike: Road, hybrid, or mountain bike

Terrain and trail surface: Hardpacked gravel that's easy to ride.

Traffic and hazards: The trail is crowded on weekends with hikers and dog walkers.

Map: USGS Lacamas Creek

Things to see: Open stretches blanked with camas (a type of lily) in April; native wildflowers in summer; interesting rock formations; waterfalls; deer, beaver, coyotes, osprey, and bald eagles; swimming spots

Getting There: By car: From downtown Portland, take I-84 east toward The Dalles, then I-205 north for 5.5 miles. Use the right two lanes to take exit 27 toward Camas, and merge onto WA 14 east for 3.3 miles. Use the middle lane to take exit 10 for SE 192nd Avenue. Turn left onto SE 192nd

Avenue, then right onto NE 13th Street. Continue onto NE Goodwin Road for 0.4 mile until you reach the intersection of NE Goodwin Road and NW Underwood Street. Park at the trailhead. Enter the trail from the parking lot, and head toward the woods. GPS: N45 38.191' / W122 27.598'

THE RIDE

Lacamas Lake is a popular recreational lake, and there are plenty of opportunities to relax around the shore. In the summertime you can rent kayaks and

Tree-lined paths wind around Round Lake for a choose-your-own adventure exploration.
PHOTO BY AYLEEN CROTTY

A gorgeous view of tree-lined Round Lake. PHOTO BY AYLEEN CROTTY

paddle on the calm lake while bold birds soar overhead—or you can just sit by the water, cool off your feet, and soak it all in.

From the trailhead, you'll jump immediately onto the smooth trail for a 3.3-mile stretch that first passes by stands of towering Douglas fir and bunches of Oregon grape. The hardpacked gravel is very easy to ride on, a firm surface with no ruts and few bumps. Along the way, the old-growth wooded trail offers a lovely ride that hugs the Lacamas Lake shoreline and affords expansive lake views. On your right at mile 1.1, large homes loom above, part of the Lacamas Shores development.

The Lacamas Lake Trail ends at the Lacamas Lake boat launch. If you're with children, this is a great spot to take a break to play on the playground and have a snack before continuing on to the next segment.

> **Bike Shop**
>
> **Camas Bike and Sport:** 403 NE 5th Ave., Camas, WA 98607; (360) 210-5160; camasbikes.com

From the boat launch you'll ride through the park on the sidewalk paths and exit at NE Lake Road. At mile 3.8, carefully cross NE Everett Street and turn

Lacamas Lake Path

immediately right into the Round Lake parking lot. Ride through the lot and onto the trail.

The 1.2-mile Lake Loop Trail will take you through the park. If you want to add additional mileage and adventure, stop by the large map kiosk to view the various signed trails you can explore within Lacamas Park. The interlocking trails feature waterfalls, a field of camas, and soaring eagles and osprey. Near the dam, look for the interesting rock formations and "potholes" made by water pounding into the sandstone rock. If you're an adept rock scrambler, lock up your bike and head down to the water to soak in any one of a number of small pools that form around here.

On the weekends and some days in the summer, this area can be crowded with families and groups out for afternoon explorations, so ride slowly and be sure to alert other trail users when you approach them.

At mile 5.0, the Lake Loop Trail ends at NE 35th Avenue, where you will return to the road and cross back over to the Lacamas Lake area. Link back up with the Lacamas Lake Trail and enjoy the easy ride back to the trailhead, where the ride started.

MILES AND DIRECTIONS

0.0 The trail begins in the parking lot.

3.3 The gravel trail ends as you enter the park by the Lacamas Lake boat launch. Continue through the park on the sidewalk.

3.9 Exit the park onto NE Lake Road, then turn left onto NE Everett Road. (**Note:** This intersection is busy. Proceed carefully.)

4.0 Turn immediate right into the Lacamas Park parking lot.

4.1 Review the trail loops and select trails to explore for additional mileage and to view modest waterfalls and other natural features. Or you can simply stay on the main lake loop.

5.0 Exit the trail and turn left onto NE 35th Avenue.

5.2 Turn left onto NE Everett Road.

5.4 Turn right onto NE Lake Road.

5.5 Turn right into the park to loop back onto the trail, which you will follow to the start of your ride.

9.1 Arrive back at the trailhead parking lot.

Lacamas Lake Path

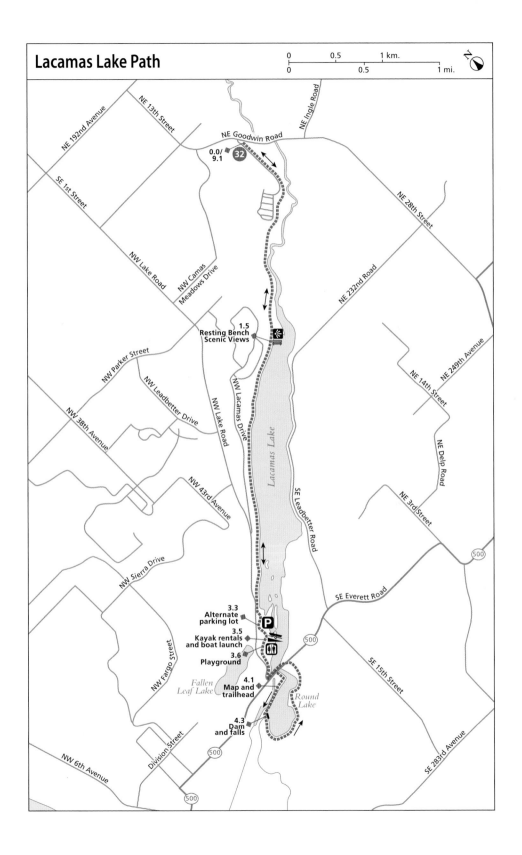

32

RIDE INFORMATION

Local Events/Attractions

Two Rivers Heritage Museum: 1 Durgan St., Washougal, WA 98671; (360) 835-8742; 2rhm.com. This cultural museum chronicles the history of the Columbia River region in Washington.

Camas Farmers Market: Wed from June through Sept, from 3 to 7p.m.; NE 4th Avenue between NE Everett Street and NE Franklin Street in Camas; (360) 838-1032; camasfarmersmarket.org.

Restrooms

Restrooms are located at the start/finish in the trailhead parking lot; at mile 3.5 (at the boat launch and park); and at mile 4.1 in Lacamas Park.

Burnt Bridge Creek Greenway Trail

This wide path cuts through the urban din of Vancouver on a trail that snakes through the city on impossibly smooth pavement, following Burnt Bridge Creek from Vancouver Lake all the way to East Vancouver. At times you'll forget you're riding through a city as you are immersed in the surprising serenity of this urban trail. This trail is great for new riders looking for a broad, safe area to practice riding, and there is almost no climbing at all. It's also a very lightly used trail, making it perfect for those who want to put their legs to the test and ride fast without interruption.

Start: Stewart Glen Trailhead at the intersection of NW Lakeshore Drive and NW Bernie Avenue in Vancouver, Washington

Length: 15.2 miles out and back

Approximate riding time: 1.5 to 2.5 hours

Best bike: Road bike or hybrid

Terrain and trail surface: Paved, smooth, off-the-road path

Traffic and hazards: You will cross busy roads at times, but the crossings have signals and are very well marked.

Things to see: Lush forested areas; Burnt Bridge Creek; expansive views of Vancouver

Map: USGS Vancouver, WA

Getting There: By car: From downtown Portland, take I-5 north for 9.0 miles. Take exit 4 for NE 78th Street. Continue 2.0 miles on NE 78th Street to the intersection of NW Lakeshore Drive and NW Bernie Avenue. Park on the street near the signed trailhead. Walk down the stairs and turn right to begin riding the trail. GPS: N45 40.412' / W122 41.418'

THE RIDE

Start your ride along Stewart Glen, just across from Vancouver Lake. At the very beginning it can be tricky to follow the trail, as many spurs and side paths exist. You will notice that most of these side routes are exits, so simply stay on the wider, main path and you'll be headed the correct way. Sections of the Burnt Bridge Creek Trail overlap with the much shorter Discovery Trail. so you will at times be following the signage for the Discovery Trail, which is extremely well marked.

You'll quickly experience the calm and serenity of this trail as you wind your way up to and over the freeway, then back down along the meandering creek. Astonishingly, there are fewer than a dozen street crossings, which makes for a very pleasant and relaxed ride. Each street crossing is well signed and safe, even when crossing a busy road.

It's easy to forget you're in the city as you travel along the Burnt Bridge Creek Greenway.
PHOTO BY AYLEEN CROTTY

The trail follows Burnt Bridge Creek, and crosses many footbridges along the way.

PHOTO BY AYLEEN CROTTY

At mile 4.4, the trail dips into a forested area that seems impossibly lush given that it's in the center of the city. Stop along the way to peer into the creek, where at times you can spot salmon and other fish, as well as bunnies and birds, all using this calm area as a refuge from the bustle of the city.

At mile 5.6, cross Devine Road and head into a broad wetland region teeming with wildlife. This important wetland area filters the water before it makes its way to the Columbia River.

Bike Shop

Kenton Cycle Repair: 2020 N McClellan St., Portland, OR 97217; (503) 208-3446; kentoncyclepdx .com

Burnt Bridge Creek Greenway Trail

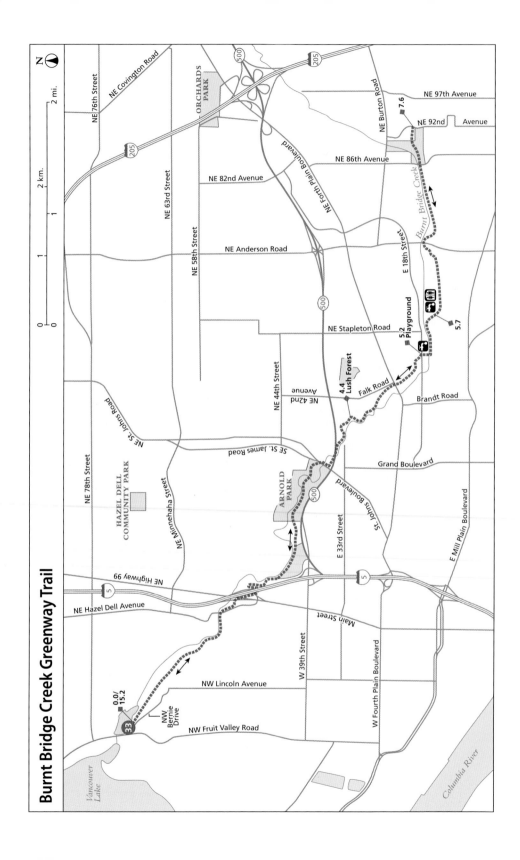

Maps and mile markers along the way will help you stay abreast of how far you've pedaled. It's easy to cut this ride short by turning around at any time.

When riding in this area of Vancouver, it's customary to swing by Bortolami's Pizzeria, a popular pizza joint. Bortolami's is located at 9901 NE 7th Ave. in Vancouver.

MILES AND DIRECTIONS

0.0 From the trailhead, walk down the stairs and turn right onto the trail. Follow the signs for the Burnt Bridge Creek Greenway or the Discovery Trail; you will see both names.

1.5 Turn right on NE Hazel Dell Avenue and use the bike lane to follow a short stretch along the road before crossing the road to continue on the trail. The trail is well marked. If you get to NW Newhouse Road, you have gone just a little too far.

4.4 Pass through lush forest.

5.2 Pass a playground.

7.6 The trail ends. Retrace the same route back to the starting point.

15.2 Arrive back at the trailhead.

RIDE INFORMATION

Local Events/Attractions

Vancouver Lake: This is a popular recreational lake with calm waters, an expansive beach, restrooms, and picnic tables. Though this ride's trailhead is very close to the lake, it is an additional 6.5 miles to get to Vancouver Lake Park, where you can access the water. The park is at 6801 NW Lower River Rd. in Vancouver.

Bortolami's Pizzeria: This popular pizza joint is completely plastered with bike racing paraphernalia, from jerseys to posters. They've even fabricated an oversize bike wheel that looms over the central dining area. 9901 NE 7th Ave., #A100, Vancouver, WA 98685; (360) 574-2598; bortolami.com.

Restrooms

Restrooms are located at the start/finish in the trailhead parking lot, and at mile 5.7 in the trailhead parking lot along the trail.

Frenchman's Bar Trail

This easy, paved, multiuse trail starts at Vancouver Lake Park and travels through rolling farmland and around the southern tip of the 2,370-acre Shillapoo Wildlife Area to Frenchman's Bar Regional Park. Both parks offer opportunities for swimming, boating, and picnicking.

Start: Vancouver Lake Park

Length: 6.6 miles out and back

Approximate riding time: 1.5 to 2 hours with stops

Best bike: Road bike

Terrain and trail surface: Paved multiuse path

Traffic and hazards: Watch for cars at road crossings.

Things to see: Vancouver Lake; wildlife; migratory waterfowl; farms; views of the Columbia River, Mount Hood, Mount Adams, and Mount Saint Helens

Map: USGS Frenchmans Bar

Getting There: From the intersection of I-84 and I-5 in Portland, drive north on I-5 for about 7 miles to exit 1D-C Mill Plain/WA 501 Highway. After the exit the road forks; stay to the right. At the stoplight, turn left onto E Mill Plain Boulevard and continue straight. (As you continue through downtown Vancouver, this road turns into E 15th Street and then W Mill Plain Boulevard.) After 1.7 miles, the road changes again to W Fourth Plain Boulevard. Continue another 3.5 miles on W Fourth Plain Boulevard, and then turn right onto NW Lower River Road at a sign for "Vancouver Lake Park." Continue 0.5 mile to a parking area at Vancouver Lake Park. Proceed through the parking area and park adjacent to the restrooms. GPS: N45 40.639' / W122 44.596'

THE RIDE

This ride starts in scenic 234-acre Vancouver Lake Park, which is located along the shores of Vancouver Lake. This lake is popular for swimming, windsurfing, canoeing, and kayaking, and also has picnic tables and volleyball courts. Frenchman's Bar Trail and the Frenchman's Bar Regional Park were named after Paul Haury, a French sailor who bought land in the area west of Vancouver, Washington, on Sauvie Island, at Kelley Point, and at the mouth of the Willamette River. Dogs are not allowed in the developed beach and turf areas from April through October.

You will start riding on the paved Frenchman's Bar Trail by turning right onto the paved path next to the restrooms. The 12-foot wide path is easy to negotiate and is mostly flat, with minimal elevation gain. After 0.4 mile, cross NW Erwin O. Rieger Memorial Highway and continue riding on the paved

Cyclists enjoy a summer ride on Frenchman's Bar Trail. PHOTO BY LIZANN DUNEGAN

Frenchman's Bar Trail

Frenchman's Bar Trail. The trail winds past open meadows and farms, where you may see migratory birds feeding in the fields or a variety of raptors flying overhead.

At 1.3 miles, you will arrive at a parking area for the Columbia River Renaissance Trailhead. Adjacent to the parking area is a path that leads to interpretive signs that describe the history of this area.

You'll continue riding on the paved path adjacent to the southern boundary of the 2,370-acre Shillapoo Wildlife Area. This wildlife area is a combination of agricultural land and developed pasture intermixed with fragmented pieces of natural habitat, and supports a variety of wildlife including Canada geese, mallards, bald eagles, Columbian white-tailed deer, and Western pond turtles.

Bike Shop

Vancouver Cyclery: 10108 NE Highway 99, Vancouver, WA 98686; (360) 574-5717; vancouvercycleryinc.com

After 2.7 miles, you'll arrive at the Frenchman's Bar Regional Park main parking area. This 120-acre park is adjacent to the Columbia River and has picnic tables, restrooms with water, volleyball courts, and a swimming beach. Continue riding on the paved path. After a short distance the paved path comes to a T intersection. Turn left and follow the path as it parallels the Columbia River. Along this section you can enjoy watching for boats and tankers on the river. The path ends at a paved turnaround that has interpretive signs that describe the history and wildlife that can be found in this area. Retrace the same route back to your starting point.

MILES AND DIRECTIONS

0.0 From the parking area, find the paved path next to the restrooms and turn right.

0.4 Cross NW Erwin O. Rieger Memorial Highway/WA 501, and continue riding on the paved path.

0.7 Cross NW River Road/WA 501 and continue riding on the paved path.

1.3 Pass the Columbia River Renaissance Trailhead parking area on the left. Turn left on the paved trail to read a historical sign and enjoy views of the Columbia River.

2.7 Arrive at the Frenchman's Bar Regional Park parking area. Continue riding on the paved path. After a short distance the paved path comes to a T intersection. Turn left and follow the path as it parallels the Columbia River.

Frenchman's Bar Trail

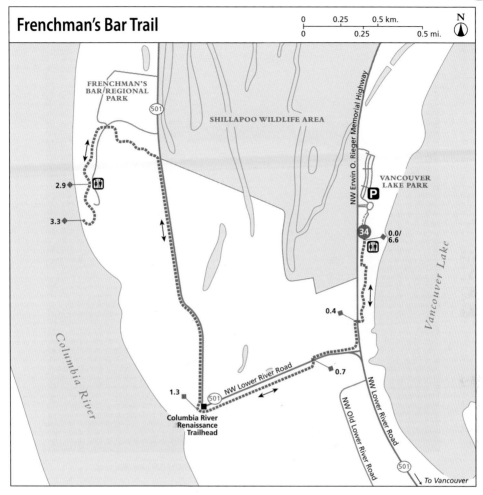

2.9 Pass restrooms on the left. There is also a swimming beach with volleyball courts here.

3.3 The path ends. You can view several interpretive signs at a turnout on the left. Retrace the same route back to the starting point at Vancouver Lake Park.

6.6 Arrive back at the Vancouver Lake Park parking area.

Frenchman's Bar Trail travels along the Columbia River in Frenchman's Bar Regional Park.
PHOTO BY LIZANN DUNEGAN

RIDE INFORMATION

Local Events/Attractions
Fort Vancouver National Historic Site: 1501 E Evergreen Blvd., Vancouver, 98661 WA; (360) 816-6230; nps.gov/fova

Restrooms
There are restrooms adjacent to the parking area at the start/finish of the ride, as well as at mile 1.3 and at mile 2.7.

West of Portland

Portland is widely regarded as a food-obsessed town, with a dedication to using local ingredients whenever possible. The abundance of farms on fertile land on the west side of Portland is a big reason the city has grown in this direction, as these farms provide the freshest ingredients just a short drive out of the city.

And it has always been this way. Since the early days of Portland, farmers would carry their goods into the city along pathways that are now heavily

You never know who might be watching as you cruise by, such as these majestic horses along a rural road. PHOTO BY AYLEEN CROTTY

trafficked roads lined with strip malls. But in this section of the book, rides will take you away from the fray of the suburbs and into the heartland, along rural roads, next to active farms, and through gorgeous scenery that's just on the edge of the city.

This section of the book contains an array of routes, from beginner mountain bike trails and off-the-road paths to short and long road rides. You're sure to find an awesome adventure for the day.

Traffic getting back into Portland, most notably along US 26, is congested at most times of the day, so plan your day accordingly.

Fanno Creek Greenway Trail

This wide, smooth trail takes you on a quiet wildlife journey through the areas of Tigard and Garden Home on the edge of Portland as it follows Fanno Creek, an important restored habitat for turtles, ducks, beaver, nutria, and other wildlife. The out-and-back trail features many offshoots, nature loops, and optional side routes so you can see different scenery on the way back to the start location. You will pass through seven parks on this very flat ride.

Start: Garden Home Recreation Center parking lot

Length: 16.4 miles out and back, including little loops

Approximate riding time: 2 to 3 hours

Best bike: Road or hybrid

Terrain and trail surface: Smooth pavement

Traffic and hazards: The path is mostly off-the-road, with a few brief stretches on the road where the trail has yet to be completed.

Things to see: Wetlands; trail art; ducks, turtles, and red-tailed hawks; elevated boardwalks; parks, playgrounds, and neighborhoods; a restored oak savanna

Map: USGS Portland

Getting There: By car: From downtown Portland, take I-5 south toward Salem for 3.6 miles. Take exit 296B for Multnomah Boulevard. Continue on SW Multnomah Blvd. for 2.5 miles. Take a slight right onto SW Garden Home Road, then a right onto SW Oleson Road. Turn into the Garden Home Recreation Center parking lot (7475 SW Oleson Rd.). Parking is free. The trail is on the wooded side of the parking lot; turn left toward the sports field to begin your ride. GPS: N45 28.019' / W122 45.133'

THE RIDE

Fanno Creek Greenway Trail is an ambitious greenway that aims to promote active recreational opportunities and access for the residents of Tigard and the surrounding areas by building trails that snake all throughout the area, following the path of Fanno Creek. A few sections have yet to be completed and additional features will be added in the future, but it is already a fantastic trail.

Neighbors of Fanno Creek once called it Drano Creek for the amount of garbage and sludge that flowed through it. Agricultural waste, industrial pollutants, and raw sewage dominated the creek in the 1960s, and was so severe that nearby residential and commercial development was halted for health

At times, the Fanno Creek Greenway Trail snakes through enchanted forested areas along a very smooth path. PHOTO BY AYLEEN CROTTY

Thanks to efforts that have restored Fanno Creek, ducks like this little guy crossing the bridge are abundant along the trail. PHOTO BY AYLEEN CROTTY

concerns. After the passage of the Clean Water Act of 1972, wetland advocates began working fervently to restore the creek to its more natural state. These days, the creek flows freely, and wildlife abounds. You'll experience this radical improvement as you meander along the water's edge for the duration of this wonderful path.

The trail starts out along a nice wooded path that wanders behind houses and neighborhoods, periodically crossing over streets. The path is lightly used, but traffic from walkers increases late in the day as neighboring residents come out for an evening stroll—exactly what the founders had in mind when they developed the trail.

At many points along the trail, you'll notice that the path splits without any signage. You can choose which direction to go; both will reach the same destination about 600 feet ahead. Occasionally these offshoot routes will take you to an area of restored natural habitat or other notable features.

At mile 3.3 you'll enter Koll Center Wetlands Park, which merges into Greenway Park, a broad swath of recreational land with a disc golf course and displays of public art and poetry. Slow down and you'll begin to notice flittering birds and other wildlife at nearly every turn.

At mile 4.9, the path passes through the broad Englewood Park wetland region, with waterways on either side of the trail. Stand calmly near the tall wetland grasses and you may spot mallards gently grazing on delicate surface-level plants, and colonies of whiskered nutria swimming through the water.

At mile 5.8, be on the lookout for signs declaring the oak savanna in Dirksen Nature Park. Less than 2 percent of historic oak savanna habitat remains in the Willamette Valley. When a grouping of oak trees was discovered along Fanno Creek, regional outdoor specialists decided to restore the habitat by thinning the surrounding area and removing invasive species. The result is a flourishing oak savanna with strong trees, important wildlife habitat, and an abundance of acorns as a food sources for animals.

Bike Shops

Santiam Bicycle: 9009 SW Hall Blvd. #104, Tigard, OR 97223; (503) 431-2644; santiambicycle.com
Western Bikeworks: 7295 SW Dartmouth Ave., Tigard, OR 97223; (503) 342-9986; westernbikeworks.com

The trail continues into downtown Tigard (mile 6.7), where an information sign explains more about the history and future of this interesting trail. Here you'll find Max's Fanno Creek Brew Pub, if you want to stop for a break.

After this point, the trail continues into a tranquil wooded area with several small footbridge crossings. Ultimately, the trail ends along a sidewalk in a neighborhood (mile 8.1), an important connection point for the residents of the area. From here, turn around and return along the same path. The ride ends back in the Garden Home Recreational Center parking lot. (***Option:*** Downtown Tigard is another natural turnaround point, which shortens the ride to 13.4 miles out and back. Other than the downtown Tigard area, there are limited opportunities for refreshments along the way, so plan accordingly.)

MILES AND DIRECTIONS

0.0 From the parking lot turn left on the Fanno Creek Trail, toward the sports field and into the woods.

1.2 At SW 92nd Avenue jog right, then immediately left onto SW Allen Boulevard.

1.3 Get into the left turn lane and turn left onto the sidewalk and into the woods to continue onto Fanno Creek Trail. (***Note:*** If you are not

Best Bike Rides Portland, Oregon

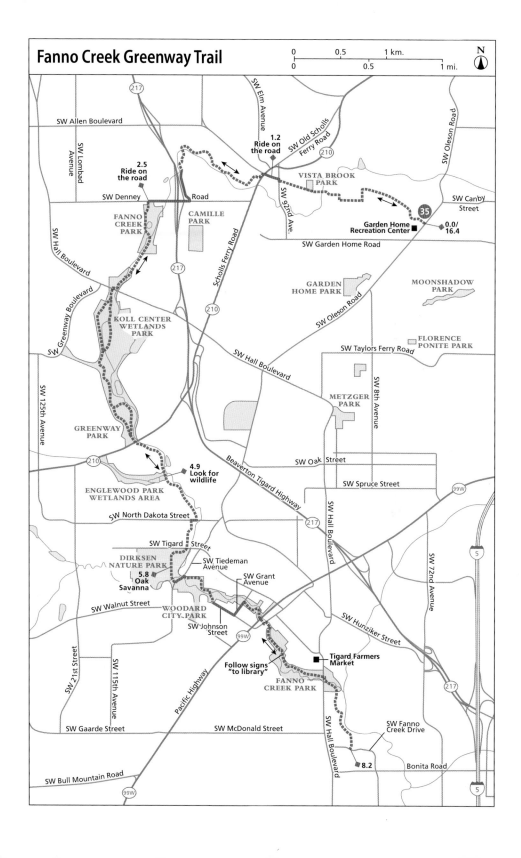

comfortable getting into the left turn lane, use the sidewalk to cross over to where you need to be.)

2.3 Turn right onto SW 105th Avenue.

2.5 Turn right onto SW Denney Road. (***Note:*** This is a busy street. Ride the sidewalk and look for the trail on the other side of the freeway.)

2.8 Turn left onto Fanno Creek Trail.

5.3 At SW North Dakota Street jog right, then left, to continue on the trail.

5.9 At SW Tiedeman Avenue jog left, then turn right to continue on the trail.

6.3 Exit the Woodard City Park and turn left onto SW Johnson Street. (***Note:*** This street is not marked. Look for a busy road and stoplight up ahead to know you are going in the correct direction.)

6.5 Turn left onto SW Grant Avenue.

6.6 Turn right on SW Main Street, then left onto the trail.

7.5 At SW Hall Boulevard jog right, then left, to continue on the trail.

8.2 The trail ends in a neighborhood. Retrace the same route back to your starting point.

16.4 Arrive back at the Garden Home Recreation Center parking lot.

RIDE INFORMATION

Local Events/Attractions

Festival of Balloons: Every summer, hot air balloons fill the sky at this celebration, which features live music and a carnival. At night, select balloons are propped up on the ground and illuminated so they can be admired at close range. The event is held in the last weekend in June at Cook Park, 17005 SW 92nd Ave. in Tigard; tigardballoon.org.

Tigard Farmers Market: Held every Sun from Apr to Oct from 9 a.m. until 2 p.m. in the public works parking lot, 8832 SW Burnham St., Tigard, OR 97223; tigardfarmersmarket.org.

Restrooms

Restrooms are at the start/finish in the Garden Home Recreation Center; at mile 4 (Greenway Park); and at mile 6.2 (Woodard City Park).

Best Bike Rides Portland, Oregon

North Plains Ramble

This ride takes you on a tour of the beautiful rolling hills of rural Washington County. Century-old farms, nurseries, and wineries are some of the many sights along this hilly route. You'll also have the chance to sample some of Oregon's award-winning microbrews and burgers at the Rogue Brew Pub in North Plains, and at the Helvetia Tavern.

Start: Rogue Brew Pub in North Plains

Length: 18.5-mile lollipop

Approximate riding time: 2 to 3 hours with stops

Best bike: Road bike

Terrain and trail surface: Paved road

Traffic and hazards: Use caution at the three railroad crossings on this route. West Union Road can be very busy. Avoid riding this route during morning and evening rush hours.

Things to see: Farms and rural countryside

Maps: USGS Hillsboro and Dixie Mountain

Getting There: From the intersection of I-405 and US 26 in Portland, head west on US 26 for about 18 miles to exit 57, signed for "North Plains." At the end of the off-ramp, turn right (north) onto Glencoe Road and continue 0.4 mile to the intersection with Commercial Street. Turn left onto Commercial Street, go 0.4 mile, and park in front of the Rogue Brew Pub on the left side of the road. GPS: N45 35.917' / W123 00.572'

THE RIDE

Rural Washington County offers premier road riding, and this route takes you on a tour through some of its most beautiful scenery. Washington County rests on an ancient bed of basalt lava. Twenty million years ago this area was covered with lava that flowed down the Columbia River basin from eastern Oregon. After the last ice age, water flooded the area and, upon receding, deposited sand, gravel, and a layer of topsoil throughout the region. These rich deposits, combined with the region's fairly mild temperatures, are perfect for growing specialty crops such as grass seed, hazelnuts, berries, hops, wine grapes, and nursery products.

The route starts at the Rogue Brew Pub, which serves local microbrews, wines, and delicious burgers. You'll pedal north for 3.0 miles on NW Shadybrook Road. This quiet rural road winds through picturesque countryside filled with grazing sheep and cattle. It serves as a good warm-up for the hill climb that begins when you turn onto NW Mason Hill Road at 4.3 miles. NW Mason Hill Road climbs more than 250 feet past fields of grapes, century-old farms, and executive homes. As you climb higher you'll have unsurpassed views of the northern Tualatin Valley, and the route becomes more forested.

Bike Shops

Olson's Bicycles: Cole Carter Building, 1904 Elm St., Ste. 1, Forest Grove, OR 97116; (503) 359-4010; olsons bicycles.com
Banks Bike Rental: 14175 NW Sellers Rd., Banks, OR 97106; (503) 680-3269; banksbicycles.com

After just less than a mile of hill climbing, you'll turn southeast onto NW Jackson Quarry Road and begin a fun, twisting descent through pockets of shady Douglas fir forest.

After a few miles of descending, the route turns east onto NW Helvetia Road and winds through more spectacular farming country. This area was settled by Swiss and German immigrants in the late 1800s. Before Prohibition it had a burgeoning wine industry and was known as Grape Hill. Near the halfway point in the ride, have lunch at the Helvetia Tavern, which features mouthwatering burgers and fries.

From the Helvetia Tavern, you'll finish by riding through more rural countryside back to the starting point in North Plains.

MILES AND DIRECTIONS

0.0   Start by turning right from the Rogue Brew Pub onto NW Commercial Street.

0.4   Turn left onto NW Glencoe Road.

0.5   Cross the railroad tracks.

0.6   Turn right onto NW Shadybrook Road.

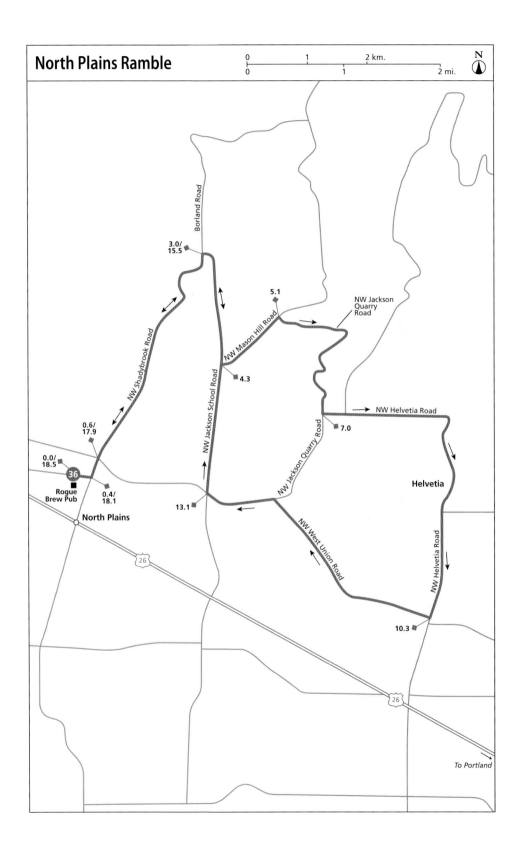

North Plains Ramble

0   1   2 km.

0   1   2 mi.

N

Borland Road

3.0/
15.5

5.1

NW Jackson
Quarry
Road

NW Mason Hill Road

4.3

NW Shadybrook Road

NW Jackson School Road

NW Jackson Quarry Road

NW Helvetia Road

7.0

Helvetia

0.6/
17.9

0.0/
18.5

36

0.4/
18.1

Rogue
Brew Pub

13.1

North Plains

NW West Union Road

NW Helvetia Road

26

26

10.3

To Portland

1.5 Turn right and keep riding on NW Shadybrook Road (NW Pumpkin Ridge Road goes left).

3.0 Turn right onto NW Jackson School Road.

4.3 Turn left onto NW Mason Hill Road and begin climbing steeply.

5.1 Turn right onto NW Jackson Quarry Road and begin a steep descent.

7.0 Turn left onto NW Helvetia Road.

9.0 Pass Helvetia Tavern on the right.

10.3 Turn right onto NW West Union Road.

13.1 Turn right onto NW Jackson School Road.

13.4 Cross the railroad tracks.

15.5 Turn left onto NW Shadybrook Road.

17.9 NW Shadybrook Road merges with NW Glencoe Road.

18.0 Cross the railroad tracks.

18.1 Turn right onto NW Commercial Street.

18.5 Arrive back at Rogue Brew Pub.

RIDE INFORMATION

Restrooms
Restrooms are located at the start/finish at Rogue Brew Pub, and at mile 9.0 (Helvetia Tavern).

Mini Farm Tour

Portland is a food-loving city that prides itself on cuisine made with locally grown produce, much of which is harvested from the rich farmland on the west side of town. This ride sends you on a lovely, flat loop to explore the farmland and take in sweeping views of the landscape. Though there is some moderate traffic, this short ride is appropriate for riders of all skill levels who are comfortable riding with traffic.

Start: At the main entrance of Rood Bridge Park at Rood Bridge Road

Length: 8.5-mile loop

Approximate riding time: 1 to 2 hours, including time to stop along the way

Best bike: Road or hybrid bike

Terrain and trail surface: Smooth pavement

Traffic and hazards: A mix of low and moderate traffic routes

Things to see: Hazelnut groves; the Tualatin River; birds; tree farms; active farming

Maps: USGS Portland; Metro Bike There! map

Getting There: By car: From downtown Portland, take US 26 west toward Hillsboro. Take exit 69A for OR 217 south. Take exit 2A for Canyon Road/OR 8. Canyon Road becomes Tualatin Valley Highway/OR 8. Continue for 8.4 miles to SE Brookwood Avenue. Turn left onto SE Brookwood Avenue, then take an immediate right onto SE Witch Hazel Road. Turn right onto SE River Road, then left onto SE Rood Bridge Road. Turn left into Rood Bridge Park and find parking. The ride begins from the main entrance of Rood Bridge Park at Rood Bridge Road. Head left on Rood Bridge Road to begin your ride. GPS: N45 29.525' / W122 57.077'

THE RIDE

In 1856, the Great Plank Road (now Canyon Road) was constructed to connect the fertile Tualatin Valley region with Portland and the Willamette River, which put Portland on the map as a major regional city. The road allowed abundant Tualatin Valley farm produce and grains to be more easily transported to the deep Willamette River port, and to export locations from there. This ride explores this rich farmland region.

This cute ride begins from Rood Bridge Park, a 59-acre park featuring a network of developed and natural areas, including paths into wooded and wetland areas, an extensive playground, tennis courts, a rhododendron garden, several ponds, a boat launch for the Tualatin River, and large lawn areas. Combine time at the park with this ride for rewarding day outside.

The rich soil of the Tualatin Valley supports vibrant farms and vineyards right outside the city.
PHOTO BY AYLEEN CROTTY

Best Bike Rides Portland, Oregon

At mile 3.3, you'll encounter the historic Lewis Pioneer Cemetery, where 280 graves mark the founders of the region. PHOTO BY AYLEEN CROTTY

This serene ride allows riders to escape the hustle and bustle of the city while being surrounded by what is still very active farmland. As you casually pedal these broad open roads, the slight dust of harvesters and farm machinery billows through the air, a constant reminder of the ceaseless work that farming requires. You'll pass many hazelnut groves, with their distinctive angled rows and stout, sturdy trees. Ninety-nine percent of the hazelnuts grown in the United States come from Oregon, where across the temperate ocean, mountain, and river climates intermingle with rich volcanic soils to create the ideal hazelnut habitat.

After heading south on SE Rood Bridge Road, your first turn is onto Burkhalter Road, where the broad landscape comes clearly into view. At mile 3.3, you'll encounter the historic Lewis Pioneer Cemetery, where some 280 graves mark the founders of the region. The earliest gravestones include those of Dolpha Howard, born in 1790, and Nancy McLendon, born in 1794. Tucked on a small hillside, this is a lovely spot to stop and explore.

Bike Shop

Orenco Station Cyclery: 1080 NE Orenco Station Pkwy., Hillsboro, OR 97124; (503) 547-0447; oscyclery.com

Mini Farm Tour

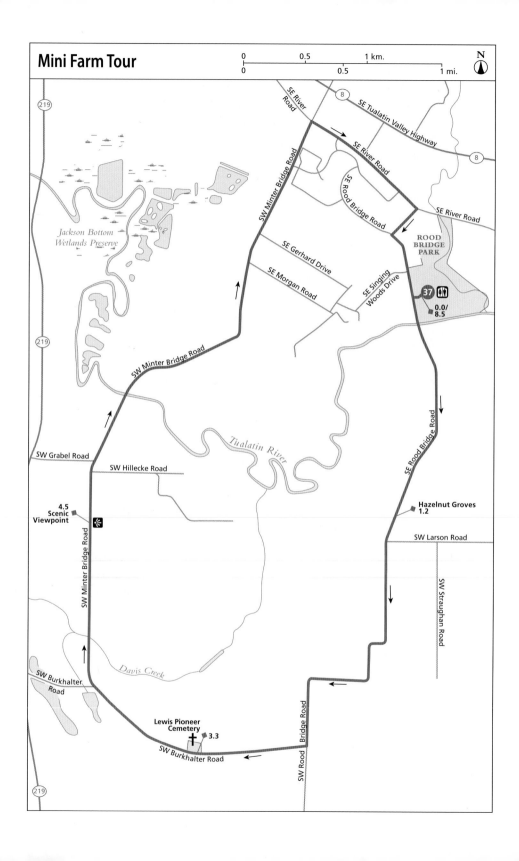

Mini Farm Tour

0   0.5   1 km.
0   0.5   1 mi.

N

219

SE River Road

8

SE Tualatin Valley Highway

SE River Road

8

SW Minter Bridge Road

SE Rood Bridge Road

SE River Road

ROOD BRIDGE PARK

SE Gerhard Drive

SE Morgan Road

SE Singing Woods Drive

37

0.0/ 8.5

Jackson Bottom Wetlands Preserve

219

SW Minter Bridge Road

SE Rood Bridge Road

Tualatin River

SW Grabel Road

SW Hillecke Road

Hazelnut Groves 1.2

SW Larson Road

4.5 Scenic Viewpoint

SW Minter Bridge Road

SW Straughan Road

Davis Creek

SW Burkhalter Road

Lewis Pioneer Cemetery

3.3

SW Rood Bridge Road

SW Burkhalter Road

219

On a clear day, as you approach mile 4.5, you can catch striking glimpses of the Cascade Mountains and the gateway to the Pacific Ocean. From here the loop continues over the Tualatin River, an important tributary of the Willamette River that drains this fertile farm region. A rich variety of wildlife, including coho salmon, steelhead trout, beaver, painted turtles, river otters, bobcat, and fox, relies upon the Tualatin River for habitat, and extensive efforts have gone into restoring and preserving the waterway.

After crossing the river, the route loops back around to the start at Rood Bridge Park.

MILES AND DIRECTIONS

0.0 Start by turning left onto Rood Bridge Road.

2.7 Turn right onto SW Burkhalter Road.

3.9 Continue onto SW Minter Bridge Road.

7.2 Turn right onto SE River Road.

7.4 Turn left onto SE Thrush Avenue.

7.5 Turn left onto SE Meadowlark Drive.

7.6 Turn right onto SE Rood Bridge Drive.

8.5 Arrive back at Rood Bridge Park.

RIDE INFORMATION

Local Events/Attractions

Rice Northwest Museum of Rocks and Minerals: 26385 NW Groveland Dr., Hillsboro, OR 97124; (503) 647-2418; ricenorthwestmuseum.org. This museum holds one of the world's finest collections of crystals from worldwide localities, including fossils, meteorites, petrified woods, oddities, fluorescents, lapidary arts, and Northwest favorites.

Jackson Bottom Wetlands Preserve: 2600 SW Hillsboro Hwy., Hillsboro, OR 97123; (503) 681-6206; www.hillsboro-oregon.gov/index.aspx?page=1256; @ci .hillsboro.or.us. This 725-acre wildlife preserve provides valuable habitat for both migratory and nesting birds.

Restrooms
Restrooms are at the start/finish in Rood Bridge Park.

Hagg Lake Ramble

This ride begins at the historic McMenamins Grand Lodge in Forest Grove, and takes you through the rural farm country of Washington County. On this route you'll have the opportunity to stop and taste fine wines at the Montinore Winery and cruise around scenic Hagg Lake, where you can stop and hike, have a picnic, or take a refreshing swim. Plan to spend some time at McMenamins, which is quite the intriguing destination.

Start: The parking lot at McMenamins Grand Lodge at the intersection of OR 47 and Pacific Avenue

Length: 28.7-mile lollipop

Approximate riding time: 3 to 4 hours with stops

Best bike: Road bike

Terrain and trail surface: Major highway with wide shoulder, and rural country roads

Traffic and hazards: Because of its close proximity to a large metropolitan area, Scoggins Valley Park can be very crowded during the summer months, and the car traffic on the lakeside road can be moderate to heavy. To avoid the crowds, ride this route in the early spring or late fall. If you visit during the summer months, try to arrange your ride on a weekday. The road around Hagg Lake is open year-round, but the park facilities are only open from mid-April through the end of October.

Be cautious of heavy traffic when you cross Pacific Avenue at 0.1 mile. This is the most congested intersection you will find on this route. US 47 has a wide shoulder, but you still need to watch for heavy traffic during peak morning and afternoon rush hours. Be cautious of logging trucks transporting logs to Stimson Mill, located off Scoggins Valley Road. Scoggins Valley Road has a 2-foot shoulder, and traffic on this road can be moderate to heavy during the peak summer season. There is also a 2-foot shoulder on the route circling the lake.

Things to see: McMenamins Grand Lodge; Momokawa Sake Brewery; Montinore Vineyards; Hagg Lake; wildlife

Maps: USGS Gaston, Gales Creek, Laurelwood, and Forest Grove

Getting There: From Portland, head 21.0 miles west on US 26 to a Y intersection with OR 6. Turn left onto OR 6 (toward Banks, Forest Grove, and Tillamook) and drive 2.5 miles to the intersection with OR 47. Turn onto OR 47 and drive 7.0 miles south to McMenamins Grand Lodge parking lot, located on the right side of the highway at the intersection with Pacific Avenue in Forest Grove. GPS: N45 31.214' / W123 05.058'

THE RIDE

This ride begins at the historic McMenamins Grand Lodge. Located on 13 acres of gardens, this Greek Revival–style lodge was originally built in 1922 as a Masonic lodge. The McMenamin brothers purchased the lodge in 1999, when the Masonic and Eastern Star Home moved to a new location. The magnificent redbrick accommodations feature seventy-seven European-style rooms that have a shared bathroom in the hall. Lodging includes a homemade breakfast served in the on-site pub. The lodge features a movie theater, restaurant and pub, soaking pool, day spa, specialty bars, local unique artwork, and live music. Even if you don't plan on staying here, it is highly recommended that you tour the building and check out the ornate artwork and grand architectural details.

Start this route by riding south on OR 47, which has a wide shoulder and can have moderate to heavy traffic during peak morning and evening rush hours. At mile 1.4 you may want to take an optional side trip to the SakéOne Tasting Room, located on the east side of OR 47, which is open daily for tours and tastings. You'll ride on OR 47 for only a few miles before turning off to pedal on rural roads that wind past fields of grapes, grass seed crops, dairies, and nurseries.

Just shy of 4.0 miles you'll pass the entrance to Montinore Vineyards on your right. This European-style winery is the fifth-largest winery in Oregon, and is situated on 711 acres. It is well known for its handcrafted pinot noir, pinot gris, chardonnay, Müller-Thurgau, gewürztraminer and Riesling. The original owner named the estate Montinore, which is short for "Montana in Oregon." The winery is open daily.

As you continue you'll pass through picturesque farm country and arrive at the small town of Dilley. This historic community was established in 1873 and was named after Milton E. Dilley, who was one of the region's original settlers. If you are working up an appetite or need to stock up on drinks, be sure to stop at the Lake Stop Store at mile 6.8. This store features deli-fried chicken, and other food and drink options.

Continue another 2.6 miles to Hagg Lake and the intersection with West Shore Drive. From here you'll begin a 10.5-mile ride around the scenic 1,113-acre lake. This much-loved lake was developed in the mid-1970s to provide irrigation water for the Tualatin Valley, and supplemental drinking water to surrounding communities. The route around the lake features rolling hills, travels past thick woods and open grassy meadows, and offers plenty of opportunities for exploration. The lake is surrounded by Scoggins Valley Park, with a 15-mile hiking and mountain biking trail that circles the lakeshore. This scenic, winding trail can be accessed from any of the lake's picnic areas or

Lizann Dunegan takes a break to enjoy the fall foliage. PHOTO BY JAN WOLFORD

from other roadside access points. Wildlife you may see includes deer, coyote, bobcat, osprey, hawks, bald eagles, songbirds, and a variety of waterfowl. If it's a hot summer day, take a refreshing plunge in the lake. Juicy blackberries can be found near the lake's edge in mid-August.

Cyclists and hikers aren't the only people enjoying this popular park. Boaters, water-skiers, and anglers also use the lake. The east end is used by motorboaters and water-skiers—the no-wake speed limit is not enforced. The west end is reserved for canoeing, sailing, and kayaking. Triathlons are held at the lake, with the Hagg Lake Triathlon being the most well known.

If you are still feeling spunky after completing the lake loop, you may want to go another round for additional mileage. For a different perspective, reverse your direction. When you're done, head back out of the park and take the same route to return to the starting point.

Bike Shops

Olson's Bicycles: Cole Carter Building, 1904 Elm St., Ste. 1, Forest Grove, OR 97116; (503) 359-4010; olsonsbicycles.com

MILES AND DIRECTIONS

0.0 Start by turning right (south) onto OR 47 from the McMenamins Grand Lodge parking lot.

0.1 Cross Pacific Avenue and continue riding straight on OR 47. Use caution at this intersection—it has heavy car traffic. OR 47 has a wide shoulder, and some sections along the highway have a separate bike path.

1.4 Pass the turnoff to the SakéOne Tasting Room on your left.

2.1 At a flashing yellow light, turn right onto an unmarked road.

2.3 Turn left onto SW Stringtown Road.

3.1 Turn left onto SW Dilley Road.

3.9 Pass the entrance to Montinore Vineyards on your right.

4.2 Turn left onto SW Dudney Avenue (SW Dilley dead-ends).

4.3 Turn right onto OR 47. Be cautious of traffic on this section of the route.

4.6 Turn right onto Old Highway 47.

Hagg Lake Ramble

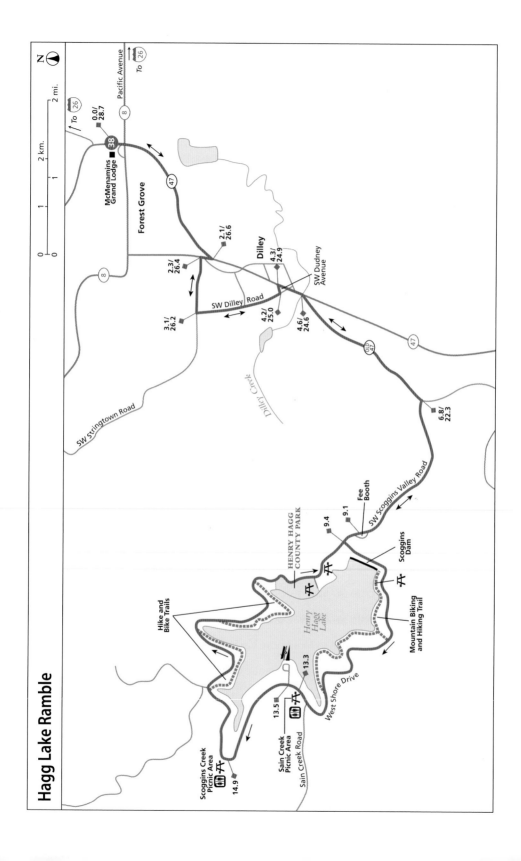

38

6.8 Pass the Lake Stop Store on the right. Just past the store you'll come to a stop sign; turn right onto SW Scoggins Valley Road. Be cautious of logging trucks heading for Stimson Mill zipping by.

9.1 Pass the Scoggins Valley Park fee booth on your left, and continue pedaling up a short hill. You won't have to pay a fee when riding a bike.

9.4 Turn left onto West Shore Drive and ride across Scoggins Dam. From this point, begin circling the lake in a clockwise direction on a series of fun rolling hills for about 10.5 miles.

10.3 Pass restrooms and a large gravel parking area on the right.

13.3 Pass Sain Creek Picnic Area on your right. This is a good place to stop for lunch. There are restrooms and picnic tables at this location. You can also access a hiking and mountain-biking trail that circles the lake from here.

13.5 Pass Boat Ramp C on your right. There are restrooms at this location.

14.9 Pass Scoggins Creek Picnic Area on your right. There are restrooms here too.

22.3 Turn left onto Old Highway 47. Be cautious of traffic.

24.9 Turn left onto SW Dudney Avenue.

25.0 Turn right onto SW Dilley Road.

26.2 Turn right onto SW Stringtown Road.

26.4 At the intersection turn right and ride 0.2 mile to the intersection with OR 47.

26.6 Turn left onto OR 47 and ride north toward Forest Grove.

28.7 Arrive back at McMenamins Grand Lodge parking lot.

RIDE INFORMATION

Local Events/Attractions
McMenamins Grand Lodge: 3505 Pacific Ave., Forest Grove, OR 97116; (503) 992-9533; mcmenamins.com/GrandLodge. This historic lodge has a theater, restaurant, soaking pool, day spa, specialty bars, and live music. The walls throughout are decorated with McMenamins' signature unique local artwork. Amenities are open to the general public without a hotel stay, though there

Hagg Lake Ramble

255

is a small fee for the outdoor soaking pool, which is well worth it after a long ride. On a cold day, cozy up by the lobby fire and enjoy a post-ride drink.

SakéOne: 820 Elm St., Forest Grove, OR 97116; (800) 550-SAKE, ext. 235; sake one.com. At this tasting room you can taste Oregon hand-crafted sake and learn more about how the sake is made.

Montinore Vineyards: 3663 SW Dilley Rd., Forest Grove, OR 97116; (503) 359-5012; montinore.com. Well known for handcrafted pinot noir, pinot gris, chardonnay, Müller-Thurgau, gewürztraminer, and Riesling. Open daily from 11 a.m. to 5 p.m.

Hagg Lake Triathlon and Duathlon: This event is held every July; visit why racingevents.com for more information. This event challenges you with a refreshing swim in the lake, riding the scenic paved road that circles the lake, and ends with a fun run.

Restrooms
Restrooms are located at the start/finish at McMenamins Grand Lodge; at mile 10.3 in the Hagg Lake parking area; at mile 13.3 (Sain Creek Picnic Area); at mile 13.5 (Boat Ramp C); and at mile 14.9 (Scoggins Creek Picnic Area).

Banks–Vernonia State Trail

This rail-to-trail route is canopied by towering trees for a lush, shady ride. Even on a hot day, the path remains relatively cool. The linear route is easy to follow, features excellent pavement, and is not too crowded. There is very little elevation gain, largely concentrated in one area, so for the most part you'll have a relaxing day. You'll enjoy the scenic mountains, fields, and forests of Washington and Columbia Counties to the west of Portland. Head out simply for a day of smooth riding, or pack your camping gear and camp at the halfway point (L. L. Stub Stewart State Park), or at Anderson Park at the end of the line. Rental bikes are available at the trailhead in Banks. This is a one-way ride, so you'll need to park a vehicle at the end of the line unless you want to earn extra points by riding back to the beginning.

Start: Banks–Vernonia State Trail trailhead parking lot at the intersection of NW Banks Road and NW Sellers Road in Banks

Length: 22.7 miles one way; shuttle required

Approximate riding time: 3 to 4 hours

Best bike: Road, hybrid, or mountain bike

Terrain and trail surface: Paved, smooth, off-the-road path

Traffic and hazards: You will need to cross gravel roads at times.

Things to see: L. L. Stub Stewart Park and mountain bike trails; the quaint towns of Banks and Vernonia; the 80-foot high Buxton Train Trestle; river swimming in Vernonia Lake

Map: USGS Vernonia

Getting There: By car: From downtown Portland, take US 26 west for 21.0 miles. When the highway turns into a smaller two-lane road, turn left onto NW Banks Road. Follow NW Banks Road to the trailhead parking lot at the intersection of NW Banks Road and NW Sellers Road. Overnight parking is not permitted. Enter the trail from the parking lot. GPS: N45 37.343' / W123 06.851'

THE RIDE

In the 1920s and 1930s, the town of Vernonia had a busy lumber mill and trains hauled wood along a rail line that ran into Portland. When the mill closed in 1957 the unused rail line began to fall into disrepair, and was completely abandoned in the 1970s. In 2010 renovations were completed to turn this once-bustling rail line into a popular trail for cyclists, hikers, and equestrians.

It's easy to hop on the trail directly from the parking lot in Banks—you can't miss it. You will begin your excursion into the woods along a smooth path with very few street crossings.

At mile 7.0, you'll cross the 80-foot-high curved Buxton Trestle, a restored train bridge with lovely views. This is one of the most scenic stretches, and makes for a nice photo opportunity. Farther along, the trail winds its way

The Banks–Vernonia State Trail travels across the impressively restored Buxton Trestle.
PHOTO BY AYLEEN CROTTY

through L. L. Stub Stewart State Park, which features 1,800 acres of rolling hills, forest glades, gleaming streams, and wildflowers, all crisscrossed with more than 25 miles of bike-friendly trails (see Ride 40 for details). If you plan to camp in L. L. Stub Stewart State Park, turn off at the Bark Spud Trail (mile 10.2) and ride the short 1,300 feet to the campground. The trailhead is well signed.

About halfway through your ride, at mile 12.1, you'll begin a series of short switchbacks that require steep climbing, but the reward is a fast descent. Other than this stretch, the Banks–Vernonia State Trail is relatively flat.

Bike Shop

Banks Bicycles: 14175 NW Sellers Rd., Banks, OR 97106; (503) 680-3269; banksbicycles.com

The Banks–Vernonia Trail quietly winds through rich farmland west of Portland. PHOTO BY AYLEEN CROTTY

Banks–Vernonia State Trail

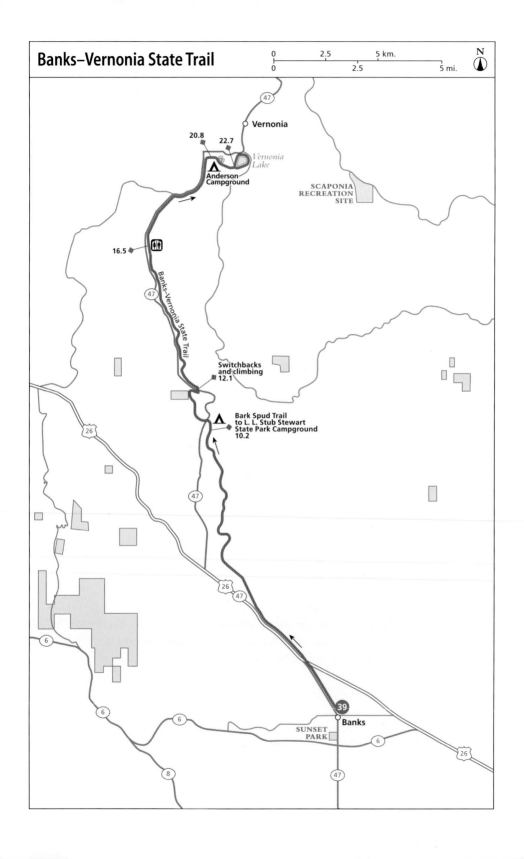

0   2.5   5 km.
0   2.5   5 mi.

N

47

Vernonia

20.8   22.7

Vernonia Lake

Anderson Campground

SCAPONIA RECREATION SITE

16.5

Banks–Vernonia State Trail

47

Switchbacks and climbing
12.1

Bark Spud Trail to L. L. Stub Stewart State Park Campground
10.2

26

47

26

47

6

6

39

Banks

SUNSET PARK

6

6

26

8

47

The ride ends at Vernonia Lake, but the swimming hole is at Hawkins Park, farther into Vernonia, where you can dip your toes in Rock Creek. The town of Vernonia features a market and several restaurants.

If you're riding in late July or early August, be sure to bring a container for harvesting blackberries. The luscious fruit is abundant all along the trail, and stopping to pick blackberries is a tradition for summertime cyclists; those who forget a container often can't resist emptying their water bottles to make room for these succulent treats.

It's easy to make this a shorter ride by starting from one of the other many trailheads along the way: Manning at 19.7 miles; Buxton at 15.7 miles; Tophill at 10.7 miles; or Beaver Creek at 5.0 miles.

MILES AND DIRECTIONS

0.0 From the parking lot, turn left onto the Banks–Vernonia Trail.

20.8 At Anderson Campground, follow the signs to Vernonia Lake on your right.

22.7 Arrive at the end of the trail at Vernonia Lake in Vernonia.

RIDE INFORMATION

Local Events/Attractions
Vernonia Friendship Jamboree and Logging Show: This three-day festival celebrates Vernonia's rich history as a logging town with competitions, an open-air market, lawn mower races, and much more. It is usually held the second weekend of August in Vernonia; vernoniafriendshipjamboree.com.

Vernonia Salmon Festival: Held every year on the first Saturday in October, this arts festival celebrates the migration of salmon as they swim through Rock Creek. For more information visit vernoniahandsonart.org/salmon-festival/.

Hawkins Park: In early summer a small dam across Rock Creek creates the "Dewey Pool," a popular swimming area. There is also a concrete kiddie pool adjacent to the creek. There is a lifeguard on duty Mon through Sat, from noon to 6 p.m. The park is at 857 Park Dr. in Vernonia.

Restrooms
Restrooms are located at the start/finish in the trailhead parking lot in Banks; at mile 6.8 (the trailhead in Buxton); at mile 12.0 (the trailhead in Tophill); at mile 16.5; and at mile 20.8 (Anderson Campground).

L. L. Stub Stewart State Park

Just on the outskirts of the Portland metro area, this woodsy playground is perfect for exploring and adventuring, featuring 1,800 acres of rolling hills, forest glades, gleaming streams, and wildflowers, all crisscrossed with more than 25 miles of trails. This trail system makes for a fun day of mountain biking for riders of all skill levels. There are ample doubletrack gravel roads suitable for riders new to trail riding, but there are also plenty of options for more advanced riders. Trails at Stub Stewart (as it is commonly known) are rated in four categories, from moderate to very challenging. The moderate trails are very easy and approachable. While some trails are shared with hikers and horse riders, there is an entire Mountain Bike Core area that allows cyclists to zoom around the trails more freely, with 6 miles of cross-country and freeride mountain bike trails reserved exclusively for bikers.

Start: At the map kiosk in the Hilltop Day-Use Area parking lot

Length: 5.7-mile triple loop; trails are 0.5 to 2.0 miles in length, with 25.0 miles of trail total

Approximate riding time: 1 to 4 hours

Best bike: Mountain bike

Terrain and trail surface: A mix of gravel doubletrack, soft cross-country trail, rugged singletrack

Traffic and hazards: Nothing notable

Things to see: Coast Range vistas; dense forest; streams; wildflowers; a freeride skills area

Maps: Consult the map kiosk in the parking lot by the restrooms

Getting There: By car: From downtown Portland, take US 26 west for 27.0 miles, then stay right at the OR 47 North split. Follow OR 47 for 4.0 miles and turn right into the park. Continue driving through the park to the Hilltop Day-Use Area. The trail map is posted by the restrooms. There is a parking fee. GPS: N45 44.494' / W123 11.162'

THE RIDE

L. L. Stub Stewart is a "choose your own adventure" ride. Most of the trails are extremely short and interconnected, so you can weave throughout the park on a quest for dirt fun. Trails converge and split constantly, so tie a handful of them together for a full day of riding. The trail system is perfect for riders new to mountain biking who want to hone their skills on approachable trails. Study the trail map at the kiosk at the parking lot to select appropriate trails.

Intermediate and advanced riders who want trails with built obstacles and challenges will love the Freeride Area, which features a variety of constructed jumps, knuckles, drops, a road gap, built terrain, and a thrilling wooden berm. The area is clearly marked and it's a challenging ride up to the top. Once there, several descents will take you back down via constructed

With broad-sky views like this, it's no surprise that L. L. Stub Stewart State Park is as popular for nighttime stargazing as it is for daytime riding. PHOTO BY AYLEEN CROTTY

L. L. Stub Stewart State Park

A mountain biker launches off a drop at the Freeride Area of L. L. Stub Stewart State Park.

obstacles. Each descent is marked with a rating, from moderate to advanced. If you've been able to ride any of the other singletrack at Stub Stewart, the most moderate descent is approachable. If you get to an area that is intimidating, you can easily dismount and walk your bike past the obstacle.

A challenging drop is positioned at the start of the most advanced descent as a filter to help you determine if you've got what it takes to ride the advanced freeride trails. It's a good idea to walk up the short trail to familiarize yourself with the obstacles before attempting the most challenging trails.

Stub Stewart is located on the Banks–Vernonia State Trail, a 40-mile paved rail-trail. You can easily leave Stub Stewart and jump on the Banks–Vernonia Trail to explore that ride as well (see Ride 39).

One great way to ride Stub Stewart is to combine a mix of the double-track gravel and some of the more introductory singletrack in a 5.7-mile loop. Start from the parking lot and head into the woods across the street. Follow the Bullbucker Trail signs and turn left onto Hares Canyon Trail, a broad, gravel, doubletrack trail. Continue uphill on the trail, which will take you past the Mountain Bike Area kiosk. Turn right onto the Unfit Settlement Trail, a loop and a bit of a climb. This is singletrack riding, but very introductory and scenic. The area is open to walkers and horseback riders also, so ride with care.

Bike Shop

Banks Bicycles: 14175 NW Sellers Rd., Banks, OR 97106; (503) 680-3269; banksbicycles.com

Descend the other side of the Unfit Settlement loop, then back down Hares Canyon to the Mountain Bike Area kiosk. Pass through to the Caddywomper Trail, a broad, flowy trail with very few technical features. This trail brings you to the uphill cutoff to the Freeride Skills Area. It's a challenging steep climb up, but totally worth it. You can stop and walk your bike at any time if the climb is too intense or the technical features are too difficult. The climb lasts for a quarter-mile.

From the top, the Freeride Area offers several routes down, and a kiosk with information will help you plan your descent. All trails come out at roughly the same point at the bottom. Hang out and watch and meet other riders, check out the tricks the skilled riders are performing, and plan your route down. Wigwam to Shoefly is a great way to go for a challenging ride, but without any of the extreme features, like drops and gaps, that exist on some of the other trails.

From the end of the descent, return to the Caddywomper Trail and take a left onto Hares Canyon. Follow this trail until you see signs for the Horseshoe Trail on your right. Make this short loop, then take a right on Hooktender Trail, and exit at the road that leads you to the parking lot. Stop to relax at the picnic

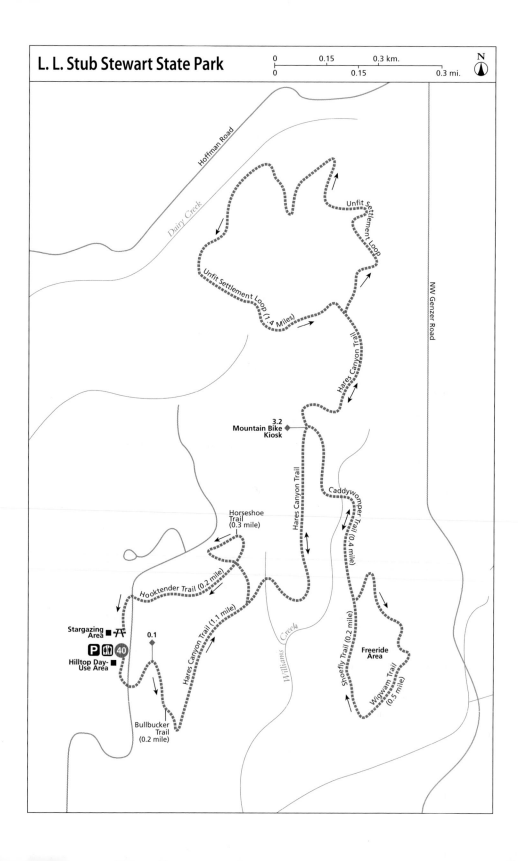

L. L. Stub Stewart State Park

0   0.15   0.3 km.

0   0.15   0.3 mi.

N

Hoffman Road

Dairy Creek

NW Genzer Road

Unfit Settlement Loop

Unfit Settlement Loop (1.4 Miles)

Hares Canyon Trail

3.2
Mountain Bike Kiosk

Hares Canyon Trail

Caddywomper Trail (0.4 mile)

Horseshoe Trail (0.3 mile)

Hooktender Trail (0.2 mile)

Williams Creek

Hares Canyon Trail (1.1 mile)

Shoefly Trail (0.2 mile)

Freeride Area

Wigwam Trail (0.5 mile)

Stargazing Area

0.1

P 🚻 40

Hilltop Day-Use Area

Bullbucker Trail (0.2 mile)

tables and celebrate a great ride while taking the views, or tuck back into the woods to ride some more.

MILES AND DIRECTIONS

0.0 Start from the map kiosk in the Hilltop Day-Use Area parking lot and head across the main road into the woods.

0.1 Follow signs for Bullbucker Trail.

0.3 Turn left onto the Hares Canyon Trail.

1.4 Turn right onto the Unfit Settlement Trail.

2.8 Return to Hares Canyon Trail and turn right.

3.2 At the map kiosk for the mountain bike area, cross over the wood hump and onto the Caddywomper Trail.

3.6 Turn left and head up the trail into the Freeride Area. Head down the Wigwam Trail, which connects to the Shoefly Trail.

4.3 Return to the Caddywomper Trail.

4.6 Take a left on Hares Canyon Trail.

5.1 Take a right on Horseshoe Trail, then turn onto the Hooktender Trail to continue back to the parking lot.

5.7 Arrive back at the map kiosk where the ride began.

RIDE INFORMATION

Local Events and Attractions
Stargazing parties: Stub Stewart is well known for its spectacular night skies. The Rose City Astronomers Club hosts stargazing parties in conjunction with the Oregon Museum of Science and Industry; for more information, check rosecityastronomers.org.

Park events: L. L. Stub Stewart Park hosts a plethora of mostly free events all summer long. See the park website for details: tinyurl.com/StubEvents.

Restrooms
Restrooms are located at the start/finish in the Hilltop Day-Use Area parking lot.

Resources

Bike Rentals

Cycle Portland: 117 NW 2nd Ave., Portland, OR 97209; (844) 739-2453; port landbicycletours.com

Everybody's Bike Rentals & Tours: 305 NE Wygant St., Portland, OR 97211; (503) 358-0152; pdxbikerentals.com

Upcycles: 909 NE Dekum St., Portland, OR 97211; (503) 388-0305; upcyclespdx .com

Organizations and Bike Event Calendars

ORbike: A statewide calendar of events and bike event news; orbike.com

Shift: A grassroots organization that promotes weekly free events and a summer bike festival; shifttobikes.org

Filmed by Bike: A film festival that features the world's best bike movies shown at a huge festival in Portland every spring. The movie collections then travel the world. Contact the organization about hosting a bike movie night where you live; filmedbybike.org

BikePortland: Bike culture and advocacy news; bikeportland.org

Bicycle Transportation Alliance: Portland's bike advocacy organization; btaoregon.org

Velo Cult Bicycle Shop: A bike shop and tavern that serves as a community gathering space for cyclists; velocult.com

Sunday Parkways: A city-sponsored event held from May–Sept where the streets are opened up for car-free enjoyment once a month; portlandsunday parkways.org

About the Authors

Ayleen Crotty is the director of Filmed by Bike, a film festival that travels the globe featuring the world's best bicycle movies. She is also the editor of ORbike.com, a resource to help people find bicycle adventures in and around Oregon. As an avid traveler, Ayleen's favorite way to discover new regions and cultures is to explore by bike. Learn more about her at AyleenCrotty.com.

Lizann Dunegan is a freelance writer and photographer specializing in writing outdoor guidebooks and travel articles about the Pacific Northwest. A Portland resident, she has been riding and exploring bike routes in Portland and the Northwest for more than 20 years. Lizann has written other cycling guides to Oregon including *Road Biking Oregon* and *Mountain Biking Oregon: A Guide to Northwest and Central Oregon's Greatest Off-Road Bicycle Rides.*